FROM MARX TO LENIN

FROM MARX TO LENIN

An evaluation of
Marx's responsibility for
Soviet authoritarianism

DAVID W. LOVELL

History of Ideas Unit
Institute of Advanced Studies
The Australian National University

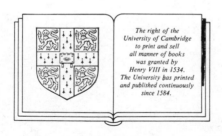

The right of the
University of Cambridge
to print and sell
all manner of books
was granted by
Henry VIII in 1534.
The University has printed
and published continuously
since 1584.

CAMBRIDGE UNIVERSITY PRESS

Cambridge
London   New York   New Rochelle
Melbourne   Sydney

Published by the Press Syndicate of the University of Cambridge
The Pitt Building, Trumpington Street, Cambridge CB2 1RP
32 East 57th Street, New York, NY 10022, USA
296 Beaconsfield Parade, Middle Park, Melbourne 3206, Australia

© Cambridge University Press 1984

First published 1984

Printed in Great Britain at the University Press, Cambridge

Library of Congress catalogue card number: 83-26276

British Library Cataloguing in Publication Data
Lovell, David W.
From Marx to Lenin.
1. Soviet Union. Politics and government
I. Title
320'.0947   JN6531
ISBN 0 521 26188 0

CE

for Sue

CONTENTS

PREFACE

Hegel has been denounced as the progenitor of modern totalitarianism, particularly Nazism, even though the National Socialists were not really guided by his thought. Karl Marx has been considered as a philosopher of freedom, even though his teachings are embraced by states whose commitment to personal freedoms is merely formal. I do not wish to labour the ironies of history, however, but to introduce the general issue of which this study treats a particular instance. That issue is the relationship between political and social theorists and the states and policies inspired by or attributed to them. What, in other words, constitutes historical continuity and legitimate application of political and social projects? This book examines whether Soviet authoritarianism was a necessary or inevitable consequence of Lenin's attempt to fulfil what he understood as Marx's project by tracing the concept of the transition to socialism through the Marxist tradition, from Marx to Lenin. This aspect of the relationship between Marx and Lenin, because of its abiding interest and political implications, has suffered no dearth of interpretations (some of which are examined briefly in the Introduction). But this work, I believe, is the first full-length study of it.

The political and social theorist who is concerned with the implementation of his ideas, rather than with study and reflection, places himself in an unenviable position. As a theorist, an employer of abstractions, he cannot hope to take account of every situation, every nuance of social life's infinite complexity. As an individual he thinks alone, and uniquely. But since an isolated reformer is virtually ineffective, he must ally himself with other like-minded, although never identical, individuals. Their motives, their points of agreement, may be limited. Indeed, if an 'ism' is a common denominator among people, it is often the lowest common denominator. If our

thinker lives to see 'his' project begun in earnest there is no guarantee
that his influence will predominate within it during his lifetime, or
endure after his death. Nor is there a guarantee that no unforeseen
obstacles will hinder or alter the project. The world is a refractory
medium for the theorist *and* the reformer. But our thinker, reflecting
upon his decease before his project is even begun, must concede
sadly that any theory can be used for almost any purpose by the
well-intentioned as well as the unscrupulous, and that if his memory
is not just politely respected his ideas and insights will be subject to
that distortion which is involved in the transmission of ideas from
one person to another, and from one generation to another. Our
thinker may simply be misunderstood by his followers. Kant was
moved by some of these considerations to pray 'May God protect us
from our friends', and Marx once declared 'I am no Marxist'.

Marx was neither widely nor fully understood by his followers.
Different aspects of his work were stressed at different times by
different of them. His ideas were often simplified, and their origins
and development obscured. He himself was partly to blame: because
he translated complex ideas into manifestos and programmes;
because he never completed a major work; and because he did not
consider, or did not make, much of his earliest work fit for publication or republication. The question is whether, despite this, he was
essentially understood. If Lenin essentially understood Marx's
project, and if that understanding was faithfully embodied in the
structure and policies of the early Soviet state, then Marx must be
held to account for Soviet authoritarianism.

My interest in the general issue of political continuity was kindled
by the question of whether Stalin was the 'rightful heir' to Lenin's
throne. Did he implement Lenin's policies or subvert them? Who
was the 'genuine Leninist': Stalin or Trotsky? But the questions
themselves were mistaken, or at least misleading. Since 'Leninism'
was the currency of political legitimacy, and thus of power, whoever
won the power struggle was the 'true Leninist'. Stalin was the
'Leninist' by virtue of his success, not by virtue of his theoretical
pronouncements within which there are evident discontinuities with
Lenin's work. Not only were the questions mistaken because they
failed to apprehend the institutional definition of 'Leninism' after
Lenin's death, but because they imply that there was a genuine
alternative to Stalin within the post-Lenin Bolshevik Party. There

may have been a 'river of blood' between Stalin and Trotsky, but on support for the authoritarian foundations of the Soviet state, and I suspect on much else, they were in basic agreement. Of course, this is not to deny that a Trotskyist Soviet Union would differ from its real counterpart; it is to deny the significance of those differences for the basic political organization of the state. Marxism, however, has yet to be institutionally defined throughout the world. It does not lend itself so readily to exclusion, and it tolerates major and fundamental divisions. Thus to ask whether Lenin was a 'Marxist' is hardly germane. But to question the relationship between Marx's project and the early Soviet state is a valid exercise, not simply because there were Marxist alternatives in 1917, but because Marx's project provides at least *prima facie* evidence for doubt that Lenin's interpretation is legitimate.

The relationship between Marx and Lenin clearly has many facets. This study is not intended to explore them all. It examines closely only the concept of the transition to socialism as it was discussed and debated in the Marxist tradition, from Marx to Lenin. It explores the changes which the concept underwent across that tradition, as well as the response by Bolshevik Marxists to the ever-present charge that their project would end in tyranny. I believe that since one of the central objectives of Marx's project is freedom, since the most important defect of the early Soviet state was its lack of freedom (now compounded), and since the most important fear inspired by Marx's project is the denial of freedom, the Marxist conception of the transition to socialism – the Marxists' immediate political objective – must be the prime subject of investigation to determine whether authoritarianism is a necessary part of any attempt to fulfil Marx's project. The relationship between Marx and Soviet authoritarianism is a complex historical and theoretical problem, unsatisfactorily explained with recourse to formulae about Marx's 'utopianism'. In an area as contentious as the study of Marxism, however, I shall count as success the revealing and illumination of some of the areas which must be examined to produce a satisfactory account of the Marx–Lenin relationship.

Many people contributed their time and talents to evaluating this work in its various stages. To my former colleagues in the Politics Discipline of the Flinders University of South Australia, where an earlier version was successfully submitted as an M.A. thesis, go my thanks for encouragement, suggestions and criticisms. To Professor Ivan Szelenyi, who assisted in its supervision, goes my gratitude for his judicious advice. Above all, my greatest debt is owed to Norman Wintrop. As main supervisor he was often critical, but always fair; as a colleague he exemplified the maxim that scholarship is a demanding task-master, earning my respect and confidence; and as a friend he was steadfast in his support. I am grateful also to Professor Eugene Kamenka, and to my other colleagues in the History of Ideas Unit of The Australian National University, for giving me the opportunity to complete the study. Professor Kamenka kindly read, and sparingly criticized, the final draft. Errors of fact or judgement which remain are entirely my own responsibility.

I dedicate this work to my wife Sue, for her patience while it was being written, and for the stability she provided while I examined, re-examined, and sometimes discarded long-cherished assumptions.

D.W.L.

INTRODUCTION

Almost from the time when Marx became a communist he was attacked for harbouring authoritarian designs on society. His disciples faced similar charges. In 1917 the first revolution to be made in the name of Marx's principles appeared to confirm the critics. This study grew from that observation. Were the political features of the early Soviet state the necessary product of an attempt to fulfil Marx's project, or a distortion of his project? For those who consider Marx's project viable, the contemporary relevance of such a question is obvious. It is perhaps fitting that we should first look at the answers given to it by one recently prominent group of such Marxists, the Eurocommunists, and by their critics, in order to assess how the question should be tackled and to uncover the mines laid for the unwary.

The Eurocommunists rejected the 'Soviet model' for achieving Marx's goals; instead, they declared themselves defenders of freedom and democracy, and legitimate contenders in the West European electoral arena. They recognized, in the words of George Urban, that 'the obstacle to Communism is Communism – Soviet style'.[1] The Italian and Spanish Communist Parties, and sections of the French Party, the bastions of Eurocommunism, appealed to voters that they would respect Western liberal democratic traditions, that there was nothing to fear from a communist, or communist–coalition government. Azcárate, a spokesman for the Spanish Communist Party, explained:

Eurocommunism ... seeks to find ways of achieving the Socialist transformation of society by means of democratic methods, and of advancing towards a new Socialist society based on full respect for human liberties, on pluralism and on a better social deal for all.... To put it another way,

Eurocommunism aims at establishing a new relationship between democracy and the Socialist transformation of society.[2]

Two issues immediately arose. First, and quite simply, could the Eurocommunists be believed? Secondly, did not any attempt to implement Marx's project involve authoritarian rule?

Having witnessed a number of communist policy changes for the sake of short-term tactical advantages, many observers were unsympathetic toward, and highly sceptical of, the Eurocommunists' new-found admiration of liberal democracy. Some questioned Eurocommunist sincerity.[3] The history of the communist movement provides grounds for this scepticism; so does Eurocommunist half-heartedness in criticizing Soviet illiberalism. More basic, however, is the fact that there are cogent theoretical grounds for suspecting that the Eurocommunists have made no fundamental break from the authoritarian traditions of Leninism. Chief among these is the inconsistency involved in Eurocommunist claims that socialism is inseparable from freedom and democracy, but that the Soviet Union and East European regimes, which they criticized for abusing freedom and democracy, are socialist. Furthermore, if the Leninist road to socialism is not categorically rejected, but merely treated as tactically unsuitable, there is no guarantee that it will not become tactically suitable once more when the Eurocommunists are in a position of more power.

If there be genuine and sustainable doubts about the Eurocommunist commitment to liberal democratic methods, there are also more fundamental questions about whether the attempt to implement Marx's project can avoid authoritarianism, and whether the attempt to avoid authoritarianism means the end of Marx's project. Critics of Eurocommunism, such as Urban, maintained that 'the progression from Marxism to Leninism, and from there to Stalinism inheres in Marxism itself'.[4] The Eurocommunists' progressive repudiation of Stalinism, Leninism, and the dictatorship of the proletariat, he argued, will lead 'inevitably to the repudiation of Marx'.[5] Amalrik agreed:

Lenin may have forced Marx, but the responsibility for Leninism and Stalinism is intellectually rooted in Marx.... The *whole* Marx leads, directly or indirectly, to Lenin.[6]

Neil McInnes demanded that the Eurocommunists explain

how Soviet collectivism came to involve tyranny, why it still does, and why any regime copied from it would not.[7]

Some Eurocommunists did indeed study closely their Soviet, and specifically Leninist, heritage to determine 'what went wrong' in the USSR. Some reviewed the Marxist theory of the state to justify their turn to liberal democracy by rejecting the need, in their states, of a dictatorship of the proletariat.

Jean Elleinstein, a Marxist historian and member of the French Communist Party (PCF), at first argued that Soviet authoritarianism 'was born ... in the nineteen-twenties *just after Lenin's death*'.[8] Lenin, he hinted, had a large share of responsibility for it. Soon after, Elleinstein became more critical of Lenin:

Far be it from me to defend Stalinism or, for that matter, Lenin's brutal onslaught on liberty and democracy in 1918.... Leninism and Stalinism can offer no guidelines for us.[9]

The Russian version of Marxism, he declared, 'was a deviation from Marx's thinking and, in extreme cases, a denial and repudiation of Marxism'.[10] Nevertheless, a dictatorship was necessary to 'consolidate' the Revolution, even though it 'constituted a danger', a danger realized when 'terror became a system of government'.[11] Elleinstein recommended to his Party that this road to socialism 'cannot and must not be taken as a model'.[12] The PCF must adopt a strategy of parliamentary gains, and renounce pre-emptive strikes for power. Leninism, he explained, was 'inevitably the product of specific historical conditions in Russia at the beginning of the century'.[13] The 'historical and cultural basis' of Western Europe would not allow the Bolshevik Revolution as a model. In his 'civilized revolution' a Communist Party government, Elleinstein claimed, would resign if confronted by an electoral reverse: 'Better the risks of democracy than the tragedy of dictatorship.'[14]

But while the Eurocommunists relied almost solely on the Russian context to explain (and justify) Soviet authoritarianism, the West European context was not their sole explanation for adherence to the democratic road to socialism. For there were possibilities for the 'democratic transformation' of the state. The question of the state, according to Santiago Carrillo, a Spanish Communist Party leader, 'is the problem of every revolution', including the Eurocommunist revolution 'by the democratic, multi-party, parliamentary road'.[15]

Neither Marx, Engels, nor Lenin, he believed, had properly understood the importance of the 'ideological apparatuses' of the state in influencing its 'coercive apparatuses'. Once bourgeois ideology is defeated in these apparatuses, the state can become more representative of the people's interests and can abandon its class and coercive character. The state can be transformed through the operation of democracy, not through its abolition. Carrillo objects to Lenin's formulation that having become a habit, democracy will 'wither away'.[16] 'What is transformed into a *habit*', he points out, 'remains and becomes *habitual*.'[17] Having thus emphasized the importance of democracy for the transition to socialism and for socialism itself, Carrillo flouts Lenin's teachings by arguing that

in the Europe of today the socialist forces can enter government and come to power through universal suffrage and they will maintain themselves in a leading position in society if they are able to keep the confidence of the people through periodical elections.[18]

If democracy is important to the socialist project, however, it is not vital. For the violence which accompanied and followed the October Revolution, and the lone rule of the Bolshevik Party were, for Carrillo, historically justified. The Rusian communists 'had no choice but to take power'.[19] But Russian conditions did not compromise the attainment of socialism. The dictatorship of the proletariat, 'a more or less lengthy period of transition during which the political rights of the defeated classes and their supporters are suppressed',[20] is to be considered a valid, even if a lesser, option. But in Russia 'the choice between proletarian dictatorship and democracy did not present itself'.[21] In general, the Eurocommunists presented the means of the transition to socialism as a choice which each particular context determined. Sadly, the democratic choice had only recently appeared, and there was no precedent to which they could point as a guarantee of its success.

On closer analysis, the Eurocommunists are much more equivocal on the role of democracy (by which they mean liberal democracy) in the transition to socialism, and in their criticisms of Soviet illiberalism, than they at first appear. In the theoretical sense they must fail because of their apparently divided commitment to the Soviet Union and to a liberal democratic transition to socialism. Nevertheless, the debate over Eurocommunism raised issues which are at least as old as the Soviet republic: is Marx's project inevitably authoritarian; and wherein lie the causes of Soviet authoritarianism? In particular, it raised the issues of the extent to which Lenin was guided by Marx's principles in leading the October Revolution; the extent to which the political physiognomy of the Soviet state was influenced by Marx's project, Lenin's interpretation of it, Russia's social, economic, and cultural heritage, or short-term tactical considerations; and the extent to which Stalin's Russia was a necessary development of Lenin's Russia, and whether in turn all this can be directly derived from Marx. The scope of this study is not quite as ambitious, but Eurocommunism brings into focus two crucial questions. If we ask whether the ideas of Marx, the ideas and political strategy of Lenin, and the socio-political order of the early Soviet state are to be conceived in terms of a fundamental continuity, or a fundamental discontinuity, we must establish not only the relationship between Marx and Lenin, but the relationship between Lenin and the Soviet state.

Was Lenin responsible for the political features of the Soviet republic until at least the end of 1918? I use that date as an end-point because, having undertaken the October coup, Lenin and his Party had by the end of 1918 made the decisions in relation to liberal democracy and dictatorship which would largely determine the character of the new regime: the coup itself, the dissolution of the Constituent Assembly, the Treaty of Brest-Litovsk, and the decisions on peasant land-tenure.[22] After this time also, nothing much remained of novel Leninist[23] theorizing which had to do with other than the exceptional situation in which the Bolsheviks now realized they had landed, how to preserve Bolshevik power, and how to overcome the exigencies of the moment. It is perhaps unfair to judge Lenin in his state of perpetual crisis, except in so far as that state was prepared and caused by him. So how far was Lenin responsible for the authoritarian nature of the early Soviet state, its abandonment of representative democracy, free elections, a free press, and civil rights? How far, that is, was Lenin's policy dependent upon, or the outcome of, his theory; how far was theory a mere rationalization, the handmaiden of a policy which had Bolshevik power at its centre, but over which Lenin had little control? Was Lenin in control and, if so, was it his theoretical concerns which determined his practice, or was Lenin being controlled by circumstances and events which overwhelmed him?

One cannot exclude or deny the effects of circumstances which attended the birth of the Soviet state, nor the effects of tasks which any government, irrespective of particular long-term social goals, had to fulfil at the time. Bertrand Russell, shortly after the Revolution, pointed out that

it may be that Russia needs sternness and discipline more than anything else.... From this point of view, much of what it is natural to criticize in the Bolsheviks becomes defensible; but this point of view has little affinity to Communism.[24]

Furthermore, Lenin did not *make* the Russian Revolution; but he utilized the opportunities which presented themselves. As Arendt reminds us: 'revolutionaries are those who know when power is lying in the street and when they can pick it up'.[25] Thus Lenin had a decisive influence on the Bolsheviks' decision to attempt a coup,[26] even if he alone could not assure its success. Trotsky embroidered on this theme in exile in 1935:

had I not been present in 1917 in Petersburg, the October revolution would still have taken place – *on the condition that Lenin was present and in command*. If neither Lenin nor I had been present in Petersburg, there would have been no October revolution.[27]

Lenin could not take power alone, nor could he retain it and administer the new republic alone. Yet he was involved in every major political decision after the *coup* until illness curbed his direct influence, and death removed it. It may be objected that the social and political development of the Soviet state was not exclusively Lenin's (or even the Bolshevik Party's) doing. Russian society was no mere victim, or nothing but a piece of plasticine. But Lenin's influence was decisive and determining. For Lenin pursued one aim above all others, and sometimes in opposition to others in his own Party (such as the Left Communists of 1918) – the retention of Bolshevik power.

The Bolshevik Party was the instrument which made Lenin's role so successful and so decisive. His role, as Trotsky perceived, could not have been filled easily by another, unlike Plekhanov's brick-dodging Robespierre.[28] Lenin's theoretically derived commitment to

Bolshevik power, based on his unshakeable, but unverifiable, notion that the Bolsheviks were the only true representatives of the proletariat's historical interests, was the crucial orientation which contributed in the first instance to the decisions to restrict the freedom of the press and to dissolve the Constituent Assembly. It contributed, along with the Civil War, to the progressive outlawing of competing political parties. The Civil War gave rise to War Communism, whose problems in turn gave rise to the New Economic Policy. No doubt the Bolsheviks reacted to these exigencies in ways peculiar to them, ways conditioned by their understanding of and adherence to Marxism; yet after about 1918 the Bolsheviks reacted in a fundamentally *ad hoc* manner on the basis of, and in consequence of, popular disaffection with and opposition to an illiberal, undemocratic political system which they (and particularly Lenin) had the major role in determining. Post-revolutionary Marxism, for which they were establishing the precedent, was an unholy alliance between necessity and theory. Lenin's commitment to Bolshevik power, determined long before 1917, lies at the base of his policies in 1917 and after. It was the commitment at the core of his concept of the dictatorship of the proletariat, and thus at the core of the major political features of the Soviet state. Lenin may have appeared to be an opportunist, and power-oriented, but only because he would never compromise on his belief that the Bolsheviks not only represented the proletariat, but that they had an historical right, even an obligation, to take power and build socialism.

The general response to the question whether Lenin responded to events he could not determine, or whether he actually determined events, and to what extent – or, as Liebman asks with broader sweep: 'Was Leninism responsible for this process [i.e., totalitarianism], or was Leninism itself among its victims?'[29] – highlights the notion of Lenin's 'will to power'. Fischer, for example, argues that Lenin's 'greatness lay in the talent to recognize an opportunity and use it. He was thus a monumental opportunist.'[30] The concentration of power in a single party, he continued, conformed to Lenin's 'principles and suited his wilful personality'.[31] I have no wish, and there is no need, to explore Lenin's personality, even if it could be done successfully.[32] It may or may not be true that, as Childs puts it, Lenin was 'an arrogant man ruthlessly pursuing his own personal power'.[33] But I dispute with Bertram Wolfe that in the study of

Leninism 'we must consider the character traits' of its creator.[34] Psychoanalytic conjectures may be suggestive, but there are more obvious and less intractable grounds for explaining Lenin's attitude towards power. I do not dispute that Lenin was obsessed by political power, its acquisition and its maintenance. P. Akselrod's observations on this score, and his feeling that in this obsession lay Lenin's effectiveness as well as his danger, is pertinent:

there is not another man who for twenty-four hours of the day is taken up with the revolution, who has no other thoughts but thoughts of revolution, and who, even in his sleep dreams of nothing but revolution.[35]

Regardless of his personality, Lenin's 'will to power' was a theoretically derived position based on his conception of the Bolshevik Party and its historical role. It was Lenin's concept of the Party in its broadest sense which prefaced the Bolshevik assault on liberal democracy in Russia. It was not, of course, the only factor in Soviet authoritarianism. In evaluating the origins of Soviet authoritarianism we must, as Kolakowski puts it in an apt analogy, determine the 'genetic versus environmental factors'.[36] Like that debate over human development, the answer is irreducible to one or the other alternative. In the literature on the Soviet state they are the variables in an equation whose result is the Bolshevik dictatorship.

Although Eurocommunism contains the suggestion of a more far-reaching diagnosis, it proposes an environmentalist weighting in this equation, an extreme example of which would argue that even the best-intentioned liberal democratic solution applied to Russia after the First World War would have been at first an authoritarian regime. The Russian scene in 1917 was certainly grim. Industry had stagnated or been destroyed; transport was in disarray and the output from agriculture continued to fall; and above all, the war continued. Whichever party took power had to deal with these problems firmly and decisively. We cannot simply assume that a democratic, liberal regime was a viable political option at this time. That it was a genuine alternative underlies much of the criticism of the early Bolshevik regime. Walkin, for example, believed that Russia was moving inexorably towards a constitutional democracy before the First World War. Thus:

8

the Soviet state is an aberration in Russian constitutional history bearing little or no relationship to its Czarist predecessors and finding its origin in the unique situation arising out of Russia's participation in World War I.[37]

Even if Walkin is correct in assessing the trend of Russian democracy, he fails to understand that the war itself created an entirely new situation in Russia, and its scale of violence created new challenges for traditional political theories. Elie Halévy perceptively noted at the time that

postwar [First World War] socialism derives much more from this wartime regime than from Marxist doctrine. The paradox of postwar socialism is that its recruits often come to it out of hatred and disgust for war, while it offers them a programme consisting of the prolongation of the wartime regime in the time of peace. At the outset, Russian Bolshevism displayed these characteristics.[38]

Conditions were so much changed by the war that the questions of how much authoritarianism and for how long was necessary to restore stability and begin rebuilding seem more appropriate. Russian society had disintegrated under the effects of the war. Thus Russian conditions must be a factor in evaluating the early Soviet regime. Lenin exploited the weaknesses and indecisiveness of his opponents in order to take power, and to justify many of his early policies. But such circumstances, and his appeals to the environmentalist argument, merely provided him with an opportunity to implement otherwise unpalatable policies which were institutionalized and extended as the Bolsheviks gained a more solid grip on power. Lenin used the cover of necessary authoritarianism to establish systematic authoritarianism. Internal crises and foreign threats (and incursions) were so many means to further his original aim of Bolshevik rule.

While environmental factors played an important part in the political organization of the early Soviet regime, they also provided a convenient justification for policies which would nevertheless have been carried out, or were implicit in Lenin's conceptions of the Party and of the dictatorship of the proletariat. Thus I side with those interpreters who, for various reasons, maintain the primacy of theoretical, or genetic, factors in the foundation of the Soviet political structure. I believe that Soviet authoritarianism is largely derived from Lenin's fundamentally authoritarian theory and practice. Yet if the environmentalist weighting of our equation is sometimes used to justify, or lessen the severity of, Lenin's policies and the authoritarian nature of his regime, the genetic weighting is often used to lay the blame for Soviet authoritarianism at the feet of Marx. Having accepted that, for the purposes of this study, Lenin's Marxism was decisive in determining the basic political features of Soviet authoritarianism, we must now ask how far Marx was responsible for his disciple. Having cleared the first hurdle, the question of Lenin's influence on the Soviet state, we can legitimately inquire: was the Soviet state the fulfilment of Marx's project?

Parenthetically, I note that it is not for me to decide herein whether Leninism was the 'totalitarian embryo', as Fainsod has described it,[39] or whether the Soviet regime until the present day embodies a fundamental political continuity. Admittedly, the issue of Lenin's Marxist-authenticity, raised by non-communist Marxists such as Karl Kautsky, was soon displaced by the dispute among Lenin's 'heirs' over whether Stalinism was the rightful and necessary continuation of Bolshevism. On the latter issue I will hazard only two points. The first point is that, at one level, whether Stalin, Trotsky, or Bukharin won the power struggle after Lenin's death is irrelevant. What is relevant, however, is the way the problem is posed, and the assumptions made about it. That three individuals could (appear to) represent such different policies; that the elevation of one of them could mean a striking change to the Soviet regime (even if only to its 'style', although these are the imponderables of history); that each could consider, or declare, the others to be class enemies: this is Lenin's legacy, the elevation of one man to extraordinary prominence within the Party and the state. Thus to say that Stalin's purges of the 1930s were a necessary or inevitable result of Leninism is true only to the extent that Leninism prepared a situation (foreseen and denounced by Trotsky as 'substitutionism') where the paranoia of one man could determine the lives and deaths of millions. The second point is that Lenin's democratic centralism, or Party organizing principle, is too much maligned. Early Soviet authoritarianism cannot be explained as democratic centralism writ large. The substitution of the Party for the working class, Soviet authoritarianism's primary cause, relied on different principles from the substitution of the leader for the Party, the major development in the Soviet regime after 1917.

The October Revolution and the Soviet republic it created have spawned a vast literature, encompassing numerous interpretations of the relationship between Marx and that republic, or more precisely, between Marx and Lenin as its architect.[40] To simplify, three major positions are taken in the assessment of this relationship. The first, and perhaps prevailing, view is that Lenin's ideas and their Soviet outcome represent the logical, rightful, and even inevitable continuation or outcome of Marx's project. Until recently, communists were defined as those Marxists who held this view, which they shared with their major opponents who sought to identify the Soviet state with the works of Marx, the better to dismiss the entire project. Apostolic succession and demoniac possession both lie neatly together on this Procrustean bed. Their tacit agreement has been challenged by Eurocommunism, which partly explains why that strategy has been denounced as a fraud by anti-communists, and as impossible by other communists.

Representative of this first view is R. N. Carew Hunt, who argued that Lenin's was 'a legitimate interpretation of [Marx's] principles'.[41] Marx, he believed, would have approved of the Bolsheviks and the October coup.[42] R. W. Postgate, writing a few years after the Revolution, makes a similar point:

The actual Bolsheviks ... are in theory rigid and undeviating Marxists. In practice also they have carried out a programme of which undoubtedly Marx would have approved.[43]

That the application of Marx's project gave rise 'to a police state' writes Carew Hunt, 'is only what might have been expected'.[44] R. G. Wesson asserts that authoritarianism is 'inherent in Marxism'. Marx's analysis of capitalism, he continues, 'was essentially illiberal'; his theory of class struggle 'was an invitation to intolerance and persecution'.[45]

The second major group of interpretations posits a certain necessary revision of Marxism, a revision made necessary by the Russian circumstances into which it was introduced, or by its shortcomings in the face of a changing world. David Shub argues, for example, that Leninism is 'somewhat of a historical mutation' of Marxism.[46] Lenin's *What is to Be Done?*, his best-known statement on Party organization presented, Shub claims, 'ideas formulated decades earlier by Peter Tkachev'.[47] Boris Souvarine's early but impressive study of Stalin represents Bolshevism as 'a Russian simplification of Marxism'.[48] Possony declares that Lenin 'eclectically synthesized Marxism with the Russian revolutionary tradition and in so doing *preserved the essence of both*'.[49] This general position, much as the first, sees Lenin as essentially a Marxist. It is in this sense that the Eurocommunists maintained that Lenin, like themselves, was a 'revisionist'. Radice, a leading Italian communist, has said that:

We are all revisionists or, if you like, Marxist–Leninists in the sense that we have all adapted, changed, or ignored the texts according to the demands of the concrete situation in which we found ourselves.[50]

The third position is by far the most varied; its coherence, however, is based on the idea of a major discontinuity between Marx and Lenin. Its adherents argue that Lenin made substantial and fundamental changes to Marx's project. Some of them see Leninism as primarily a modernizing ideology for pre-industrial societies. John Kautsky, a descendant of one of Lenin's major post-1917 antagonists, argues that Leninism is

not merely ... a perversion or misunderstanding of Marxism but more specifically ... an adaptation of an ideology born in an industrial environment to the conditions of an underdeveloped one.[51]

Maximilien Rubel considered the Bolsheviks to have been 'objectively bourgeois' in substituting themselves as industrialists during what he believed should have been the capitalist phase of Russian historical development.[52] Others suggest that Lenin was influenced above all by Russian factors, and particularly by the Russian revolutionary tradition. T. H. Von Laue maintained that Lenin remained 'a secret Slavophile in the Marxist ranks',[53] while Nicolai Berdyaev, in his speculative but fertile work on Bolshevism, stressed the 'national roots of Russian Communism and the fact that it was Russian history which determined its limits and shaped its character'.[54] For Russian communism, he argued, was the 'transformation and deformation of the old Russian messianic idea'.[55] Fülöp-Miller's early study described Lenin as 'the real executor of the political testament which Peter the Great left to Russia'.[56] Robert Daniels is one who has repeatedly argued that Marxism has little responsibility for the October Revolution or for the Soviet state. 'At the very outset', he writes, 'Soviet Communism had a relation to Marxist doctrine that was emotional rather than logical.'[57] The Soviet political system, he explains, is a complex of many factors, including ideology. Once the Revolution had been made, however, considerations of Marxist theory gave way to the question of retaining power which 'became for Leninists a point of doctrine'.[58] Lenin may have appealed to Marxism, but he 'radically transformed his Marxian heritage ... in the direction of the ideas espoused by the Russian revolutionaries who preceded him'.[59] Lenin, Daniels argues, was a *Russian* revolutionary, and his Revolution 'yielded an intrinsically Russian result'.[60]

Still others of this third group treat the discontinuity between Marx and Lenin in terms of a major difference in theory. Gray considered Leninism 'a one-sided restatement of certain aspects of Marx'.[61] Adam Ulam claims that 'Lenin revised the doctrine of the Master as much as Bernstein did'.[62] C. Wright Mills also argued that Leninism 'though in several ways "based on Marx" differs profoundly from others of his theories and from the range of political action expected and from the policy most clearly derivable from him'.[63] In one of his later works, Sidney Hook argues that

the conception of the dictatorship of the Party over the proletariat, confirmed by the whole history of the Soviet Union, marks an absolute break with all the democratic traditions of Marxism.[64]

Drachkovitch suggests that the post-October regime 'represents a huge effort of improvisation and experimentation, an effort made in the name of Marx but certainly not according to Marx'.[65] Raymond Aron considers that the Bolshevik leaders 'believed themselves sincere Marxists even as they were scrapping essential portions of Marx's thought'.[66] Marxism, he continues, should have prevented the Bolsheviks from assuming power in 1917; they 'took power and built their allegedly socialist system *in spite of their doctrine*.'[67]

Some want to 'save' Marx; some to 'implicate' him; and others to do neither. What they generally share is a lack of clarity over the type of questions, and their manner of expression, which must be asked to establish the relationship between Soviet authoritarianism (for this is their chief concern with Lenin) and Marx's project. I contend that it is mistaken, or unproductive, to ask, what is the relationship of Leninism to Marxism, or, was Lenin a Marxist? There have been any number of attempts to define Marxism to make it operational in the sense of excluding individuals and groups: from Lukács's insistence that orthodoxy refers to method,[68] to Leszek Kolakowski's belief that the intellectual content of Marxism is unimportant, Marxism having become a formal, institutionally defined concept.[69] Rather than arbitrarily excluding some Marxists from a 'pure' Marxism, it seems more fruitful to consider Marxism as a historical movement whose self-proclaimed agents themselves determine its contents by selecting from a number of leading ideas to which Marx tried to give coherence and equal importance. Thus it is not my aim to construct 'what Marx *really* meant', or the 'essence' of Marxism, as a standard by which to measure all contenders for the title. Marx's work is a synthesis of competing strains of thought; its essence is that it doesn't have 'an essence'.

Adhering consistently to this approach to Marxism may result in the disconcerting phenomenon that an original complexity becomes transformed into a caricature. Nevertheless, not to prosecute the case for any one variant of Marxism (or none!) as the true Marxism would be quixotic. It is not to the point of this work that Lenin was or was not a Marxist. He claimed that he was; I will accept that he was. My willingness to countenance the widespread and divergent uses of 'Marxism' is rarely shared by Marxists; Lenin himself usually denied this appellation to his opponents even if they considered themselves Marxists. Lenin held a declamatory and prescriptive, if highly idiosyncratic, conception of Marxism. For my purposes, on the contrary, a Marxist is one who claims to adhere to Marxism as he himself conceives it. Of course there are major theoretical and political disagreements between Marxists; my approach is adopted because there are such disagreements. 'Marxism' here is used not to mean a set of substantive doctrines, but to evoke the idea of a unity and diversity something like that of a family: members share some characteristics, but they may not all share any one characteristic. To say Lenin was a Marxist is to move no closer to answering the real problem of whether his theory and its Soviet consequence have a relationship to Marx's project which is logical and necessary.

Neither should we ask what Marx 'would have thought' of Leninism, the early Soviet regime, or its present-day counterpart. This injunction prohibits expressions of whether Marx 'would have approved' of the Soviet state, or whether he 'would turn in his grave', or other such colourful colloquialisms. Asking what Marx would have thought if he were transplanted into the twentieth century calls for too many adjustments to lead to anything but idle speculation. But it is certainly not idle to ask in what relation Leninism and the early Soviet state stand to Marx's principles.

Nevertheless, it may be argued that this study falls into an equally vicious trap by employing the notion of Marx's 'responsibility' for Soviet authoritarianism. But it is not my intention to haul Marx before some imaginary bar of history, to bring him to account morally for the actions of his disciples. Marx's disciples were independent moral agents, for whose actions Marx cannot properly be held morally responsible. Yet Marx's work was a causal factor in the actions of his disciples. Marx's responsibility, in the morally neutral sense intended herein, is simply a question of causal nexus. Was Marx's thought, or the acceptance of Marx's thought, a primary cause of the political complexion of the Soviet state? I have no intention to exhume Marx: to get his opinion or to castigate him. These are misguided objectives.

In classifying interpretations of the relationship between Marx and Lenin, I omitted an important group which, while it pays due respect to the quality of the questions it poses of this relationship, raises a different order of problems. It is a group whose members seek formulae, or underlying causes, for what they believe to be the inevitable translation of Marx's thought into Soviet authoritarianism. The intellectual stature of its leading representatives is beyond doubt; but this study, by contrast with theirs, is based on the belief that only a systematic pursuit of concrete historical and theoretical links between Marx's thought and Leninism can yield the foundation for a judicious assessment of their relationship. I shall explain why the formulae are no substitute.

The formulae seek to show that Marx's project was inherently flawed. Their inventors believe that beneath the actual links between Marx and Lenin there lies a 'weak link', or an 'original sin', which makes the transition from Marx to Lenin, and thence to an authoritarian state a necessary, inevitable, and logical one. Thus one does not have to assume that the Bolsheviks, or Marx, were evil men. According to those who devise the formulae, good intentions are not worth a jot, and what has happened before by necessity will happen again if Marx's project is attempted. Kolakowski, for example, rightly argues that Marx's project contains 'a degree of tension between heterogeneous strains of thought',[70] and that Lenin's (and

Stalin's) interpretation of it was based upon only one of the ideas of freedom which it contained: freedom as social unity. But despotism, Kolakowski continues, 'is the only known technique' for establishing such unity.[71] Freedom and social unity, in other words, are competing values, one realizable only at the expense of the other. Their incompatibility 'is empirical, not logical',[72] and Kolakowski concludes that

> every attempt to implement all basic values of Marxian socialism [is] likely to generate a political organization that would bear marks unmistakably analogous to Stalinism.[73]

Such an approach is not entirely new. Lord Acton believed that the French Revolution endangered liberty because of its quest for equality: 'The finest opportunity ever given to the world was thrown away because the passion for equality made vain the hope for freedom.'[74] Jacob Talmon considered that coercion was the likely result of Marx's project since it relied on a 'too perfectionist' concept of man,[75] and envisaged a complete social harmony without the need of force, although brought about by force.[76] It may be wondered, incidentally, how Talmon distinguished between 'too perfectionist' and merely 'perfectionist' views of man. Karl Popper makes similar points about the utopianism of Marx's goal, and argues that since it is impossible to determine or choose between ends scientifically,[77] there can only be violence between competing utopias:

> the Utopian engineers must ... become omniscient as well as omnipotent. They become gods. Thou shalt have no other gods before them.[78]

Others have attempted to link Marx with the authoritarianism of Lenin's regime, and subsequent Soviet regimes, by arguing that large-scale state ownership and economic planning necessitates dictatorship.[79]

These formulae raise at least two important issues. The first is the idea that Marx's project is based on competing values, that its message is not monolithic, and that Lenin's is thus a legitimate and necessary interpretation of it. The second is that Marx has utopian goals of a perfect man and a harmonious society, and that a preoccupation with ideal ends is necessarily linked with a thorough indifference towards even the basest means.[80]

The relationship between utopianism and violence, authoritarianism, or totalitarianism is not a necessary one. It has been argued that utopianism leads to a stress on ends, with a corresponding indifference towards the means; yet it is neither necessary nor obvious that utopians are Machiavellians, nor that those who concern themselves solely with means cannot be Machiavellians. Utopians are not necessarily oblivious to the relationship between means and ends. Marx certainly was not. 'An end which requires an unjustified means', he wrote in 1842, 'is no justifiable end.'[81] Clearly in Marx's view not all means were justified. Those who seek the roots of authoritariansim in Marx's utopianism overlook the commonplace fact that many who are motivated by the highest ideals, and who have the highest goals, do not resort to any means in the attempt to realize their goals. The doctrine of the perfectibility of man, for example, pre-dates Marx. It was one of the foundations of early–modern liberalism, although liberalism is not charged with attempting to create a tyranny. For this is a twentieth-century criticism, and specifically a post-First World War and post-Bolshevik Revolution criticism. Halévy noted the influence of the First World War on socialists, particularly on Leninists. If the scale of destruction and human losses called for an immediate end to the system they believed was responsible for the war, it also called for a reappraisal of some fundamental ideas about man by the supporters of that system. The Second World War and the Holocaust reinforced the notion that man's rationality, his innate goodness, and his perfectibility, ideas associated with liberalism, should be abandoned or greatly modified. In the midst of the Second World War, in his *Open Society and Its Enemies*, Popper argued that we must come to terms with man's imperfect, sometimes bestial, nature and reject those theories based on the assumption of man's perfectibility. He contrasted large-scale utopian social engineering with 'piecemeal' social engineering to remedy specific abuses (even though 'abuse' suggests 'ideal'). In short, the twentieth century has witnessed the end of man's thoroughgoing optimism about man.

To explain the basis of this criticism concerning ends and means, however, is in no way to dismiss it. There is no doubt that Leninism was end-directed, and that it justified its rather base means in terms of its declared ends. But why should we take Leninism at face value on this question when it is notoriously deceptive on so many others? The presuppositions of Marx's project were not those of a predominantly peasant society. Lenin was compelled to stress ends, otherwise his attempt at power in a backward society would have been pointless. Lenin attempted to become history incarnate, to force history. It was this, and not Marx's utopianism, which bred Leninism's end-directedness. And Leninism's end-directedness was a justification for taking power, for lack of concern with means, not a necessary ingredient. The argument is two-fold: that utopianism does not necessarily lead to a stress on ends; and that a stress on ends does not necessarily lead to Machiavellianism. We should also note that Popper's motif, Kant's dictum that man should never be treated as a means, but always as an end, is contradicted by most purposive human behaviour, within and across generations. We continually, and often voluntarily, make ourselves a means to an end: individually and socially. We sacrifice ourselves for wealth and status; we sacrifice ourselves in war for the continued existence of the nation; and we sacrifice ourselves for our children. Whether or not we ought to, we all at some time use ourselves and others as a means to an end without falling victim to authoritarianism.

We can admit that Marx's project is utopian, that it is based on the perfectibility of man – ideas which tell against it – without thereby agreeing that it is doomed to produce authoritarian regimes. Furthermore, pre-First World War criticism of Marx's project as the precursor of authoritarianism did not rely on the supposed effects of utopianism. It was very practical criticism which could be answered, or argued about, without recourse to different views of man. Indeed, most critics of Marx and Marxism shared many of Marx's presuppositions, particularly about man's perfectibility. Some of the major critics of Marx and Lenin were themselves socialists and Marxists. It is to these critics we must turn for an appreciation of the dangers of Marx's project. The pursuit of utopia, or the adherence to utopian ideals before about the time of the First World War was not considered to be inherently dangerous to the utopian project, partly because some generally accepted doctrines, such as the perfectibility of man, were not considered 'utopian', in its pejorative sense: that is, impossible.

Kolakowski charges that Marx's project is utopian because it is based on competing values of freedom and social unity. Certainly, one of the major strands of Marx's concept of freedom was the idea of freedom as social unity. But true social unity, Kolakowski objects, can only be achieved by despotism. Thus Lenin was consistently applying Marx's concept of freedom when he imposed social unity in Russia; thus Lenin's was a legitimate interpretation of Marx's project. Two questions arise here. The first is whether despotism constitutes a legitimate interpretation and application of Marx's conception of social unity, or rather Marx's conception of universality. The second is the larger question of whether, if Marx's project is based on different and competing intellectual traditions, if it presents major ambiguities (as I believe it does), any solution of these ambiguities which relies on only one of the traditions which Marx attempted to synthesize constitutes a legitimate interpretation. Marx himself never accepted despotism as freedom; he was a consistent critic and opponent of despotism as a matter of biographical fact. But this is not the issue. If freedom can be conceived of as social unity, can an enforced unity, a despotism, be conceived of as freedom? We must here distinguish between social unity and conformity, that is, between a situation in which there are no fundamental conflicts and a situation in which there are (apparently) no conflicts at all. Marx's project envisages the end of all fundamental conflicts within society; despotism, however, is the epitome of conflict. Despotism can never achieve unity, only conformity. It cannot therefore be a legitimate interpretation of Marx's concept of freedom, or of his concept of universality. Furthermore, Kolakowski errs in his belief that despotism is the 'only known technique' for social unity. War is particularly effective for binding the people of a nation against a foreign antagonist. It may well be argued that Marx's concept of the universal interest realized in a communist society is hopelessly romantic, and that particular interests will always reign supreme except in such emergencies as war. The community, in other words, will always be a collection of individuals pursuing their own interests, rather than a unit pursuing common interests, except where the existence of the community itself is threatened. This is perhaps why a 'siege mentality' is fostered in the Soviet Union, why a 'war', in Hobbes' rather broad terms, exists between the Soviet Union and the West. It is a tacit admission that despotism continually threatens to break into open conflict between rulers and ruled.

In Marx's project there are significant ambiguities and unresolved problems. Kolakowski uses Marx's concept of freedom to illustrate this point. But to argue that a one-sided solution to such problems as Marx set his disciples is a legitimate and even a necessary development from Marx, as Kolakowski claims for Lenin's interpretation, is to be unable to account for the other varieties of Marxism which competed with Leninism around the turn of this century. A legitimate interpretation of Marx's project, then, is not to be found by relying on 'one' Marx rather than 'another', but by appreciating the problems for which Marx believed his project to be a solution, and by openly coming to terms with the ambiguities and problems of that project. Otherwise by Kolakowski's logic, defence of one of the other concepts of freedom which Marx's project contains must also constitute a legitimate and necessary development from Marx. I make no argument against the view that Marx's project contained within it the seeds of Leninism; such a proposition reveals little. That Marx's texts of 1848–52 were largely amenable to Lenin is an obvious and much-repeated point. Some go so far as to claim that Marx was a Leninist *avant la lettre*.[82] But that they caused Leninism, or made it inevitable, is not at all obvious. The opposite is just as true: Marx's work contained other important and non-Leninist seeds which Kautsky, for example, based his ideas upon. And Leninism also had roots in the Russian revolutionary tradition, the Russian conditions it had to face, as well as the effects, both moral and physical, of the First World War. The solutions to the problems of Marx's project, if there be solutions, must be found by openly confronting the problems.

To assess the continuity, or otherwise, of theory, policy, and implementation, as the problem of the relationship between Marx's project and Soviet authoritarianism suggests we must, is a complex and difficult task. Barrington Moore Jr. has written by analogy: 'one cannot put the Roman Empire in a test tube, add a little Christianity, and watch whether it declines and falls'.[83] Between Marx and the Soviet state were a number of significant mediators, among which were the European Marxists including Engels, and the Russian Marxists including Lenin, as well as the circumstances attending the Revolution: notably the effects of the First World War and Russia's industrial and general economic backwardness. I have tried to limit the problems involved by discounting the importance of Russian conditions in determining the fundamental features of

Soviet authoritarianism. Further, I shall examine only the concept of the transition to socialism, particularly the roles of liberal democracy and dictatorship within it, as it was discussed and debated in the Marxist tradition, from Marx to Lenin. We can move toward resolving our problem by studying the development of a theme in Marxist thought.

The absence of liberal democracy in the Soviet state almost from its inception (when it was not so much the lack of desire, but the tenuous ability to enforce their dictatorship which compelled Bolshevik toleration of opposition) is a major part of that obstacle to communism faced by communists today, and for which Eurocommunism was one response. It is also the area over which there is a continuous tradition of criticism. That Marx's project will culminate in a dictatorial, oppressive state is a criticism which dogged Marx and Lenin, and which continues growlingly to pursue present-day Marxists. Finally, the question of liberal democracy and dictatorship is one which can, from the viewpoint of implementation, be fairly quickly and easily assessed. By liberal democracy I mean, essentially, the political organization of society which embodies and guarantees the right to opposition, combined with a commitment to democratic leadership which is representative and accountable. By itself, democracy is an inadequate term of reference for, as John Dunn has pointed out, today everyone is a democrat:

Democratic theory is the public cant of the modern world; and cant is the verbal medium of hypocrisy; and hypocrisy is the tribute which vice pays to virtue. All states today profess to be democracies because a democracy is what it is virtuous for a state to be.[84]

If it is difficult to determine how representative of the people's will a political system may be, it is easier to assess the level of civil liberties which obtain. How does the Marxist tradition, from Marx to Lenin, respond to the right to opposition: within the transition to socialism, and under socialism itself? By dictatorship I mean the arbitrary authority of a single political force. Is this the logical outcome of Marx's project?

I have argued above that until at least the end of 1918 the Soviet state in its basic political features represented an outcome consistent with Lenin's theory, specifically with Lenin's theory of the dictatorship of the proletariat. As a theorist Lenin must be taken seriously, if cautiously. Lenin's theory, or theories, are on the whole a reliable guide to his practice. Thus the question of the relationship between Marx's project and the Soviet state is here reformulated as the question of the relationship between Marx's conceptions of the roles of liberal democracy and dictatorship in the transition to socialism, and Lenin's conceptions of these roles as embodied in the theory and practice of the October Revolution and its immediate aftermath. If Lenin, more than anyone else, represents the influence of an interpretation of Marx's project upon Russia, what was the quality of his interpretation? We must be wary of attempts to turn the Soviet regime under Lenin into a 'golden age'. It is no defence of Leninism to say that in the early years of the Soviet regime the Cheka or the revolutionary courts may not have acted within the principles of liberal democracy, but they at least, with a few unfortunate exceptions, shot the right people. No doubt Lenin's rule operated within the bounds of a sort of primitive and summary justice, but as the basis of a system it was open from the first to arbitrariness and manipulation. The real issue is about the system established by Lenin, and the place that system accorded to opposition.

I shall examine those areas of Marx's work which relate directly to the question of the state and its transcendence, to discover the problems which fuelled the discussions about the transition to socialism among Marxists. Engels' idea of the proletarian dictatorship will be examined separately, as well as the contribution of the Revisionist controversy within German Social Democracy. All contributed directly to Lenin's political education. But Lenin received some of his first political lessons in the Russian revolutionary tradition. I shall also examine whether, and to what extent, traditional ideas were reflected in Lenin's conception of the transition. The study ends with the articulation of two competing Marxist conceptions of the transition to socialism, those of Lenin and Kautsky. Marx had bequeathed a crucial problem to his disciples, the importance of which even he seemed unaware. Stojanovic declares that

the growth of revolutionary dictatorship into socialist democracy is not simply one of the problems of socialism; it is *the problem of socialism*.[85]

Schumpeter wrote earlier in this connection:

Socialism in being might be the very ideal of democracy. But socialists are not always so particular about the way in which it is to be brought into being.[86]

Can Marx's principles clarify the two essential problems of the identity of the revolutionary power, and the identity of its post-revolutionary form?

What are the historical and theoretical links between two figures of whom Schapiro has written that

the difference of doctrine between Lenin in practice and Marx in theory is at any rate sufficient to raise serious doubt whether the political doctrines of the two men were really one and the same.[87]

How substantial were these differences, and how could this doubt be substantiated? This study seeks to contribute to the answering of these questions.

2

MARX AND THE TRANSITION TO SOCIALISM

I propose in this chapter to examine Marx's notion of the transition to socialism, particularly his concept of the 'dictatorship of the proletariat', to answer what is perhaps the most fundamental question that must be asked of it in the context of this study: does the transition allow for the existence of opposition and the protection of opposition rights? The major obstacle to this task is that Marx was never clear about the constitution of his 'transition', and was sometimes even evasive about it. Characteristically, Marx was long on criticism and short on precise remedies, for what he thought were good reasons. Marx's project was formed at a time when detailed, and sometimes fantastic, plans for harmonious communities were being proposed by socialists such as Fourier and Cabet. Marx determined to avoid such a method. As he wrote many years later in the only volume of *Capital* he completed, he had always refused to write 'receipts ... for the cook-shops of the future'.[1] In itself, Marx's commitment reveals a good deal about his project and its implementation, and it will be examined later. But it also relieved him from being specific and detailed on those very points on which his followers most needed direction. Marx's contemporary critics, particularly the anarchists, were never mollified, for he refused to answer them directly. In the face of his general reticence we must attend to the context of his writings on the 'transition', and to the context of the 'transition' itself.

Much of the early criticism of Marx's project, by socialists and anarchists, was bound up with suggestions of improper personal ambitions: Marx's project was seen by many as Marx's vehicle to power. Mikhail Bakunin, the Russian anarchist who became Marx's chief rival in the International Working Men's Association (IWMA), for example, detested Marx, believing that 'As a German and a Jew he is authoritarian from head to heels.'[2] Elsewhere he wrote:

Marx will never forgive a slight to his person. You must worship him, make an idol of him, if he is to love you in return; you must at least fear him, if he is to tolerate you. He likes to surround himself with pygmies, with lackeys and flatterers.[3]

Marx reciprocated, charging that Bakunin himself had dictatorial ambitions within the IWMA:

Bakunin represents *le collectivisme anarchique*. The anarchy is indeed in his head, wherein there is room for only one clear idea, that Bakunin must play first fiddle.[4]

Quite apart from the question of the veracity of these charges, it must be acknowledged that intra-socialist criticism of this period, and perhaps even until today, was often of this type. But there is further evidence against Marx, adduced by scholars as well as scatologists. Karl Vogt, a socialist and contemporary of Marx, in a polemic against him cited a letter from a Lieutenant Techow, an exile from continental Europe after the failures of the 1848 Revolutions. On the basis of a conversation with a drunken Marx, Techow had 'gained the impression that his [Marx's] personal domination is the aim of all his activities'.[5] In 1853 a police agent reported that

Marx is jealous of his authority as head of the Party; he is vengeful and implacable towards his political rivals and opponents; he does not rest until he has brought them low; his dominant characteristic is a boundless ambition and desire for domination.[6]

Although the 'impartial observer' seems impossible to find, one might readily concede that, despite some notable diplomacy in the IWMA, Marx was a difficult and imperious man. He pursued Herr Vogt, for example, to inordinate lengths.[7] But this is not simply a point about Marx's personality, for as I argued above Marx's personal motives and intentions are not relevant to the assessment of his responsibility for Leninism and its Soviet consequences. Marx was a curious potential dictator indeed: nowhere does his project endorse the pre-eminent role of any individual; nor did he ever seek to translate his leading role (i.e., his exercise of intellectual authority) in organizations such as the IWMA into a programmatic postulate; nor did he continually seek to foster organizations in which his will would be primary. Marx was a potential dictator, if we can assume so much from certain disagreeable traits, in spite of his project. Like many an intellectual convinced of the correctness of his views, he was intolerant of others'.

The obvious foil to Marx was Ferdinand Lassalle, the first successful organizer of the German workers' movement. Marx wrote to Engels in 1863, with considerable justice, that Lassalle 'behaves ... altogether like a future labour dictator'.[8] Lassalle himself corroborated this obervation. Demanding the presidency of the General German Workers' Association, he explained his requirements thus: 'Whoever is President, his powers must be dictatorial. Otherwise nothing will get done. We can leave mass talking to the bourgeois.'[9] In June 1863 he described the statutes of the Association to the German Chancellor Bismarck as

the constitution of my kingdom which perhaps you will envy me! But this miniature will be enough to show how true it is that the working class is intrinsically inclined to dictatorship if it feels that such will be exercised in working-class interests.[10]

The real dictator betrays himself too easily, if 'betray' is the appropriate term for one who had so little respect for the political abilities and potential of the working class. Bismarck recalled in 1878 that Lassalle, with whom he had had some discussions,

was ambitious, on a large scale, and there is perhaps room for doubt as to whether, in his eyes, the German Empire ultimately entailed the Hohenzollern or the Lassalle dynasty.[11]

Lassalle had his own role mapped out. With the advent of universal suffrage, for which he worked, working-class representatives could vie with representatives of the wealthy class in a parliament. When universal suffrage comes, he promised the working class,

you can depend upon it, there will be at your side men who understand your position and are devoted to your cause – men, armed with the shining sword of science, who know how to defend your interests. And then you, the unpropertied classes, will have only yourselves to blame if the representatives of your class remain in a minority.[12]

For Lassalle, the task of emancipation was not the task of the workers themselves, but of their representatives – educated men such as Lassalle himself. Can these representatives be held accountable to the working class, whose interests they purport to represent, if the working class does not, and perhaps cannot (who can put a limit to Lassalle's contempt for working-class abilities?), know and defend its true interests?

Lassalle was a statist. He believed that the state could be a neutral umpire in the contest between classes, and that universal suffrage would ultimately produce a microcosm of society in a parliament. He conceived the rule of working-class interests through a state. Marx opposed him not only, although at the time it seemed primarily, because of his dissemination of the theory of the 'iron law of wages', but also because of this statism. Marx was considered in turn, by P.-J. Proudhon and Bakunin, as a statist. Both of these critics, while they displayed concern or irritation over Marx's personality, were primarily concerned that his project, and indeed any communist project, would create a new system of oppression because it relied on the existence of a post-revolutionary state. They believed that the continued existence of any state was inherently authoritarian, for the state, whatever its political form, was simply organized coercion against the ruled. So-called representatives of the working class in a socialist state would, of necessity, become detached from their class, and the old authoritarian relationship between rulers and ruled would be re-established. The state was ineradicably evil. It highlighted rulers' authoritarian characteristics and corrupted their most democratic characteristics. Where Marx saw a danger in Lassalle's paternalism, operating through and reinforced by his proposed control of the state, anarchists believed that Marx's project, whatever its attitude towards the working class, would end in the tyranny of a 'workers' state'.

Even had Marx been a statist, as they claimed, the anarchists' critique of the state as necessarily authoritarian is not convincing. Their conception that all states are resolved into rulers and ruled is superficial; their conception that all relations between rules and ruled are authoritarian is absurd. The anarchists cannot accept that one man may be able to have a legitimate authority over another. Bakunin, however, accepted the authority of 'science' over man. He did not question whether Marx had founded a science of society and history. But he objected that if Marx had discovered the natural laws of history, why would a state be needed to enforce them after a revolution made in accordance with them?

The liberty of man consists solely in this: that he obeys natural laws because he has *himself* recognized them as such, and not because they have been externally imposed upon him by any extrinsic will whatever, divine or human, collective or individual.[13]

Bakunin opposed the Marxists as statists, not as scientists.

The government of science and of men of science ... cannot fail to be impotent, ridiculous, inhuman, cruel, oppressive, exploiting, maleficent.[14]

Both Proudhon and Bakunin believed, in the words of Proudhon, that communism was 'the exaltation of the State, the glorification of the police'.[15]

Marx's relations with Proudhon and Bakunin were, generally, not happy or fruitful ones. Proudhon, who in the 1840s was one of the best-known French socialists, even if his political influence began to thrive in wider circles only after his death in 1865, was asked by Marx to join and contribute to an international association to link European socialists by regular correspondence. 'In this way', Marx wrote in May 1846, 'differences of opinion will come to light; ideas will be exchanged and impartial criticism arrived at.'[16] Proudhon replied that although he would cooperate, his contribution would be limited by other commitments. He then charged Marx with attempting to establish his own socialist dogma:

Let us set the world an example of wise and farsighted tolerance. Let us not set ourselves up as the apostles of a new religion, even if it be the religion of logic or of reason.[17]

For the postscript to Marx's invitation was a sharp attack on the German 'true socialist' Karl Grün, with whom Proudhon was at that time associated. Not written by Marx, but presumably with his knowledge and assent, it evinced the very opposite of Marx's declared intentions. Proudhon's reply effectively ended direct contact between them. The next year Marx made a sustained, but ineffective, attack upon Proudhon's reputation in his *Poverty of Philosophy*, a 'reply' to Proudhon's recent (1846) *Système des contradictions économiques, ou Philosophie de la misère*.

Bakunin, unlike Proudhon, mounted a direct political challenge to Marx in the IWMA. Marx considered Proudhon's followers in the

IWMA merely a nuisance; he engineered its destruction so that it might not fall into the hands of Bakunin. Bakunin resented Marx's influence over the General Council of the IWMA. He charged that the International had become divided: 'the majority as blind tools and the minority of learned savants who do all the directing'.[18] Having entered the International with his supporters, Bakunin sponsored the 1872 Sonvillier Circular which declared that the IWMA had been turned 'into a hierarchical and authoritarian organization'.[19] He was expelled from it at the 1872 Hague Congress. The General Council, on Marx's initiative, was removed from London to New York, where it effectively perished. Marx resented Bakunin's growing influence within the International, particularly within the Spanish and Italian sections. He realized that his influence over the International's leadership was tenuous and insecure:

Their [the Bakuninists] announced watchword is that Pan-Germanism (i.e., Bismarckism) dominates the General Council. This, of course, is a reference to the unforgivable fact that I am a German by birth and exercise a decisive intellectual influence on the General Council.[20]

He could also be tolerant and accommodating when the situation warranted it. Indeed, the diverse coalition which was the IWMA often demanded it of him, and Marx believed often warranted it. For the IWMA was revolutionary, sometimes despite itself, according to Marx. To a request by the Bakuninists to enter the International Marx was magnanimous:

The General Council replied: It is not its function to sit in theoretical judgement on the programmes of the various sections. Its only task is to see to it that the latter are *not in direct contradiction with its Statutes and their Spirit.*[21]

His later implacable hostility towards the Bakuninists, although in some measure to be explained by the campaign against him, raised nevertheless the spectre of dogmatism.

In 1843 Marx had protested against dogmatism:

we do not confront the world in a doctrinaire way with a new principle: Here is the truth, kneel down before it! We develop new principles for the world out of the world's own principles.[22]

But he himself was ambivalent about the status of his theoretical project: did the real movement of the working class embody Marx's project; or did it have to adopt his project? The relationship between his project and the working-class movement, between theorists and leaders and the mass of the movement, was neither clearly formulated nor resolved. In his *Poverty of Philosophy*, Marx argued that when the proletariat had constituted itself as a class, and when its struggle was clear, socialist theorists move from being mere utopians who 'improvise systems and go in search of a regenerating science' to become the 'mouthpiece' of the proletariat's struggle.[23] G. D. H. Cole summarized Marx's ambivalence within the IWMA:

Marx had indeed insisted, in the earlier years of the First International, on the need for building on actual movements rather than constructing a dogma into which movements were then required to fit. But when the actual movements took forms which he disliked, as they largely did in Spain and Italy, in Germany under Lassalle's influence, and in Great Britain as soon as the Trade Unions' most immediate demands had been met, he was apt to forget his own precepts and to become the grand inquisitor into heretical misdeeds.[24]

Marx responded, more theoretically, to both Proudhon's and Bakunin's charges against his project. In his *Poverty of Philosophy*, Marx denied that his project would result in a new class domination or a new state domination. In 1875, in his private notes on Bakunin's *Statism and Anarchy*, Marx made a similar denial. But this is to anticipate. For Proudhon, Marx was just another communist, just another statist, representing all the dangers he believed that position entailed. We shall see first how Marx responded to Proudhon's charges, and from this base reconstruct Marx's conception of the state under socialism and during the transition to socialism. From the transition we shall return to Marx's response to Bakunin to see whether, with the passing of almost three decades from his reply to Proudhon, he had ultimately a compelling case against the interpretation of his project as tyrannical.

Marx replied only briefly to Proudhon's charges in his *Poverty of Philosophy*. 'After the fall of the old society', Marx asked directly, will 'there ... be a new class domination culminating in a new political power? No.'[25] The state, according to Marx, is a political power, that is, a power which expresses the division of civil society into classes and the struggle between those classes. But Marx's socialism was a classless society. Hence there was no need, or basis, for a state. Marx's *Poverty of Philosophy* is significant as the first public presentation of what became known as the 'materialist conception of history',[26] which he and Engels had first formulated around 1845. It stressed the (antagonistic) class character of capitalism; it stressed that the development of capitalism was bound up with the development of classes; and it stressed that the working class would introduce socialism, which would be classless. If some of these points were only dimly perceived by Marx's socialist contemporaries, his stress upon them was unique. Class analysis emerged and began to flourish after the 1830 Revolution in France. But socialism, which grew with it, was at first committed to the union of classes in their common interest until, and sometimes still in spite of, the bourgeoisie's determined resistance to it. The socialists' quandry was how to preserve the goal of a united and fundamentally harmonious society, how to preserve their universal goal, while finding support almost solely among the working class. How could socialism avoid becoming the banner for particular, that is selfish, interests, which socialists had decried as the source of society's ills? Marx resolved this dilemma (to his own satisfaction, at least) in his Introduction to the *Contribution to the Critique of Hegel's Philosophy of Law*, first published in the 1844, and only, edition of the *Deutsch–französische Jahrbücher*. Here he identified the 'proletariat' as the 'universal class', embodying society's true (i.e., universal) interest. It was Marx who laid the theoretical foundation for socialism to become an unashamedly working-class movement and project.

Thus did Marx stress the inherently class-oriented nature of all discussions about socialism as a protest against capitalism and as a goal in his *Poverty of Philosophy*. In bourgeois society, he declares, the mass of people have become workers, and these workers form a class.

The domination of capital has created for this mass [of workers] a common situation, common interests. This mass is thus already a class as against capital, but not yet for itself. In the struggle ... this mass becomes united, and constitutes itself as a class for itself. The interests it defends become class interests.[27]

Marx's concept of 'class' is resolved into two aspects: the class in itself (*an sich*), the class defined by its objective position in the process of production; and the class for itself (*für sich*), the same class, but defined now by its self-consciousness, and thus by its revolutionary, anti-capitalist, bearing. It is the working class itself which will make the socialist revolution and the socialist society. In the proletariat's self-emancipation, the role of socialists and communists ('the theoreticians of the proletarian class')[28] becomes redundant, or they become simply the proletariat's 'mouthpiece', as class consciousness is achieved. Furthermore, Marx does not accede, and never acceded, to the anarchist programme for a state-less society, except in a superficial sense. Marx wrote:

The working class, in the course of its development, will substitute for the old civil society an association which will exclude classes and their antagonism, and there will be no more political power *properly so-called*, since political power is precisely the official expression of antagonism in civil society.[29]

Marx's socialism was state-less only in so far as the state was an expression of class society. Marx did not share the anarchists' indiscriminate prejudice against leadership. His conception of socialism had a place for leadership, authority, and for 'politics' in a non-class sense. In the *Manifesto of the Communist Party*, first published in early 1848, he wrote that under socialism 'the public power will lose its political character',[30] meaning its class character. But a public power would remain. Why and how this is significant will become clear as we pursue Marx's concept of the transition to socialism, a concept which, until the *Manifesto*, he had nowhere discussed.

The imminence (and for Marx the immanence) of the 1848 Revolutions compelled Marx to consider closely the practicalities of his project and its implementation. In the *Manifesto of the Communist Party* he raised, *inter alia*, two important issues: the question of leadership, or the relations between proletarians and communists; and the question of the transition to socialism, or the first steps of the socialist revolution. As for the communists, they are

on the one hand, practically, the [most advanced and] resolute section of the working-class parties of every country, that section which pushes forward all others; on the other hand, theoretically, they have over the great mass of the proletariat the advantage of clearly understanding the line of march, the conditions, and the ultimate general results of the proletarian movement.[31]

Marx recognized that the working class contained within itself different degrees of class consciousness. Although he believed that the development of the class 'for itself' was ineluctable, having described its various stages in the *Poverty of Philosophy*, Marx now pointed out the role which class-conscious workers must play in this development. Their 'immediate aim' is the 'formation of the proletariat into a class'.[32] Meanwhile, they were representative of the interests of the working-class movement as a whole. But it was only on the basis of Marx's conviction that working-class rule was historically necessary that the communists were representative; they were not elected, nor were they (at least immediately) accountable to the working class. Marx was sure that they would be confirmed as representative once the class 'for itself' was formed. Nevertheless, it was a type of representation which raised novel problems. Chief among these is the question of the extent to which communists can take decisions for and act on behalf of the working class. Perhaps Marx never formulated the question; he certainly never answered it. Yet his remarks on conspirators and conspiracies, which we shall examine later, reveal his hostility towards substitution for the working class. If they are its representatives, the communists are not the working class.

Marx recognized also that socialism would not simply appear on the morrow of the revolution. Rather, there was a number of transitional steps to socialism:

the first step in the revolution by the working class is to raise the proletariat to the position of ruling class, to win the battle of democracy. The proletariat will use its political supremacy to wrest, by degrees, all capital from the bourgeoisie, to centralise all instruments of production in the hands of the State, *i.e.*, of the proletariat organised as the ruling class; and to increase the total of productive forces as rapidly as possible.[33]

Marx adds a rather moderate, ten-point plan designed to begin the proletariat's 'despotic inroads on the rights of property'.[34] The central concept here is undoubtedly the proletariat 'as a ruling class'. What does it mean? Marx offers two definitions, or two aspects of a definition: first, the winning of the 'battle of democracy'; and second, the control of 'the State'. Marx argued, in the *Manifesto*, that the proletarian movement was a movement of 'the immense majority',[35] even though the working class was in no country a majority. On the basis of universal (manhood) suffrage which Marx, like many other socialists, supported, he believed that the representatives of the proletariat would naturally constitute a parliamentary majority in the advanced European countries. Engels' draft of the *Manifesto*, the *Principles of Communism*, was less mysterious about the 'battle of democracy', and more realistic about its outcome, than the *Manifesto* itself:

In the first place it [the revolution] will inaugurate a *democratic constitution* and thereby, directly or indirectly, the political rule of the proletariat. Directly in England, where the proletariat already constitutes the majority of the population [*sic*]. Indirectly in France and in Germany.... Democracy would be quite useless to the proletariat if it were not immediately used as a means of carrying through further measures directly attacking private ownership and securing the means of subsistence of the proletariat.[36]

Engels appears to have considered democracy as a stage in the development of communism, as the transition period itself. Elsewhere in 1847 he had argued that 'The industrial proletariat ... has become the vanguard of all modern democracy',[37] and that the communists 'for the time being ... take the field as democrats'.[38] For Engels believed that in Europe, 'democracy has as its necessary consequence the political rule of the proletariat',[39] and thus the transition to communism. Even in *The German Ideology* Engels had referred obliquely to the revolutionary and working-class potential of democracy:

the struggle between democracy, aristocracy, and monarchy, the struggle for the franchise, etc., etc., are merely the illusory forms ... in which the real struggles of the different classes are fought out among one another.[40]

The demand for universal manhood suffrage was indeed a radical one, having been taken up by the Chartists, among others. Universal manhood suffrage was untried, and was feared as much by conservatives as it was savoured in anticipation by radicals. In the event, the operation of universal suffrage in France in December 1848 returned a conservative government, although it was not simply the result of a preponderance of peasants.

The 'battle of democracy' in which Marx trusted seems unlikely to have been won by the proletariat in 1848: not simply on account of its lack of numbers, but also because the proletariat had not yet fully recognized its distinct class interests. The revolutionary appeal and application of the *Communist Manifesto* remained unimpaired, incidentally, because of its careful confusion of tenses. The first of its new editions, in 1872 after Marx had achieved a certain notoriety because of the Paris Commune, contained few changes of substance. But would success in the 'battle of democracy' have meant that the proletariat was in control of the state? Did Marx and Engels both assume that the existing state, working in the interests of the bourgeoisie, could be taken over by the proletariat (primarily through the mechanism of universal suffrage) and used to implement the proletariat's economic programme? Did they discount the idea of bourgeois resistance, or its effect upon a democratic transition to communism?

Two important aspects of the transition to socialism are adumbrated in the *Manifesto*. The first, about which there is more, and which is clearer, than the second, is the economic tasks of the transition: the centralization of the means of production and credit in the hands of the state; abolition of the right of inheritance, and of property in land; a heavy, progressive income tax; and so on. The second aspect is the political task of the transition: the political supremacy of the proletariat through winning the 'battle of democracy'; and the gradual transcendence of 'politics' in its class-struggle sense and context. Marx fails to discuss the defence of the gains of the revolution against the dispossessed bourgeoisie; he fails to discuss the dangers of the state organization itself for the transition, and relies instead on an instrumental notion of the state; and he fails to give any idea of the duration of the transition period. Even so, within those aspects of the transition that are discussed, there seems to be a conflict between the strengthening of the state, the class instrument of the proletariat in its struggle to reorganize the economy, and the disappearance of the state as a class instrument. On the one hand the class features of the state are strengthened; on the other hand its class features are progressively diminished. How could these imperatives be achieved at the same time?

The 1848 Revolutions destroyed whatever lingering hopes socialists had harboured about the basic good-will of the bourgeoisie towards the workers' plight and ambitions. From 1830 many socialists had appealed to the bourgeoisie to show the way to socialism; the idea of a fundamental antagonism between classes, if not unique to Marx, found its most consistent and forceful advocate in him. The socialists were progressively embittered and disillusioned by a bellicose bourgeoisie. The June Days of 1848 in Paris, when a workers' uprising was bloodily suppressed, were a turning-point for socialism. Marx claimed to have been vindicated; other socialists began to adopt his position on class antagonism. But even Marx seemed surprised by the brutality of the bourgeoisie's response to the workers' demands (which were not preponderantly socialistic). In his reflections on the 1848 Revolutions, Marx drew the lesson that the proletarian revolution needed to defend itself against the flowering of self-interest it would encourage amongst the bourgeoisie, and its blossom of violence. He argued that the proletariat's victory must lead to a dictatorship of the proletariat.

The concept of the 'dictatorship of the proletariat' is crucial for this study. For it was the concept which Lenin used to justify Soviet authoritarianism. We must try to determine what Marx meant by it, as well as (later) what interpretation Lenin gave to it. If it was, for Marx, a 'model' of the transition to socialism, was it a complete model, or was it the only model of the transition he held? Some scholars attach little importance to the role which the concept of 'the dictatorship' plays within the corpus of Marx's thought,[41] while others, such as Ralph Miliband, argue that it was 'a concept to which Marx attached supreme importance', yet paradoxically, one 'which he never defined in any detail',[42] and rarely used. Miliband's assessment of its importance seems to me the more just; his appreciation of some of the problems involved in determining its meaning is well-founded. Despite these problems, and because of them, we can only construct a conception of the dictatorship of the proletariat which is plausible, not indubitable.

Marx's use of the concept 'dictatorship of the proletariat', its frequency and its contexts, have already been studied in some detail by Draper,[43] used by Wolfe,[44] and amplified by R. N. Hunt.[45] I see no need to follow these familiar and generally accepted paths. But their major points should be noted. Marx or Engels, it has been established, used the expression 'dictatorship of the proletariat' in three different, but distinct, periods of their careers: in the 1850–2 period; in the 1872–5 period; and in the 1890–1 period, which Draper characterizes as an 'echo' of 1875.[46] The term 'dictatorship', as our three authors above point out, has its origins in the *dictatura* of the Roman Republic, which designated a constitutionally envisaged, temporary, emergency regime summoned primarily for the purpose of military defence. Wolfe claims that the *dictatura*/dictatorship corresponds properly 'to the modern institutions of temporary *state of siege*, proclamation of *martial law* in a distress area, or some other form of *crisis-and-emergency government*'.[47] Dictatorship, Draper adds, only assumed its present meaning – arbitrary rule, or rule without legal constraints – in the decade following the First World War.[48]

As much as it might be suggested, however, it does not follow that 'dictatorship', when used in the nineteenth century, retained the meaning and connotations of the Roman *dictatura*. Even though Robespierre tried to legitimate his 'revolutionary dictatorship' by reference to the *dictatura*,[49] fundamental differences remain between his (and Marx's) conception of 'dictatorship' and the *dictatura*. In essence, the *dictatura* was a defensive institution, a voluntary closing of ranks in order to preserve society from the military threat which challenged its continued existence. The revolutionary dictatorship, whatever else it might be, is a constructive institution, dedicated to effecting change, which splits society rather than uniting it. The very novelty of the situation in which a revolutionary dictatorship arises (in the modern sense of 'revolutionary'), raises problems for a dictatorship which did not arise in the three centuries of the *dictatura* system. The Roman dictator could suspend laws, but he could not create new ones; when the *dictatura* was ended (that is, when the threat was over), he was accountable for his actions as dictator.[50] There seem to be no such guarantees against the abuse of a revolutionary dictatorship, which by its very nature is outside the scope of a constitution, instead of an integral part of one.

To shift the focus of the debate over the dictatorship of the proletariat to the etymology of 'dictatorship' clarifies very little; in fact, it raises more questions than it solves. Grant for a moment that the dictatorship of the proletariat is an emergency regime, a condition of martial law (which, tellingly, was not until recently the 'rule of law' in any recognizable sense): how will it be constituted; who will make the decisions; against whom will the dictatorship's force be deployed; whence comes the threat? And assurances about the dictatorship's temporary status notwithstanding, how long must it last? Furthermore, he who suggests that the now-accepted meaning of 'dictatorship' arose only at the beginning of this century overlooks the ways in which Marx and Engels used the term which ring familiar, and fails to specify how different nineteenth-century usage was from twentieth-century usage. Not least of all, he fails to account for Marx's use of the expression: the 'dictatorship of the bourgeoisie'. If we attend more closely to the context of Marx's discussions of 'dictatorship', I believe that we can form a better idea of his meaning.

Marx first used the expression 'dictatorship of the proletariat' in his articles, written between January and November 1850, which were collected as *The Class Struggles in France*. The 1848 Revolutions stimulated both Marx and Engels to record numerous dictatorships in their, primarily journalistic, works of the period. Marx took the opportunity to draw this lesson:

> Every provisional political set-up following a revolution requires a dictatorship, and an energetic dictatorship at that. From the very beginning we blamed Camphausen for not having acted in a dictatorial manner, for not having immediately smashed up and removed the remains of the old institutions.[51]

Marx was not even recommending a proletarian dictatorship, for Camphausen was the (eventually deposed) leader of the Prussian liberal bourgeoisie. But was Marx recommending a bourgeois dictatorship? Before answering this question, let us examine further the uses of 'dictatorship'. Engels, in particular, used the term a number of times in this first period, in formulations such as 'military dictatorship',[52] and 'individual dictatorship'.[53]

The June 1848 insurrection by Paris workers signified, for Marx, a civil war between classes. In *The Class Struggles in France*, he reflected that 'doctrinaire Socialism', which tried to wish away the class struggle, was by-passed by the proletariat, which

> increasingly organizes itself around *revolutionary Socialism*, around *Communism*, for which the bourgeoisie itself has invented the name of *Blanqui*. This Socialism is the *declaration of the permanence of the revolution*, the *class dictatorship* of the proletariat as the necessary transit point to the *abolition of class distinctions generally*.[54]

That Marx waxes lyrical over what he considered the demise of other ('bourgeois' and 'petty bourgeois') socialisms is perhaps understandable. They had been exposed theoretically for neglecting the class antagonisms and class dynamics of modern society; and, according to Marx, they had been deserted by the proletariat. But that he should link (his) 'revolutionary Socialism' with the arch-conspirator of the nineteenth century, Auguste Blanqui, is curious.

Blanqui, it is interesting to note further, came in for none of that venomous criticism which Marx directed against other socialists and communists in the third section of the *Communist Manifesto*.[55] It was more curious still to place the 'class dictatorship of the proletariat' adjacent to the name of Blanqui. Certainly Blanqui, who is sometimes credited with originating the expression, did not use 'dictatorship of the proletariat' before 1850.[56] Indeed, it is uncertain whether he ever used it. What can Marx have meant? Is he inviting us to equate the dictatorship of the proletariat with Blanqui's conspiratorial methods and Blanqui's conceptions of a post-revolutionary dictatorship of the revolutionary elite? Although Marx and Blanqui never met, they had a high regard for each other; Marx even formed tactical alliances with the Blanquists during certain revolutionary periods.[57] The Blanquists formed one of the few revolutionary groups which Marx rarely criticized. Nevertheless, as we shall see, Marx was implacably opposed to conspiracy and the dictatorship of a revolutionary elite. Marx's reference to Blanqui in *The Class Struggles* remains a mystery. Perhaps Marx saw the name of Blanqui as the only consistently revolutionary banner in France during the 1848 Revolution towards which workers could be drawn (his own name was virtually unknown); and perhaps he believed that, having begun to struggle, the workers would quickly out-pace their conspiratorial leaders. But this is conjecture.

Elsewhere in *The Class Struggles in France*, Marx claims that during the June insurrection

there appeared the bold slogan of revolutionary struggle: *Overthrow of the bourgeoisie! Dictatorship of the working class!*[58]

He described the bourgeoisie's reaction to this insurrection as a 'bourgeois dictatorship'. After the June Days, Marx relates, there was formed a 'military dictatorship and a state of siege in Paris'.[59] Cavaignac, the leader of the repression, represented 'the dictatorship of the bourgeoisie by the sabre'.[60] Marx was not indifferent to the various forms of bourgeois rule, and his use of 'dictatorship' in this context signifies the bourgeoisie's repressive reaction against the proletariat.

Marx next used the concept of 'proletarian dictatorship' in the statutes of the Universal Society of Revolutionary Communists, drafted in April 1850, where it took its place as an aim of the

Society.[61] In June 1850, Marx wrote to the editor of the *Neue Deutsche Zeitung*, equating the '*rule and the dictatorship of the working class*',[62] and claiming that it was quite consistent with the abolition of class differences. He declared he had held the same position since at least his polemic against Proudhon, the *Poverty of Philosophy*, in 1847.[63] It was not the expression 'dictatorship', however, which perplexed the editor of the *Neue Deutsche Zeitung*; rather it was the idea that the rule of the working class would result in an end to classes. Marx's philosophical conception of the proletariat as the universal class, the genuine representative of society's interests, was not understood. Consequently, Marx defended the rule of the working class, but did not explain why he should describe that rule as a dictatorship. The last time Marx used the 'dictatorship' concept in this first period was in his well-known letter to Weydemeyer of 5 March 1852, in which Marx claims among his discoveries:

(2) that the class struggle necessarily leads to *the dictatorship of the proletariat*, (3) that this dictatorship itself only constitutes the transition to the *abolition of all classes* and to a *classless society*.[64]

Hunt claims that the phrase reappears here because Marx was prompted by the title to Weydemeyer's article in the New York *Turn-Zeitung* of 1 January 1852, 'The Dictatorship of the Proletariat', which he received a few days before he wrote this letter.[65]

It was almost twenty years before Marx revived the expression. In September 1871, he spoke of the necessity of a 'proletarian dictature' to end class rule.[66] Marx no doubt remembered the unnecessarily savage suppression of the Paris Commune a few months earlier. The Commune had been poorly organized for defence; its very existence as an amorphous body was possible only in the power vacuum created by French defeats in the Franco-Prussian War. For Marx this confirmed the lesson of the 1848 Revolutions: that the proletariat must expect armed retaliation by the bourgeoisie to its attempts for power. We shall examine later his qualification of this belief. Among the six uses of the expression 'the dictatorship of the proletariat' in the 1871–5 period, the most important (for later disputes and interpretations) is that contained in Marx's *Critique of the Gotha Programme* (April–May 1875):

Between capitalist and communist society lies the period of the revolutionary transformation of the one into the other. Corresponding to this is also a political transition period in which the state can be nothing but *the revolutionary dictatorship of the proletariat.*[67]

Engels made use of this source in the 1890–1 period. With the German Social Democratic Party (SPD) preparing a new Party programme, it seems likely that Engels re-read Marx's unpublished *Critique*, and revived the 'dictatorship' concept which it contained in a letter to C. Schmidt.[68] Karl Kautsky published the *Critique* in February 1891, with Engels' complicity, but the SPD's Reichstag deputies immediately dissociated themselves from it. Annoyed by their reaction, Engels included the offending expression in his twentieth-anniversary introduction to Marx's *Civil War in France*, written in the wake of the Paris Commune:

Of late, the Social-Democratic philistine has once more been filled with wholesome terror at the words: Dictatorship of the Proletariat. Well and good, gentlemen, do you want to know what this dictatorship looks like? Look at the Paris Commune. That was the Dictatorship of the Proletariat.[69]

Whether or not Engels calmed the SPD, his equation of the Paris Commune and the dictatorship of the proletariat has no direct support in Marx's works, and is an unwarranted liberty with Marx's concept of the dictatorship. Engels' final, and equally unwarranted, interpretation of the 'dictatorship of the proletariat' occurs in his critique of the SPD's draft programme of 1891:

If one thing is certain it is that our Party and the working class can only come to power under the form of a democratic republic. This is even the specific form for the dictatorship of the proletariat, as the Great French Revolution has already shown.[70]

Engels' problem is understandable. Faced with a growing social democratic movement which seemed likely to be soon confronting the question of power, he had to begin the very practical task of specifying immediate political tactics and objectives, while trying to keep the Social Democrats faithful to Marx's broad project. His advice, given the existence of universal (manhood) suffrage in the advanced European countries and the existence, in some, of parliaments which held real power seems, on the whole, quite sound if we recall his warnings to be alert to bourgeois resistance. But to claim

that the democratic republic is Marx's 'dictatorship of the proletariat' is illegitimate and perhaps unnecessary. For Marx's 'dictatorship' highlights that aspect of working-class rule, based on the
experience of 1848 and 1871, which Engels considered no longer
central: the defence of the proletarian revolution against bourgeois
resistance. In one sense, Engels reverts to (or perhaps he changed
little from) his position of 1847, when he argued that the proletarian
revolution would inaugurate a democratic constitution which
would lead to the rule of the working class directly where it was a
majority.[71]

Having briefly summarized the major uses of the concept 'dictatorship of the proletariat' by Marx (and Engels, although he cannot and
does not speak with Marx's authority), we must be more specific
about what Marx meant and did not mean by it. The obvious
difficulty, as pointed out above, is that Marx himself was never
specific about its organization and characteristics. A further difficulty is that we cannot simply assume Marx's consistency; we
cannot assume that when Marx used 'dictatorship' he always meant
the same thing. Should we accept Sartori's claim that 'dictatorship,
for Marx, was simply another word for "revolution", it only meant
the use of force'?[72] Or was the dictatorship of the proletariat
intended to denote the dictatorship of a revolutionary elite? Marx's
'relationship' with Blanqui, and the eventual use made of his concept
by Lenin, suggest such a question. But Marx consistently opposed
conspiracy and revolutionary elites. And commentators such as
Draper and Engels distinguish sharply between a Blanquist dictatorship and a class dictatorship. Engels wrote, for example:

Since Blanqui regards every revolution as a coup de main of a small
revolutionary minority, it automatically follows that its success must
inevitably be followed by the establishment of a dictatorship – not, it should
be well noted, of the entire revolutionary class, the proletariat, but of the
small number of those who accomplished the insurrection and who themselves are at first organized under the dictatorship of one or several
persons.[73]

But it is a distinction based on the breach of the rules of the 'class
dictatorship', rather than on their observance, for the real problem
of specifying those rules is not tackled.

Nevertheless, Marx spoke against conspiracy not only because of its elevation of a revolutionary elite, but because it ignored the objective historical determinants for socialism, factors closely united in Marx's view. Engels, in his *On the History of the Communist League* (1885), recalled that he and Marx had joined the League in the 1840s only after it had abandoned conspiracy.[74] Marx, in his *Revelations Concerning the Communist Trial in Cologne* (1853), dissociated himself and the Communist League from conspiracy.[75] In March 1850, Marx condemned conspirators for their neglect of organizing the proletariat, and helping it to develop:

It is precisely their business to anticipate the process of revolutionary development, to bring it artificially to crisis-point, to launch a revolution on the spur of the moment, without the conditions for a revolution. For them the only condition for revolution is the adequate preparation of their conspiracy. They are the alchemists of the revolution.[76]

Conspirators, he continued, were occupied entirely with incendiary bombs and the latest instruments of violence, and were contemptuous of the 'theoretical enlightenment of the proletariat about their class interests'.[77] Six months later, Marx made similar points against the Blanquists. For them,

the revolution is seen not as the product of realities of the situation but as the result of an effort of *will*. Whereas we say to the workers: You have 15, 20, 50 years of civil war to go through in order to alter the situation and to train yourselves for the exercise of power, it is said: We must take power *at once*, or else we may as well take to our beds.[78]

Marx's conception of the preconditions for the socialist revolution will be examined more closely later. For now it is enough to suggest that Marx believed that the transition to socialism had to be achieved by the workers themselves exercising power. If that is so, the problem of dictatorship remains: how will that power be organized. Some have argued that Marx's concept of 'dictatorship' gives us no precise description of the type of rule of the proletariat, since 'dictatorship' is synonymous with 'rule'. This, it is sometimes tacitly held, rescues Marx from the allegation that by 'dictatorship' he meant dictatorship, in the now accepted political sense. It attempts to rescue Marx from such claims as Kolakowski's, that 'there was nothing obviously wrong in taking the word "dictatorship" at its face value'.[79] Thus Hunt believes that Marx intended, whether he used 'dictatorship' or its synonym 'rule', 'a democratic governmental structure'.[80] But David McLellan argues, from a similar equation, that 'it is difficult to read any particular political implications into the term "dictatorship"'.[81] In both Hunt's and McLellan's works the result is the same: Marx is spared the responsibility for the authoritarian uses to which his 'dictatorship' concept was put. I too believe that Marx can be spared this responsibility; but it is not this simple.

There is no doubt a basis in Marx's works for the claim that 'dictatorship' is synonymous with 'rule'. Did we not see above that Marx equated the *'rule and the dictatorship of the working class'* in June 1850?[82] Shlomo Avineri presents the case for this equation clearly when he argues that the dictatorship of the proletariat represents the political power, that is, the class rule of the proletariat. His argument deserves extended quotation as the model of its type:

For Marx, every form of political power is class power, and thus dictatorial with regard to the other classes of society that do not share it. *Hence, every state, whatever its class-base, is dictatorial.* The political rule of the bourgeoisie is a dictatorship of the bourgeoisie even if it is cloaked in parliamentary garb, and, consequently, the political rule of the proletariat is *always* a dictatorship of the proletariat. Political rule *as such* is dictatorial, and therefore the ultimate aim of socialism is not merely to substitute the class rule of the proletariat for the class rule of the bourgeoisie, because in that case just one form of dictatorship would be replaced by another: the aim of communism is the *abolition* of political power *qua* political power, because all political power is dictatorial. ... 'Dictatorship' in this way as it is used by Marx refers directly to the class nature of political rule, not to the way in which any form of government is being carried out.[83]

There is a splendid and inexorable logic behind this well-expressed argument. It shifts the discussion away from that frankly annoying 'dictatorship' concept towards the issue of what political form (best?) corresponds to the political rule of the proletariat. If, as Avineri maintains, 'dictatorship' refers to the class nature of political rule, a class nature which in bourgeois society is based on private ownership of the means of production and which can coexist with political forms as diverse as parliaments and individual dictators, how can the class nature of the political rule of the proletariat be determined when the state owns the means of production, and what political form corresponds to it? Trotsky, for one, used a variant of

44

this argument (when in opposition) to call for the 'reintroduction' of Party and Soviet democracy: since the state owned the means of production, it could only be a true workers' state if the workers themselves were in control of the state, which they could be if the Party was more democratic and thus more representative of the workers. Trotsky will be examined, with Lenin, in chapter 6 below, but his intrusion here serves to illustrate the rather sterile debates about democracy that this approach to dictatorship leads to. Trotsky never renounced his defence of the rule of the Bolshevik Party over the Soviet state as democratic, for he believed that the Party under Lenin was (somehow) truly representative of the working masses' interests. Under Stalin, the Party changed. Freed of the Stalinist bureaucratic deformation, according to Trotsky, the Party would again (again somehow) be truly representative, and thus democratic. This explains why Trotsky, when he was not identifying with the Old Bolsheviks, for it was a cruel joke of history that this incarnation of the Party only joined it in 1917, stressed that Stalin had destroyed the Old Bolsheviks. The debates about the dictatorship of the proletariat, in other words, should not be debates about democracy, but about liberal democracy. Does Marx's dictatorship offer us any illumination on the question of the treatment of opposition?

Neither by appealing to the etymology of 'dictatorship', nor by equating 'dictatorship' with 'rule', can we reach a proper understanding of Marx's 'dictatorship of the proletariat' and, in particular, its response to the rights of opposition. But both of these positions contain an element of truth. To put it simply, Marx used the concept of 'dictatorship' in two, irreconcilable, ways. The first, what I would call the foundation, meaning is to be found in Marx's 1848 contention that 'Every provisional political set-up following a revolution requires a dictatorship.'[84] Marx would have had Camphausen set up a bourgeois dictatorship to protect the gains of the Revolution from the soon-triumphant reaction. The proletarian dictatorship must protect the gains of the proletarian revolution. The frenzied bourgeois response to the workers' demands and actions during the 1848 Revolutions (and following the 1871 Paris Commune), by which he was taken aback, was not lost upon Marx. And, it seems to me, this right of the socialist (or any) revolution to protect itself must be conceded, if one is a socialist, or any other type of revolutionary. The second, what I would call the spurious, meaning of dictatorship is to be found in Marx's characterization of bourgeois states as 'bourgeois dictatorships', and in the characterization of the transition to socialism as the 'proletarian dictatorship'. Why is this second meaning spurious? Quite simply because politics, in the non-class sense, is important to Marx and Marx's project; because Marx is not as crude an analyst of states as this concept of dictatorship would suggest; and because the transition to socialism in Marx's project is a complex one in which dictatorship plays only a small and an early role. I do not mean to imply that dictatorship in this second sense does not appear in Marx's work, for it obviously does; I mean to imply that logically it should not appear. Why this is so, I shall now explain.

Marx's theory of the state has long been a source of contention. In the opening pages of the *Communist Manifesto*, Marx declared that 'the *executive* of the modern state is but a committee for managing the common affairs of the whole bourgeoisie'.[85] The only other discussion of the state in the *Manifesto* is contained in section II, 'Proletarians and Communists', where Marx explains that the postrevolutionary state, 'the proletariat organized as the ruling class', must centralize the means of production, credit, and so forth. The problem of the state's executive is not confronted. It seems to be assumed that, with no modifications other than the introduction of democracy, the proletariat can use the state to fulfil its objectives. And if the proletariat as ruling class can use the state for universal ends, as Marx suggests and Avineri argues,[86] what is the purpose of the state's transcendence? For, as in his recent *Poverty of Philosophy*, Marx wrote in the *Manifesto* of the 'association' which would replace the state:

When, in the course of development, class distinctions have disappeared, and all production has been concentrated in the hands of a vast association of the whole nation, the public power will lose its political character. Political power, properly so called, is merely the organized power of one class for oppressing another.[87]

Marx thus argued in the *Manifesto* that the existing state must be used by the proletariat to implement its immediate objectives, which measures would destroy the basis for classes and thus for the state itself, as a class instrument.

In his evaluations of the 1848 Revolutions, by contrast, Marx sought to explain why universal suffrage had not produced working-class political power, and why the state bureaucracy had played such an important role in defending and ultimately in reconstituting the bourgeois *status quo*, by arguing that the state had a certain independence from all social classes. In the *Eighteenth Brumaire of Louis Bonaparte* (1852) in particular, Marx argued that 'This executive power with its enormous bureaucratic and military organization, with its extensive and artificial state machinery', this parasite on society, seemed under 'the second Bonaparte ... to have made itself completely independent'.[88] For on 2 December 1851 Louis Bonaparte, who had been elected as French President on 11 December 1848, led a coup against the parliamentary regime of the bourgeoisie. It was, according to Marx, the end of bourgeois rule[89] and the victory of the executive power.

Marx was well aware of the problem of bureaucracy as early as 1843. In his *Contribution to the Critique of Hegel's Philosophy of Law*, Marx argued that bureaucracy was based upon the modern division between state and civil society.[90] Bureaucracy had the state 'in its possession, as its private property';[91] in contrast to Hegel's conception, Marx considered the bureaucracy to be a particular interest, not the embodiment of the universal interest. The bureaucracy would be abolished, and real universality achieved, when the antithesis between state and civil society was overcome, when individuals ceased to separate the general interest from themselves as something alien and over-arching.[92] For Marx, the division between state and civil society was a 'modern' problem, completed only in France when the French Revolution transformed social differences, that is, differences within civil society, into differences without political significance.[93] Thus bureaucracy might logically appear to be a 'modern' problem as well. Yet Marx believed, in the 1840s, that bureaucracy was a particularly difficult problem only in Germany, and ironically because that country was not fully 'modern'. In *The German Ideology*, for example, Marx writes that

The independence of the state is only found nowadays in those countries where the estates have not yet completely developed into classes ... where consequently no section of the population can achieve dominance over the others. This is the case particularly in Germany.[94]

On this account, bureaucracy is a product of the incompleteness of the separation of civil and political spheres. This is confirmed later, when Marx ascribes the 'abnormal independence' acquired by the German bureaucracy to the impotence of the separate spheres of German social life '(one can speak here neither of estates nor of classes, but at most of former estates and classes not yet born)'.[95] Thus did the particular German ethos of the bureaucracy develop, an ethos reflected in Hegel's *Philosophy of Right*. Engels, in 1847, even attributed the power of the German bureaucracy to a compromise, or balancing, between the political forces of the nobility and the petty bourgeoisie.[96] Engels was only being consistent when he went on to argue that

From the moment the state administration and legislature fall under the control of the bourgeoisie, the independence of the bureaucracy ceases to exist.[97]

It may, therefore, have come as something of a surprise to Marx to see a bureaucracy flaunting its independence and power in 'modern' France: a country in which since 1830, he believed, the bourgeoisie had held political sway. Where one might previously have tried to reconcile Marx's views on bureaucracy by arguing that the existence of bureaucracy was a 'modern' problem (bound up with the existence of a modern, separate state), but its power was a product of the incompleteness of 'modern' development, this reconciliation would no longer do. Marx responded by adapting Engels' idea: the executive of the state could achieve a certain independence from classes only if the opposing powers of those classes were balanced, if the power of one cancelled out the power of the other. The question of the relations between the state and social classes, as Marx had conceded in 1844, was a complex one.[98]

Marx's 'reorientation' after the 1848 Revolutions, his inclusion of a recognition of the executive power as a force not to be neglected in considering the state, has fostered the idea that he operated with two theories of the state.[99] Miliband, for example, writes that Marx's view of the state up to about 1850 was that set down in the *Communist Manifesto*: the idea that the state was an instrument of the bourgeoisie, or the ruling class.

This is the classical Marxist view on the subject of the state, and it is the only one which is to be found in Marxism–Leninism. In regard to Marx himself, however ... it only constitutes what might be called a primary view of the state. For ... there is to be found another view of the state in his work, which it is inaccurate to hold up as of similar status with the first, but which is none the less of great interest.[100]

This 'second view' is that the state has a certain independence from social classes, and can in some instances dominate them. An interpretation of Marx which argues that these different theories of the state coexist within his work must face the difficulty, which John Plamenatz pointed out, that the two theories are incompatible. 'If the state is an instrument of class oppression', Plamenatz explained, 'then anything that rises superior to all classes is not a state.' But if the state 'is a parasite superior to all classes in society, there is no reason for supposing that when society becomes classless the state will disappear'.[101]

Nevertheless, there is a way to reconcile these apparently conflicting views of state, if we can establish that there is only one theory of the state in Marx's political philosophy, of which these two views are but expressions. Marx's ideas on the state and bureaucracy are to be found in his writings from at least 1842 and 1843. His only real excursion into political philosophy, the *Contribution to the Critique of Hegel's Philosophy of Law*, established motifs which recurred throughout his later writings, especially in relation to the concept of the state. This critique of Hegel by Marx identified a major weakness in Hegel's advocacy of constitutional monarchy. Marx intended, as he told Arnold Ruge in a letter of March 1842, to expose '*constitutional monarchy* as a hybrid which from beginning to end contradicts and abolishes itself'.[102] Marx effectively turned Hegel against himself primarily by clarifying and deepening the distinction between state and civil society, a distinction which Hegel had inherited from an eighteenth-century French tradition of political thought. Hegel, Marx insisted, had inverted the proper relationship between state and civil society: 'Family and civil society are the premises of the state',[103] not its products or '*spheres of the concept* of the state'.[104] According to Marx, Hegel had correctly described the modern separation of state and civil society and the hostility between these spheres,[105] but had nevertheless 'expounded it as a *necessary element of the idea*, as absolute rational truth'.[106] Marx rejected the necessity of this division:

The abstraction of the *state as such* belongs only to modern times, because the abstraction of private life belongs only to modern times.[107]

Marx's hostility to this division was based on the argument that modern man must 'effect a *fundamental division* within himself'[108] as a citizen of the state and a member of civil society. The political state is the separation of 'the *objective* essence of the human being from him as merely something *external*';[109] it is an illusory universality. Yet given this modern separation of state and civil society, and thus the end of the direct influence of property, wealth, religion, etc. in the political sphere, the notion of constitutional monarchy was a contradiction in at least the sense that primogeniture is 'the power of *abstract private property* over the *political state*',[110] that 'The political constitution at its highest point is . . . the *constitution of private property*.'[111]

The basic problem with Hegel's political philosophy lay not in his appreciation of the division between the state and civil society, itself a fruitful notion, but in his acceptance of the coexistence of particularity with universality. Hegel's civil society was a *bellum omnium contra omnes*, a sphere in which particularity reigned; over this stood the state, the sphere of universality. But genuine universality, logically, must consist in the abolition of particularity. The political state, Marx argued, is 'the *abstraction of civil society from itself*';[112] true universality consists in civil society raising itself to '*political* being as its true, general, essential mode of being'.[113] True universality, the true expression of man's essential nature, would mean the dissolution of the abstract political state and civil society.[114] Marx persisted in his view that the sham universality of the political state was asserted against the particularist elements of civil society, and that political emancipation – effectively the emancipation of the political state from civil society, the hallmark of 'modernity' – frees civil society from any directly political character,[115] even if it could not free man from the limitations of property, religion, etc.[116] True universality would be achieved by a human emancipation, by the abolition of the distinction between state and civil society.

For Marx, the modern state was an alienated expression of man's universal nature. A system that corresponded to man's nature was described by Marx as a 'true democracy', and the case for 'true democracy' was developed in his first critique of Hegel. Democracy, he declared,

is the solved *riddle* of all constitutions. Here, not merely *implicitly* and in essence but *existing* in reality, the constitution is constantly brought back to its actual basis, the *actual human being*, the *actual people*, and established as the people's *own* work. The constitution appears as what it is, a free product of man.[117]

In a democracy, Marx explains, the constitution and the law are acknowledged as human products; humans are not legal manifestations, created by the constitution. 'Only democracy ... is the true unity of the general and the particular.'[118] Yet despite Marx's declaration: 'Sovereignty of the monarch or sovereignty of the people – that is the question',[119] he is not, or not solely, a political democrat. He used the terms 'democracy' and 'true democracy' to denote the truly human society, man's universal community. This community might better be proclaimed the sovereignty of the human; in what relation it stood to the sovereignty of the people is a contentious question. Certainly, in his *Contribution to the Critique*, Marx envisaged nothing more outrageous than that elections unlimited 'both in the respect of the franchise and the right to be elected' would put an end to the distinction between man's competing civil and political roles:

Electoral reform within the *abstract political state* is therefore the demand for its *dissolution*, but also for the *dissolution of civil society*.[120]

But Marx differs profoundly from the conventional democrat, not only in that he rejects republicanism, but also in the fact that he rejects the idea of republican representation. To coin a phrase from Marx's rejection of 'crude communism' in the *Economic and Philosophic Manuscripts of 1844*, republicans are 'crude democrats', since:

The struggle between monarchy and republic is itself still a struggle within the abstract state. The *political* republic is democracy within the abstract state form.[121]

The true democrat, Marx argues, works for the 'true unity of the general and the particular',[122] not for the establishment of an abstract sphere of generality. Because the division between state and civil society will no longer exist, the true democrat is not delegated by civil society to represent general concerns (and hence really to represent particular interests), but is a representative by virtue of being human. 'He is here representative not because of something else which he represents but because of what he *is* and *does*.'[123] Universality becomes an essential quality of each individual.[124] The universal nature, or promise, of the state is thus fulfilled and the state itself is transcended (*Aufhebung*), as civil society is *Aufhebung* by raising itself to political being 'as its true, general, essential mode of being'.[125] Universality can only be realized when the institution of illusory universality, the state, is transcended.

Avineri argues that 'a close inspection of the *Critique* has shown that Marx arrived very early indeed – in the summer of 1843 – at his ultimate conclusion regarding the *Aufhebung des Staats*'.[126] This *Aufhebung* must involve the abolition of the bureaucracy.[127] Marx rejected Hegel's claim that the bureaucracy was the universal class, while retaining the notion that such a class was necessary to establish universality. In his Introduction to the *Contribution to the Critique of Hegel's Philosophy of Law*, first published in 1844, Marx identified this universal class as the proletariat. It had 'a universal character by its universal suffering'.[128] The proletariat would effect the transcendence of the state and civil society. Marx's *On the Jewish Question*, first published at the same time as the Introduction, clarified the position Marx had developed in his unpublished, and fragmentary, *Contribution to the Critique*. With the abolition of the property qualification for suffrage, Marx argues, goes the last '*political* form of giving recognition to private property'.[129] But property itself, and other distinctions of civil society, are not thereby abolished when the state abolishes their political recognition. Distinctions of birth, social rank, education and, of course, property, still

exert the influence of their *special* nature. Far from abolishing these *real* distinctions, the state only exists on the presupposition of their existence; it feels itself to be a *political state* and asserts its *universality* only in opposition to these elements of its being.[130]

The state is the illusory expression (or expression in fantasy, not reality) of man's true, political nature. Political emancipation in the abstract, alienated sense of 'political' is for Marx the last step towards real human emancipation possible within existing society. Human emancipation will be accomplished when man 'no longer separates social power from himself in the shape of *political* power'.[131] True democracy, or communism, will be accomplished when the distinctions within civil society itself, the basis for the reign of particular interests, are abolished.

With the benefit of these early texts, not widely known until only a few decades ago, we can see that Marx conceived of the state as an illusory universality, as the alienation of man's political nature from himself. The state, therefore, is an institutionalized form of man's alienation, just as capital, for example, is an alienated social relationship. For Marx, man was a political animal. Man's political nature was the foundation for universality, a distorted expression of which, the state, already existed. Marx believed that the state could be overcome 'by the general interest *actually* ... becoming the particular interest, which in turn is only possible as a result of the *particular* actually becoming the *general* interest'.[132] But if the dominant particular interest of civil society, the bourgeoisie, is defended by the state, the bureaucracy, the state apparatus itself, has a particular interest in perpetuating an alienated relationship between men of which it is the institutionalization. Marx's state is founded upon a class-divided society. It is this claim, rather than any notion of direct class influence on the state's operation, or the state's relative independence from this influence, which is central to Marx's conception of the state. Paul Thomas calls this conception 'the theory of alien politics'.[133] Marx's project was political emancipation, in the sense of emancipating politics from the state and returning it to man.

What are the implications for this study of Marx's conception of the state as a form of alienation? First, it indicates that Marx was sensitive to political forms: that not all rule, even if it was predominantly class rule, was dictatorship. Secondly, it indicates that Marx believed that a parliamentary democracy in a bourgeois state was the most complete form of 'alien politics', and therefore the prelude to the abolition of this alienation. And thirdly, it suggests that for Marx the transition to socialism must involve the reappropriation of politics, and thus the attempt to destroy the state's institutions. That Marx apprehended this last consequence, after having neglected it in the *Communist Manifesto*, is confirmed by his reactions to the 1848 Revolutions in *The Eighteenth Brumaire* and to the Paris Commune.

Writers such as Robert Tucker have argued that 'Marx's normative position with regard to the state was anarchism'.[134] This view misses the point that Marx, unlike the anarchists, believed the modern state to be a product of the relations between classes in civil society; it misconstrues Marx's aim of the *Aufhebung* of the state, which may be nominally similar to the anarchists' aim, but the product of which is a 'public power' which perhaps represents something akin to the classical Greek *polis*; and finally, it introduces an element of crude reductionism into Marx's political philosophy which was not there. Marx did not believe that the state was simply or primarily an instrument of force or coercion; nor did he believe that political forms such as parliamentary democracy were merely masks for this reality. This is not to deny that Marx saw an element of coercion in existing states, nor to deny that Marx conceived an element of coercion necessary during the transition of socialism. It is merely to deny that he saw coercion as the primary feature of states and their continued existence, and politics as a diversion. But when Marx decried the 'dictatorship of the bourgeoisie', and when he did not intend by it to describe the bourgeoisie's attempts to protect by force their material and political predominance, he fell prey to simple frustration. Marx generally realized that the modern state was a function of the existence of antagonistic classes, that the bourgeoisie's influence over the state was not necessarily political or direct, and that the notion of the bourgeoisie as the 'ruling class' was not entirely political, or state-related. His concrete historical investigations, particularly *The Eighteenth Brumaire*, bear out this interpretation. Even the *Communist Manifesto*, the *locus classicus* of the theory of the state as an instrument of the ruling class, despite its simplifications, is not simplistic. Marx argued that the bourgeoisie had 'conquered for itself, in the modern representative State, exclusive political sway'.[135] 'Political sway' in this context is ambiguous, but it seems simply to mean that the bourgeoisie faces no fundamental political and social challenge in the representative institutions of the modern state. The following sentence, furthermore, is carefully qualified: 'The *executive* of the modern State is but a committee for managing the *common* affairs of the *whole* bourgeoisie.'[136] But if there is a certain reduction in Marx's widespread use of terms such as 'bourgeois state' and 'bourgeois republic', it is not the same gross reduction of the worth of political forms Marx sometimes indulged in when he wrote of the 'dictatorship of the bourgeoisie'.

That Marx was aware of the possibilities which different political forms of the modern state allowed is evident from his 1872 speech at The Hague. The speech, which raised the issue of the peaceful transition to socialism, has been interpreted as a comment on the relative bureaucratization of modern states: the greater the degree of bureaucratization, the greater the amount of coercion needed to overthrow it.[137] I see it rather as a comment about the extent of suffrage, of sovereign representative government, and of the liberal tradition. Marx had said:

We know of the allowances we must make for the institutions, customs and traditions of the various countries such as America, England, and I would add Holland if I knew your institutions better, where the working people may achieve their goal by peaceful means. If that is true, we must also recognize that in most of the continental countries it is force that will have to be the lever of our revolutions.[138]

For Marx, England had long been a model of the possibility of universal suffrage yielding power to the class-conscious workers. In 1852 he declared:

Universal Suffrage is the equivalent for political power for the working class in England, where the proletariat forms the large majority of the population [*sic*], where, in a long, though underground civil war, it has gained a clear consciousness of its position as a class.... Its inevitable result, here, is the *political supremacy of the working class*.[139]

In 1880, Marx wrote similarly to Hyndman, a British labour leader and sometime follower, that 'if the unavoidable evolution turn into revolution, it would not only be the fault of the ruling classes, but also of the working class'.[140] In Germany, by contrast, he claimed that proletarians were 'fully aware from the beginning of their movement that you cannot get rid of a military despotism but by a Revolution'.[141] The same issue was raised in July 1871, when Marx informed a journalist that the IWMA did not fix strategies for its affiliates. In England, he explained, 'insurrection would be madness where peaceful agitation would more swiftly and surely do the work'.[142]

Marx's sensitivity to political forms is also revealed by the second implication of his conception of the state: that the modern political state was the most complete expression of man's universality alienated from him, and thus the prelude to man's reappropriation of his political nature. Until about 1845, Marx's project was unashamedly based in philosophy. Some of its major problems, such as the tension between freedom and determinism, arise from the translation of Marx's philosophical conception into a political programme. The materialist conception of history did not give rise to the problem of freedom versus determinism, it inherited it. Marx was committed to universality, understood as the unity of appearance and essence. One of the virtues of Epicurus, Marx argued in his *Doctoral Dissertation* (1838–40), was that he 'was the first to grasp appearance as appearance, that is, as alienation of the essence, activating itself in its reality as such an alienation'.[143] For Marx, alienation was the cause of a development which necessarily culminates in the unity of appearance and essence. As early as the *Dissertation*, he had held the world of men to be at odds with the essence of man. In succeeding years he isolated the division between state and civil society, and then the divisions within civil society itself, as forms of alienation. Although they were social divisions, they expressed a division between man and his universal essence. And as early as the *Dissertation*, Marx held that the achievement of universality required the active intervention of man: universality was at once logically necessary and inevitable, and yet contingent upon man (the 'party of the concept' in the *Dissertation*, which had become the 'proletariat' by 1844).

The importance of Marx's concept of alienation, however, is enhanced by its alliance with a historical (and perhaps logical) framework which posits that before alienation can be overcome it must be perfected. This perfection of alienation represents the clearest contrast between appearance and essence. In his *Economic and Philosophic Manuscripts of 1844*, Marx argued that industrial capital was 'the accomplished objective form of private property',[144] that is, of human self-estrangement. In *The German Ideology* of 1846, which he jointly authored with Engels, Marx repeated that under capitalism, alienation 'has assumed its sharpest and most universal form'.[145] He rephrased the point in the *Communist Manifesto*:

The bourgeoisie, wherever it has got the upper hand, has put an end to all feudal, patriarchal, idyllic relations. . . . In one word, for exploitation, veiled by religious and political illusions, it has substituted naked, shameless, direct, brutal exploitation.[146]

Thus, bourgeois society tears away the illusions from men's relations with each other, 'and man is at last compelled to face with sober senses, his real conditions of life, and his relations with his kind'.[147] Marx's conception of 'social class' itself, despite his occasional use of it in the generic sense of any major historical social grouping,[148] was intended to denote the most estranged social relation in which men can stand to each other. For 'class' 'assumes an independent existence as against individuals'.[149] And so it is in the political sphere. The modern representative state which, in the formal sense, isolates politics from the material factors of civil society, also clearly isolates man's essential, political being from his real life. Political emancipation, the clear division between state and civil society, between man as citizen and man as bourgeois, was, according to Marx, the prelude to human emancipation.

For these reasons, Marx paid great attention to the material and political preconditions of the socialist revolution. He emphatically rejected the idea that political will could create the conditions necessary for the abolition of capitalism, even if it could precipitate insurrection: insurrection is timeless. Marx declared:

The first direct attempts of the proletariat to attain its own ends, made in times of universal excitement, when feudal society was being overthrown, these attempts necessarily failed, owing to the then undeveloped state of the proletariat, as well as to the absence of the economic conditions for its emancipation, conditions that had yet to be produced, and could be produced by the impending bourgeois epoch alone.[150]

Marx's respect for the Jacobins was tempered by his appreciation that, for Robespierre, 'the principle of politics is the *will*'.[151] The perfection of the political mind, Marx argued, leads to its belief in the '*omnipotence* of the will' and to its corresponding blindness 'to the *natural* and spiritual *limits* of the will' and thus its blindness to the real source of social ills.[152] In *The German Ideology*, Marx had argued that

this development of the productive forces ... is an absolutely necessary practical premise [of communism], because without it privation, *want* is merely made general and with *want* the struggle for necessities would begin again, and all the old filthy business would necessarily be restored.[153]

In his speech to the September 1850 meeting of the Communist League, Marx made explicit his opposition to the premature seizure of power. We must tell the workers, he declared, that they have fifteen, twenty, or even fifty years of civil war ahead to train them for the exercise of power.[154] Karl Schapper, Marx's major opponent at this meeting, countered by claiming that 'if we come to power we can take such measures as are necessary to ensure the rule of the proletariat'.[155] Marx replied

We are devoted to a party which, most fortunately for it, cannot yet come to power. If the proletariat were to come to power the measures it would introduce would be petty-bourgeois and not directly proletarian. Our party can only come to power when the conditions allow it to put *its own* views into practice. Louis Blanc is the best instance of what happens when you come to power prematurely.[156]

Blanc was a well-known and popular French socialist during the 1840s, whose association with the Provisional Government in 1848 brought him into disrepute and soon consigned him to political oblivion. Marx's regard for material preconditions for socialism led to his criticism of 'primitive communism', where 'The category of *worker* is not done away with, but extended to all men';[157] his regard for the political preconditions for socialism led to his opposition to Lassalle's overtures to Bismarck. As Avineri has written:

For Marx, socialism grows out of the contradictions inherent in bourgeois society and political liberalism. A socialism that would grow, like Lassallean socialism, out of an alliance with the Right after both have overthrown political liberalism, will necessarily carry with it some of the characteristics of its authoritarian ally.[158]

For Marx, the politics of the pre-revolutionary state was an important factor in the success of the revolution.

Marx's regard for politics, in the sense that political emancipation within the modern state was a precondition for socialist revolution, and in the sense that socialism meant the emancipation of politics from the state, had important political consequences for his conception of the transition to socialism. In particular, the state itself had become an obstacle to socialism. The transition, besides having to destroy the state, had to create the basis for a non-state politics. These were the logical requirements of Marx's transition period, even though he did not at first perceive them. *The Eighteenth Brumaire* was one of his earliest works to adumbrate the idea that the state machine must be smashed by the socialist revolution.[159] Writing of the French state, Marx declared: 'All revolutions perfected this machine instead of breaking it.'[160] But the confirmation of Marx's idea came in 1871 with the existence of the ill-fated Paris Commune.

After the short, but for the French disastrous, Franco-Prussian War in 1870, the 'little people' of Paris rebelled and proclaimed Paris a Commune in March 1871. For two months the Communards held out against the Republican government of Thiers, which had taken up France's defence after the surrender by Napoleon III to the Prussians. In September 1870 Marx, through an Address by the IWMA, had urged the French workers not to rise against the new Republic:

Any attempt at upsetting the new Government in the present crisis, when the enemy is almost knocking at the doors of Paris, would be a desperate folly. The French workmen must perform their duties as citizens.... Let them calmly and resolutely improve the opportunities of Republican liberty, for the work of their own class organization.... *Vive le République!*[161]

Ten years after the Commune's suppression, Marx wrote that it

was merely the rising of a city under exceptional conditions, the majority of the Commune was in no way socialist, nor could it be.[162]

Indeed, the Commune's declarations were rhetorical rather than practical, and it was only after much discussion that night work for bakers was abolished. The Bank of France continued its operations. The intentions of most of the Commune's members were not socialist, nor were its initiators *proletarians* in Marx's sense. But for Marx, the Commune's importance lay not so much in what it did, as in what it represented. He believed that it was an expression of the transcendence of the state, the abolition of existing state institutions and their replacement by organs of real politics, of authentic universality.

The Paris Commune was, in its political form, a body elected by universal suffrage which combined both the legislative and administrative functions of the conventional state. Marx described it as 'the political form at last discovered under which to work out the economic emancipation of labour'.[163] It rekindled in Marx's writings his views on the modern state as alienated politics, and his views on socialism as man's reappropriation of politics. As he had put it in 1850:

in bourgeois countries the abolition of the state means that the power of the state is reduced to the level found in North America.[164]

And in 1875, Marx argued that: 'Freedom consists in converting the state from an organ superimposed upon society into one completely subordinate to it.'[165] Marx's draft manuscript of *The Civil War in France*, his evaluation of the Commune, exemplifies this general conception of the state and its transcendence:

The Commune – the reabsorption of the State power by society as its own living forces instead of as forces controlling and subduing it, by the popular masses themselves, forming their own force instead of the organized force of their suppression – the political form of the social emancipation, instead of the artificial force (appropriated by their oppressors) . . . of society wielded for their oppression by their enemies.[166]

And even though Marx described the Commune as a 'revolution against the *state* itself',[167] his evaluations of it do not represent an embrace of anarchism, as some have claimed.[168]

The *Aufhebung* of the state and the preservation of politics, which the Commune represented for Marx, were bought at an ultimately fatal cost. As Eugene Kamenka has observed, the Commune's political forms were possible only because of 'its total isolation from the real business of transforming or of governing a nation'.[169] Even Engels remarked in 1872 that 'it was the lack of centralization and authority that cost the Paris Commune its life'.[170] Yet in so far as the Commune was unable to ensure its continued existence against the attacks of its enemies, it was no dictatorship of the proletariat in the strict sense.

I have suggested that Marx used the expression 'dictatorship of the proletariat' in two senses: the first, strict, sense denoted the defence of the socialist revolution's gains against its enemies; the second, broader (and I maintain, inconsistent), sense denoted the entire transition period between capitalism and socialism. The second sense is inconsistent because it denies the important role of politics during the transition, the role which was emphasized by Marx in his assessment of the Paris Commune. It is in this second sense that 'dictatorship' equates with 'rule', but the problems of the 'rule of the proletariat' are not solved by giving it a new name. The proletariat must still defend its rule against class enemies who would destroy it; it must still overcome alienated politics to advance to a society where man's political nature can find true expression. Nevertheless, most interpreters of Marx's concept of the 'dictatorship of the proletariat', when they recognize that it seems to have competing connotations, tend to conflate the dictatorship and the transition to socialism. Miliband, for example, argued that:

In its proper Marxist meaning, the notion of the 'dictatorship of the proletariat' disposes much too easily, and therefore does not dispose at all, of the inevitable tension that exists between the requirement of *direction* on the one hand, and of *democracy* on the other, particularly in a revolutionary situation.[171]

Karl Korsch perceptively noted an ambivalence in Marx towards the (generic) 'dictatorship of the proletariat' upon a close reading of Marx's *The Civil War in France*. While Marx considered the Paris Commune as providing a model of the political form under which the necessary tasks of the proletariat's economic liberation could be carried out, elsewhere in his pamphlet he praised the Commune's openness, its indeterminate form.[172] Many have argued that Marx was fundamentally a democrat. Draper declared that Marx's socialism represented '*the complete democratization of society*'.[173] The 'dictatorship' must therefore be democratic, as Leonhard, for example, claims.[174] But as Talmon has stubbornly, but rightly, pointed out, there is democracy (liberal) and democracy (totalitarian).[175] Because they do not separate the legitimately illiberal functions of the 'dictatorship of the proletariat' proper from Marx's broader conception of the transition to socialism, such democratic interpretations of Marx's transition (the generic 'dictatorship') as Draper's, Leonhard's, and even Lenin's, simply invite Talmon's scorn. They also avoid the real stumbling-blocks to Marx's project: how are the legitimate tasks of the protection of the socialist revolution to be undertaken, to be effective only against genuine enemies, and to be ended; most importantly, how are these tasks to be integrated with the re-politicization of society?

Marx himself never fully resolved the questions which his conceptions of the 'dictatorship of the proletariat' and the 'transition to socialism' raised. This is evident from one of his few discussions on the transition: a response in the form of private, marginal notes made in 1875 to Bakunin's *Statism and Anarchy*. Bakunin claimed that Marx's project would culminate in a new form of state oppression:

the ruling of the majority by the minority in the name of the alleged stupidity of the first and the alleged superior intelligence of the second.[176]

It was bound to produce, he continued, a new political and economic enslavement of the majority. If there is to be a post-revolutionary state, Bakunin asks rhetorically, over whom will it rule? Marx jotted down that the state power will be used against the class enemies of the proletariat, the bourgeoisie in particular, 'as long as the proletariat fights against them'.[177] Bakunin, however, answered the question himself quite differently, conjecturing that the new state might rule over the peasant rabble, or perhaps institute a new form of national oppression with German workers ruling over Slavs. 'A State without slavery, overt or concealed', he maintained, 'is unthinkable – and that is why we are enemies of the State.'[178] He proceeded to the central point:

What does it mean: 'the proletariat raised into a ruling class'?[179]

Marx replies:

It means that the proletariat, instead of fighting individually against the economically privileged classes, has gained sufficient strength and is sufficiently well organized to employ general means of compulsion in its struggle against these classes. It can, however, use only economic means designed to abolish its own distinctive trait as a wage-earner, and hence to abolish itself as a class. Its complete victory is consequently also the end of its domination, since its class character has disappeared.[180]

Marx's response is consistent with his conception of 'dictatorship' as defence of the socialist revolution by the proletariat against the bourgeoisie. But Marx misses Bakunin's point. How, Bakunin asked, is the proletariat's 'domination' to be organized? What role, for example, would a communist party play?

Further probing by Bakunin along these lines leads to Marx's retort that by the rule of the proletariat he means self-government.[181] But in order to support this notion, Marx slides from proletarian rule to classless society. He replies too sharply, in fact, to Bakunin's denigration of elections and representatives embodied in the notion of self-government:

The nature of elections is determined not by the name, but by the economic basis, the economic interrelations of the voters, and from the moment when the functions have ceased to be political ones (1) government functions no longer exist; (2) the distribution of general functions becomes a routine matter and does not entail any domination; (3) elections completely lose their present political character.[182]

This is quite beside the point for, as Marx has just finished explaining to Bakunin: 'when class rule has disappeared a state in the now accepted political sense of the word no longer exists'.[183] Thus Marx is defending elections in a classless society, not in the period of the transition. Marx merely reaffirms his longstanding position that under socialism there will be a public power which will administer 'general functions', and to which there will be elections. The state–civil society distinction will have been eliminated, as will the economic basis for particular interests.

Bakunin maintains his attack; he has perceived a certain weakness in Marx's armour. Why should a society conforming to general scientific laws which can be elaborated independent of the masses need to consult the people?

... this would-be people's State will be nothing else but despotic rule over the toiling masses by a new, numerically small aristocracy of genuine or sham scientists. The people lack learning and so they will be freed from the cares of government, will be wholly regimented into one common herd of governed people. Emancipation indeed! The Marxists are aware of this

[Marx interjects: !][184]

contradiction, and, realizing that government by scientists

[Marx interjects: *quelle rêverie*][185]

(the most distressing, offensive, and despicable type of government in the world) will be, notwithstanding its democratic form, a veritable dictatorship – console themselves with the thought that this dictatorship will be only temporary and of brief duration.[186]

While Marx indulges in exclamation marks and asides, this criticism is very much to the point. Marx's tone changes; this is all a slight misunderstanding, he seems to say. '*Non, mon cher!*' he replies:[187]

the *class rule* of the workers over the resisting strata of the old world can only continue until the economic basis that makes the existence of classes possible has been destroyed.[188]

Taken as a whole, Marx's comments have dodged the issue.[189] Bakunin is clearly grappling with the problems of Marx's transition period, in particular the problem of leadership, while Marx refuses to discuss the political form of what must be (at least in part) class rule by the proletariat. It is all very well to deny the anarchist claim that elections can never be meaningful acts of political decision-making by the masses, that is, to affirm that political forms are important; but to avoid the complex political questions raised by the transition thereby is to take shelter behind the familiar. For the transition is class rule, and is not class rule. It is Janus-faced. It must present its class face towards the bourgeoisie, that is to say its alienated face, not necessarily a dictatorial face; it must present its non-class face towards the proletariat and its allies. This is the central tension in Marx's concept of the 'transition to socialism'. It is a tension between the state as alienated politics, as a product of the continued existence of classes, and the state as the reintegration of politics and man, the forward-looking face of the transition. The role of coercion against the bourgeoisie, where warranted, of the dictatorship of the proletariat in the strict sense is a part of the state's continuing alienated existence. In Marx's other terms, where the state is an expression of class rule, the transition is a tension between a state and a non-state. The 'dictatorship of the proletariat' in its strict and in its other sense serves merely to cloud this tension and the issues it raises: above all, how are this state and this non-state to be accommodated under the one roof? Marx sometimes displayed an admirable caution about the precise structure of socialism. As Avineri points out, Marx's method was not to isolate a model of transition, or construct a blueprint, but to anticipate the actual development of society. Reviewing the Russian revolutionary Sergei Nechaev's *The Fundamental Principles of the Future Social Order*, Marx noted that 'the leaders have arranged everything in advance'.[190] Nechaev, the sometime ally of Bakunin, had some definite ideas about the future. Marx commented:

What a beautiful model of barrack-room communism! Here you have it all: communal eating, communal sleeping, assessors and offices regulating education, production, consumption, in a word, all social activity, and to

64

crown all, *Our Committee*, anonymous and unknown to anyone, as the supreme director. This is indeed the purest anti-authoritarianism.[191]

But Marx took caution to extremes; he offered us few clues about his socialism.

Even granted that the dictatorship of the proletariat is but one aspect of the transition to socialism, there remain such questions as: how and by whom the dictatorship will be organized, and against whom it will direct its force? It is a question not only of *quis custodiet custodes?*, but of who are the guardians? For some this remains a recipe for authoritarianism. For did Marx not stress the leadership of the communists in the *Communist Manifesto*, and did he not stress the inevitability of socialism in passages such as this, from 1845:

It is not a question of what this or that proletarian, or even the whole proletariat, at the moment *regards* as its aim. It is a question of *what the proletariat is*, and what, in accordance with this *being*, it will historically be compelled to do.[192]

The context of this declaration, however, tempers the tone of this historical necessity. While it may at first conjure up for us the all-too-familiar image of commissars compelling proletarians 'to be free', in fact it was uttered with precisely the opposite intention. *The Holy Family*, from which it is derived, is a lengthy – some might say a prolix – attack upon the Critical Critics: Bruno Bauer and his group. The Critical Critics developed a sharp theoretical distinction between themselves and 'the Mass'. They believed that they alone held the key to social progress, and that 'the Mass' was the chief stumbling-block to progress. They, as philosophers, held the universal standpoint; 'the Mass' was concerned only with its particular interests and limited standpoint. Edgar Bauer wrote that 'The modern worker thinks only of himself.'[193] Bruno Bauer rejected 'the Mass' as 'the true enemy of the spirit', and as the enemy of historical progress.[194] In his Third Thesis on Feuerbach, Marx rejected this distinction between enlighteners and darkened minds:

The materialist doctrine concerning the changing of circumstances and upbringing forgets that circumstances are changed by men and that the educator must himself be educated. This doctrine must, therefore, divide society into two parts, one of which is superior to society.[195]

He was also concerned to defend the idea that the proletariat had an objectively universal interest which would ultimately be translated into à universal standpoint, despite the fact that at present its standpoint was narrow.

The position Marx developed in *The Holy Family* is quite consistent with his insistence, in the *General Rules* he drafted for the IWMA, that 'the emancipation of the working classes must be conquered by the working classes themselves'.[196] Yet Marx does not seem to have considered seriously the structure and problems of the dictatorship, or indeed of the entire transition. The major problem of the dictatorship is the problem of opposition to the socialist revolution; the major problem of the transition is to subordinate the state to society by making man's existence political, in the non-class sense. The problem of the transition is to liberate politics from a separate sphere of activity, so that there will be no politicians, simply political people.[197] The problem of combining the dictatorship and the transition is the problem of whether all or any opposition is bourgeois opposition: when is opposition within the transition opposition to the transition? This is *the* question of the transition, and Marx's failure to answer it suggests either that he did not consider it, or that he could not answer it.

There is not much mileage to be had from Marx's supposed contempt for the proletariat. His commitment to the proletariat's self-emancipation was consistent at least from his Third Thesis on Feuerbach, cited above, to his 1879 'Circular Letter' addressed to the SPD leadership through August Bebel. He consistently opposed the ideas expressed, for example, by Buonarroti, a survivor and publicist of Babeuf's Conspiracy of Equals during the French Revolution:

The experience of the French Revolution ... sufficiently demonstrates that a people whose opinions have been formed by a regime of inequality and despotism is hardly suitable, at the beginning of a regenerative revolution, to elect those who will direct it and carry it out to completion.[198]

Marx scorned these self-appointed educators who had somehow escaped the effects of 'a regime of inequality and despotism'. As he and Engels wrote to Bebel in 1879, reminding the SPD of the IWMA's position on the proletariat's self-emancipation:

We cannot, therefore, co-operate with people who openly state that the workers are too uneducated to emancipate themselves and must first be freed from above by philanthropic big bourgeois and petty bourgeois.[199]

But Marx's conception of opposition within the transition to socialism is largely unexplored. Johnstone has argued that 'there are no grounds for arguing that they [Marx and Engels] would have favoured the suppression of political opposition and dissent as a normal feature of the dictatorship of the proletariat'.[200] Yet, apart from the implication that had they not 'favoured' it they would have 'acquiesced' in it, this statement has little textual support, or challenge. A revolution, whether or not it is violent, is intrinsically illiberal. It defines a new centre of power which must protect itself, at least initially, against the power it has displaced. It must therefore curtail the rights and, if necessary, the lives of its opponents. These may be unpleasant facts; but these are facts. Now, putting the question of the justification of the socialist revolution completely to one side, we must admit that the socialist revolution (on its own terms) has the right to survive. Thus it must be illiberal towards its opponents. Who are its opponents? The bourgeoisie. But the transition is not simply, nor even primarily, a question of defence of the revolution. It is primarily a question of the establishment of socialism in an economic sense and of the transcendence of the state. By conflating Marx's two senses of dictatorship of the proletariat so that the dictatorship in synonymous with the transition itself, the illiberalism of the transition is moved from the periphery to the centre. All opposition is condemned as 'bourgeois', even that opposition within the new centre of power which is necessary for the development of the transition. How could the transition distinguish between its opponents? Marx did not resolve this problem, although it would seem a logical problem to encounter given the two faces of the transition. Of course, it could be argued that revolution itself, because of its illiberalism, and not the transition, is the basis for authoritarianism, and that any project that is revolutionary is fundamentally authoritarian; but historical experience does not support this view. Revolutions are illiberal, but their illiberalism is limited. Marx failed to tell us how the illiberalism of the socialist revolution should be limited. Nevertheless, because of his belief in the primacy of politics in socialism, Marx's project implies – perhaps demands – that there must be a limit. In general, Marx seemed to believe that if the working class was sufficiently conscious and organized, and if it came to power when economic conditions were mature, illiberalism against its opponents could be reduced to minor proportions. Marx's project relied upon stringent attention to pre-condition, as well as considerable faith in the proletariat.

The inclusion of a 'transition period' in any political or social project is an admission that the changes that project advocates will result in a fundamentally different society; it is an approximate indication of the degree of change desired. Nevertheless, the inclusion of a 'transition period' raises a number of important problems independent of those which may beset the ultimate goal: in particular, are any means justified within the transition? The problem with Marx's project is not so much that he failed to provide some general guidelines of his ultimate goal, but that he failed dismally to explain the purposes and structure of his 'transition period', and even confused the issue by his inconsistent use of the concept of the 'dictatorship of the proletariat'. Any transition, however, must bear a logical relation to its ultimate destination. Marx's goal entailed the abolition of the distinction between the political state and civil society, the achievement of true democracy or universality. While Marx never specified the concrete relations between the individual and the species when the individual was an unmediated representative of man's species-essence (*Gattungswesen*), universality did not mean conformity or the absence of individuation. The abolition of particularity did not mean the abolition of particulars. Marx's universality was a fundamental social unity within which there is a role for politics and thus for difference. Men will, in the words of Aristotle, be in harmony, not in unison. It may have been that because differences under Marx's socialism were not conceived of as fundamental, because politics in the sense of being extraneous to man and factious would no longer exist, Marx did not believe that the right to opposition was needed. Lockean liberalism had its proper place only in class society. Yet the transition period was in some senses still a class society, and Marx nowhere spoke of the right to opposition under it. For fundamental opposition would come from the bourgeoisie, and the transition had a greater right to protect itself. But the suppression of fundamental opposition in the transition had, logically, to coexist with the flowering of non-fundamental opposition, so that socialism could develop. How were these two types of opposition to be distinguished? This was the fundamental problem of Marx's transition, about which he said nothing.

Marx's treatment of the concept of the 'dictatorship of the proletariat' highlights the problem of opposition. I agree with those who argue that Marx's dictatorship is what it says it is: a dictatorship in the conventional sense. But I differ from them in arguing that to this core meaning of the 'dictatorship of the proletariat' as the defence of the socialist revolution against bourgeois opposition, Marx added a spurious meaning of the 'dictatorship of the proletariat' which was inconsistent with his presuppositions: 'dictatorship' as the (undifferentiated) rule of a class. The core meaning undoubtedly has its problems: for example, how will the proletariat be organized in order to defeat the bourgeois counter-attack? But it is only one aspect of the transition to socialism, and it is not the most important aspect. It suggested that a state power was still needed to thwart the bourgeoisie. The second meaning of the 'dictatorship of the proletariat', however, identifies the 'dictatorship' with the entire transition. Not only does it suggest that defence of the revolution against the bourgeoisie is the primary task of the transition, to which all else must be subordinate, but it makes no distinctions between class rules. If all class rule is dictatorship, as Marx himself sometimes implied, then the political forms of class rule are unimportant. But this was far from Marx's considered opinion on the matter of political forms. He held that the political forms of bourgeois rule were of great consequence for the socialist revolution, and that liberal democracy was the prelude to the revolution. Indeed, for Marx liberal democracy increased the likelihood of a peaceful revolution. Politics is important to Marx for the pre-revolutionary period as well as for the ultimate fulfilment of man's nature. It was thus important for the transition to socialism. The central aspect of the transition was its fostering of politics as an activity integral to man's existence, not separate from him as under the system of 'alien politics' embodied in the existence of a state. It was this aspect of the transition, the effective dissolution of the state, which fired Marx's enthusiasm for the Paris Commune.

Marx's 'transition period', apart from the confusions of language which surround it and the little space he devoted to its exegesis, contains a central tension between the continued existence of a state (in the transitional regime's dealings with the bourgeoisie), and the abolition of the state (in the attempt by the proletariat and its allies to move towards socialism). Marx evidently believed that, where the bourgeoisie would offer resistance to the transition, the resistance would be short-lived. Faced by a class-conscious proletariat and by material conditions which would facilitate the speedy construction of socialism, bourgeois resistance would have little support.

It seems that Marx did not consider the problems of opposition, of bourgeois and working-class opposition, to and within the transition to socialism, not because he intended the indiscriminate suppression of all opposition, but because he believed that his project had transcended liberalism by transcending class society. Of course, he believed that the socialist revolution had the right to defend its own existence against its class enemies who had no rights, but opposition would afterwards cease to be class opposition and would need no rights to protect it. As Sartori explains:

Marx rejected representative democracy because he wanted *more* democracy, liberalism because he wanted *more* liberty, and laissez-faire because he wanted an economic system which would attain perfect retributive justice. . . . It is the grievous gaps in his doctrine and the total lack of foresight which have turned Marxism into quite another thing.[201]

Because the socialist revolution is illiberal, and because Marx's project does not endorse liberalism, there is no compelling reason to conclude that Marx's project entails the abolition of all opposition. Despite his lack of direction on this question, there are good grounds for believing that Marx saw the transition to socialism, once it had disposed of bourgeois opposition, as the flowering of oppositions.

3

ENGELS, DEMOCRACY AND REVOLUTION

Frederick Engels played a decisive role in systematizing and extending Marx's project or, as McLellan writes, in transforming 'Marx's views into a *Weltanschauung*, a philosophical system, an interpretation of the world'.[1] This role began a few years before Marx's death, when Engels published a polemic against Eugene Dühring, whose theories were then in vogue among German socialists, taking the opportunity to set down Marx's ideas in a popular and systematic form. Engels' later pamphlet *Socialism: Utopian and Scientific*, culled from *Anti-Dühring*, became the standard introduction to Marxism for vast numbers of Social Democrats, many of whom were not even familiar with the *Communist Manifesto*. In his last and most productive period, which coincided with the period after Marx's death in 1883, Engels undertook the defence and explication of the Marxism of *Anti-Dühring*. In the field of political economy he edited the last two volumes of Marx's *magnum opus*, *Capital* (volume II was published in 1885, and volume III in 1894); in the field of philosophy he wrote *Ludwig Feuerbach and the End of Classical German Philosophy* (1888), and the notes published after his death as the *Dialectics of Nature*; in the field of history (and anthropology) he wrote, *inter alia*, *The Origin of the Family, Private Property, and the State* (1884); and his letters abound with practical political advice to Social Democrats in many parts of the world.

Engels' modesty in evaluating his role as Marx's collaborator notwithstanding,[2] many writers – from Marxists such as Karl Kautsky and Lenin, to anti-Marxists such as R. N. Carew Hunt – have treated Marx and Engels as though they were one person, and as though what came from the pen of one would have been wholly endorsed by the other. They assumed, that is, that Engels always spoke with the authority of Marx. The repercussions of this view were particularly significant in the period from 1883–95, when Engels, as an undisputed authority on Marx and Marxism, gave a pronounced direction of his own to Marx's project.

Some recent works have examined closely the Marx–Engels relationship, the orthodox view of which, adumbrated above, had been questioned at least as early as the 1920s.[3] Chief among these is Norman Levine's *The Tragic Deception: Marx contra Engels*,[4] although Lichtheim[5] and F. L. Bender,[6] among others, have also contributed to this side of the debate. Levine argues not simply that Marx and Engels were not completely unanimous, but that 'major differences of thought' existed between them. Engels, he claims, was 'the first revisionist'.[7]

Levine's work concentrates on the philosophical level of the Marx–Engels relationship:

without the notion of *praxis*, Engels saw history as unfolding according to laws extrinsic to man, while Marx saw history as unfolding according to powers intrinsic in human labour. Marx believed in immanence; Engels in emanation.[8]

His argument relies primarily upon the idea that Engels had little understanding of the Hegelian origins, and the continuing Hegelian legacy, of Marx's central concepts. 'Unlike Marx', Levine explains, 'Engels did not see the state as a form of alienation.'[9] They differed also, he maintains, in their conceptions of communism and freedom. Communism for Engels, Levine argues, was 'industrial puritanism';[10] for Marx, it was the fulfilment of a truly political existence:

Communism, for Engels, meant the end of political existence. Such was not the case with Marx. For Marx, communism meant the triumph of society. Thus, political life was possible for Marx under communism as long as it was expressive, or as long as it was subordinate to human social life, or species being.... That is, for Marx communism meant species and anthropological life becoming political life – the unanimity and harmony of natural and political man.[11]

I am concerned, however, with whether or how these differences are related to those of a practical political kind, particulary in relation to the question of the transition to socialism. Levine argues on the one hand that Marx and Engels differed 'on the philosophical and speculative level', and that their agreements were 'of a practical, strategic kind'.[12] On the other hand, his charge that Engels was a revisionist recognizes that there were differences in practical and strategic areas:

the tactics of Engels led to the replacement of the revolution by mechanistic determinism, to the replacement of conscious *praxis* by the faith in inevitabilism, to the replacement of class warfare by parliamentarism. Engels was directly responsible for the evolutionism and accommodationism of the Second International.[13]

While many may agree that Engels' *Dialectics of Nature* does not represent Marx's historical, society-based dialectic,[14] and that in general he may have philosophically misunderstood Marx, does this necessarily entail the political differences and changes which are described here? Levine contrasts Marx the Jacobin with Engels the reformist. 'In situations where revolutionary conditions existed, Marx's devotion to Jacobin politics was clear';[15] a devotion evident, he claims, during the 1848–50 period, and at the time of the Paris Commune.[16] A commitment to force and coercion in effecting a revolution, he implies, was absent in Engels, or at least in the Engels of 1883–95.

Yet Engels maintained a revolutionary political orientation until his death, even if his legacy was misinterpreted or misused by European social democracy. To blame Engels for the shift in political strategy undergone by some parties in the Second International, furthermore, is to exaggerate his influence over these parties as well as to distort his real position. The SPD, for example, did not change its strategy or practice because of a supposed change in Engels' theory, or even because of Eduard Bernstein's theoretical revisions. If anything, Bernstein and his Revisionism served to reflect and to signal an already changed strategy generated by the SPD's successes in the electoral and trade-union areas. In re-evaluating the relationship between Marx and Engels, we must not try to correct the extremes of an earlier position simply by establishing an opposite extreme. Thus, for the purposes of this study, I shall consider Marx and Engels, despite significant differences on philosophical issues, to have shared a fundamental political agreement. Their lengthy period of collaboration would not have been possible otherwise. Having established this, however, I shall devote the remainder of this chapter to exploring a political area in which there was some difference between Marx and Engels which emerged fully only after

Marx's death: the transition to socialism. It was Marx's reticence on this increasingly important issue which contributed as much to the urgency of the need for clarification as to the authoritativeness of Engels' interpretation.

In 1873 Engels made an interesting contribution to the discussion of 'authority' and 'authoritarianism' in the means of achieving socialism and in socialist society itself. *On Authority* is directed against the anarchist critics of Marx's project. Engels' first move in it is to declare that all organizations presuppose authority. Under socialism, therefore, authority will not have disappeared, but will merely have changed its form. Socialism, he explains, is founded upon large-scale industry: 'wanting to abolish authority in large-scale industry is tantamount to wanting to abolish industry itself'.[17] The demands of industry are paramount:

> We have thus seen that, on the one hand, a certain authority, no matter how delegated, and, on the other hand, a certain subordination, are things which, independently of all social organization, are imposed upon us together with the material conditions under which we produce and make products circulate.[18]

Such a case misses the point entirely, even if it reveals a good deal about Engels' vision of socialism. To begin with, the anarchists were primarily concerned with political authority and subordination, not that obtaining in industry. Next, Engels' casual aside about authority 'no matter how delegated' relegates the chief area of concern to obscurity. Engels' error is his assumption that authority equals authoritarianism; consequently, he does not consider that authoritarianism can be conceived of as an abuse of authority. If the anarchists assume that all authority constitutes an abuse, Engels is not obliged to accept this; his argument would be stronger for an explicit rejection of it. Engels avoids two crucial problems in his polemic. The very manner of his treatment of the central terms means that he cannot examine whether authority could be abused in a socialist society, and what sort of safeguards would prevent it. Secondly, he does not address the problem of organizing power in a socialist society.

Engels, however, can claim one major victory against the anarchist critics. The anti-authoritarians, he writes,

74

demand that the first act of a social revolution shall be the abolition of authority. Have these gentlemen ever seen a revolution? A revolution is certainly the most authoritarian thing there is; it is an act whereby one part of the population imposes its will upon the other part by means of rifles, bayonets and cannon ... [and the victorious party] must maintain this rule by means of the terror which its arms inspire in the reactionaries.[19]

Should we not have reproached the Paris Communards, he asks, for not having used this authority freely enough? Engels' paper victory, his fearless grasp of an essential part of the idea of 'revolution', is at once his defeat. How is this ample use of force and violence, this authoritarianism, to be limited, and ended? How will it be controlled and directed, and by whom? What is to stop the revolution's authoritarianism from becoming institutionalized? Engels did not consider these to be problems. As early as 1844 he had written that

the role of talent is to convince the masses of the truth of its ideas, and it will then have no need further to worry about their application, which will follow entirely of its own accord.[20]

Engels cannot conceive that anything might go wrong. Surely, he asks, mankind is 'not passing through democracy to arrive back eventually at the point of departure [i.e., aristocracy]'?[21]

Engels was particularly forthcoming on the nature of the state, and about the changes it would undergo during the transition to socialism. Lenin's *The State and Revolution* relies much more heavily upon the work of Engels than of Marx. In a letter written to August Bebel around the time of Marx's *Critique of the Gotha Programme*, Engels too criticized the new programme's adoption of the term 'free state' as inferior even to the expression 'free people's state':

Taken in its grammatical sense, a free state is one where the state is free in relation to its citizens, hence a state with a despotic government. The whole talk about the state should be dropped, especially since the [Paris] Commune, which was no longer a state in the proper sense of the word.[22]

At a time when Marx was writing of the transitional state as nothing but the revolutionary dictatorship of the proletariat, Engels independently wrote of the Commune as 'no longer a state in the proper sense of the word'. Why would any form of state still be necessary? According to Engels:

75

so long as the proletariat still *uses* the state, it does not use it in the interests of freedom but in order to hold down its adversaries [by force], and as soon as it becomes possible to speak of freedom the state as such ceases to exist.[23]

But this view differs slightly from Marx's, as Lenin seemed to realize when he wrote that it was 'one of the most, if not *the* most, remarkable observation on the state in the works of Marx and Engels'.[24] Previously, Marx had written of the state power losing its political, that is, its class, character;[25] and his *Critique of the Gotha Programme* had not envisaged a state-less communism. Most importantly, Marx had never spoken of the 'withering away' of the state. Lenin too noticed the difference between Marx's letter to Bracke of 5 May 1875 (the *Critique*), and Engels' letter to Bebel of 28 March 1875, but argued that to contrast them would be 'superficial', and that 'Marx's and Engels' views on the state and its withering away were completely identical'.[26] But there were two important differences. For Marx, the struggle against the socialist revolution's enemies went on at the same time as an increasing liberty for the proletariat: the state and non-state elements of the transition coexisted, and were not simply before-and-after. And freedom, for Marx, was not the absence of a state, but the subordination of the state to society. To argue that freedom and the state cannot be reconciled is the foundation for arguing that political forms are of no importance.

Engels went on to develop his views on the state and its 'withering away' in later years. In *Socialism: Utopian and Scientific*, he declared:

As soon as there is no longer any social class to be held in subjection; as soon as class rule, and the individual struggle for existence based upon our present anarchy in production, with the collisions and excesses arising from these, are removed nothing more remains to be repressed, and a special repressive force, a state, is no longer necessary.[27]

The state, for Engels, is reduced to an instrument of repression; its last independent act is to take possession of the means of production for society, and in the Saint-Simonian formulation, beloved by Engels, the 'government of persons is replaced by the administration of things'.[28] Engels provides no explanation or detail of such a change. But by far his most thorough considerations on the subject of the state are contained in his working-up of notes left by Marx on Lewis Morgan's anthropological research into North American

Indian social organization. This work, *Origin of the Family*, further illuminates Engels' notion of the state. Historically, he argues, the division of labour in society led to the division of society into classes, which culminated in the development of the state. The state,

while ostensibly standing above the classes struggling with each other, suppressed their open conflict and permitted a class struggle at most in the economic field, in a so-called legal form.[29]

If the state was a unifier, it was evidence nevertheless of 'irreconcilable antagonisms' in society,[30] and worked for the benefit of the economically dominant class. 'The modern representative state', he continued, 'is an instrument of exploitation of wage labour by capital.'[31] But the state and the economically dominant class are not coextensive; that class must somehow enter the state's arena to become politically dominant:

it is, as a rule, the state of the most powerful, economically dominant class, which, through the medium of the state, becomes also the politically dominant class....[32]

Engels often allows the state more independence from the economically dominant class than he would care to admit. This is revealed in his discussion of the democratic republic:

The highest form of state, the democratic republic, which under our modern conditions of society is more and more becoming an inevitable necessity, and is the form of state in which alone the last decisive struggle between proletariat and bourgeoisie can be fought out – the democratic republic officially knows nothing any more of property distinctions. In it wealth exercises its power indirectly, but all the more surely.[33]

Marx confronted the same problem in 1843, yet he did not scour for the mechanisms through which the bourgeoisie controlled the state; in the democratic republic politics was the alienated expression of man's political nature brought to completion. Engels, however, argued that the bourgeoisie exercised power by the direct corruption of officials, as well as the alliance between government and Stock Exchange (i.e., the public debt). The bourgeoisie rules, furthermore, through universal suffrage. Universal suffrage, cautioned Engels, 'is the gauge of the maturity of the working class', it cannot be anything more.[34]

Engels' analysis of the democratic republic seems to afford it significant independence from the bourgeoisie. The bourgeoisie has, for the moment, the upper hand in this arena, but by allowing the working class to have political expression the bourgeoisie prepares its own downfall. Building upon the research in his *Origin of the Family*, Engels concluded in 1891 that

Society had created its own organs to look after its common interests, originally through simple division of labour. But these organs, at whose head was the state power, had in the course of time, in pursuance of their own special interests, transformed themselves from the servants of society into the masters of society.[35]

The state arose, Engels argued, because the organs which safeguarded society's common interests came to express particular interests under the guise of universality. Did it thereby give up performing its useful social and administrative functions? There is a logical flaw in Engels' reasoning about the state's 'withering away'. Even if we accept that the state arose with the division of society into classes (in Engels' rather broad sense of that term), it does not follow that the state is necessarily an instrument of class rule, nor that the state will not outlive class divisions. The causes of the state and its functions, as John Plamenatz pointed out, are not necessarily the same;[36] if the causes are overcome, it does not follow that the functions can be dispensed with.

On these points Marx and Engels must be clearly distinguished. For Marx, the proletariat must use the transitional period to overcome the economic basis for particular interests, and begin to construct that democracy which will truly express the universal interest. Necessary social functions will exist as before, but the new 'state' will be completely subordinate to society. For Marx, the transition must inaugurate the process of the *Aufhebung* of the state, its transformation from the expression of particularity to the expression of universality. Yet Engels' formulation of the fate of the state stresses the idea of repression and coercion, and their disappearance. If the state is simply a repressive institution, then its proletarian version must be repressive against the bourgeoisie. Marx had also considered repression to be an aspect of the state, and the concept of the 'dictatorship of the proletariat' was deployed by him to express this aspect under the transition. But Marx never considered repression to be the essence of the state; the essence of the political state was its separation of politics from the life of man.

If the expression 'withering away of the state' was Engels' contribution to Marxism, did he differ from Marx in conceiving the outcome of the transition to socialism? Marx rarely claimed that the state would be 'abolished' under socialism. He wrote in 1844, however, that:

If the modern state wanted to abolish the *impotence* of its administration, it would have to abolish the *private life* of today. But if it wanted to abolish private life, it would have to abolish itself, for it exists *only* in the contradiction to private life.[37]

Again in 1850, Marx wrote that 'in bourgeois countries the abolition of the state means that the power of the state is reduced to the level found in North America'.[38] For communists, he continues, the abolition of the state follows the abolition of classes. 'Abolition' is perhaps not the most appropriate term to use in this context, and Avineri suggests that Marx's view of the state's future is best expressed as 'transcendence'. He claims:

While Engels ... speaks about the state 'withering away' (*der Staat wird nicht 'abgeschafft', er stirbt ab*), Marx always refers to the abolition and transcendence (*Aufhebung*) of the state.[39]

While the claim is not entirely correct,[40] the generally existing difference of terminology between Marx and Engels on this issue highlights their differing conceptions of the state and its counterpart under socialism. In the first draft of his *The Civil War in France*, for example, Marx described the Paris Commune as 'a revolution against the state itself ... a revolution to break down this horrid machinery of class domination itself'.[41] The state, he explained, had become 'the master instead of the servant of society'.[42] Marx's concern from at least the time he became a communist was to transcend the division between state and civil society. He envisaged a 'state', or public power, which would be subordinated to society through universal suffrage. Engels did not grasp Marx's essential point: that the state was an alienated expression of man's universality. The fact that he most often spoke of it as an instrument of coercion, as something which the proletariat could use to hold down its adversaries, demonstrates that he had taken the appearance of the state, or one part of its appearance, for the essence.

That there were differences between Marx and Engels on the question of the state and its 'withering away' was discerned as early as 1946. Solomon Bloom recorded that the theory of 'withering away' was propounded by Engels, not Marx, and that it had important but misleading consequences for the interpretation of Marx's project. 'The weight of evidence', he contended, 'is rather against an anarchist interpretation of the doctrine of Marxism, as that doctrine was defended by its principal author [Marx].'[43] Bloom, in fact, believed that Marx's project was closer to liberalism than to anarchism. Almost a quarter of a century later, Adamiak reconsidered Bloom's novel interpretation. Adamiak agreed with Lenin, however, that on the 'withering away' of the state 'the views of Marx and Engels ... were identical'.[44] The idea, he maintained, was really a 'facade' to cover their statist aspirations: 'what lay behind Marxism's anti-state rhetoric was statism',[45] and the rhetoric was conjured up to eliminate the theoretical threat from anarchist rivals. That an ostensibly anti-statist ideology produced an intensified statism in the Soviet Union Adamiak regards as no paradox, but the result of a verbal juggling which treats the state in which is concentrated all the means of production as no state at all.

But Adamiak forgets the transition period which is so vital for the success of Marx's project. The proletariat needs the state to defend itself but must, at the same time, begin to break down the barrier between state and civil society. But this was not the dissolution of the civil society into the state, for, as Rudolph Bahro argues, statification is *socialization in a totally alienated form*.[46] Communism, for Marx, was the transcendence of all forms of alienation, not least of which was the modern state. That the attempt at the transition to socialism begun in 1917 has not led to the transcendence of the state, in so far as the failure is a consequence of some theory, is due less to Marx's theory of the state than to Engels', with its anarchist-like denigration of politics. Despite Bloom's inspired analysis, he is unaware of the fundamental transformation which Marx expects in communist society in relation to the expression of true universality, and thus makes the more familiar distinctions between 'spheres' or 'realms' in which the individual and the state will operate in communist society. By relegating the communist 'state' to a subordinate position in society (as Marx does in the *Critique of the Gotha Programme*), Bloom assumes that Marx is fulfilling the liberal project, while in fact Marx is arguing for a changed conception of the entire relationship between individuals and the determination and execution of their 'common interests'.

Coexisting with that aspect of Engels' work in which politics is presented as a peripheral component of the state, as a deception, there is an important strain in which liberal democracy is argued to be the political regime most favourable for the assumption of power by the working class. During the 1890s, Engels was increasingly confronted by the question of a violent versus a peaceful transition to socialism. In 1891 he declared:

One can conceive that the old society may develop peacefully into the new one in countries where the representatives of the people concentrate all power in their hands, where, if one has the support of the majority of the people, one can do as one sees fit in a constitutional way: in democratic republics such as France and the U.S.A., in monarchies such as Britain. . . . But in Germany where the government is almost omnipotent and the Reichstag and all other representative bodies have no real power, to advocate such a thing in Germany ... means removing the fig-leaf from absolutism and becoming oneself a screen for its nakedness.[47]

Engels' analysis of the state in a democratic republic, where wealth exercises its power 'indirectly but all the more surely', is lost here. The democratic republican state seems to consist only of represent-ative institutions, or at least, these are the only institutions that count. Engels adds:

If one thing is certain it is that our Party and the working class can only come to power under the form of a democratic republic. This is even the specific form for the dictatorship of the proletariat, as the Great French Revolution has already shown.[48]

This appears to mean that the proletarian dictatorship will take the political form of the democratic republic, although it sits uncom-fortably with Engels' earlier assertion that the proletarian state existed only to repress the bourgeoisie, unless repress loses its earlier connotation of overt coercion. Altogether, Engels' remarks on the dictatorship of the proletariat serve to confuse the issue, and Marx's intent. Engels argued that the Paris Commune was such a dictator-ship, although its efforts to suppress bourgeois resistance were half-hearted at best. He argued that the state existed after the socialist revolution only so long as it was needed to suppress the bourgeoisie, and implied that its political form, if not immaterial, could not achieve freedom. And he argued that the democratic republic was the 'specific form' of the dictatorship. Engels made some attempt to integrate these views in his last major piece of work, in 1895, in which he essentially argued that the democratic republic could be a guarantee against premature revolution and was an appropriate organization of the transition because it minimized the risk and the seriousness of bourgeois resistance.

By far the most consequential statement by Engels on revolution was his 'testament', the March 1895 Introduction to a new edition of Marx's *The Class Struggles in France*. When it was first printed in Germany in 1895, the SPD leadership made certain deletions from Engels' text, about which he was livid.[49] The sense of Engels' work, however, was not lost in the editing. In essence, Engels argues that while conditions for the assumption of proletarian power had changed considerably since 1848, and must be exploited to the full, the use of violence may still be necessary for its success. The major change in his approach is the emphasis on defensive violence – violence to defend the proletariat's gains rather than violence to initiate the revolution.

In 1848, Engels writes, he and Marx had been 'under the spell' of the previous French Revolutions (1789 and 1830). Since that time, history had 'completely transformed the conditions under which the proletariat had to fight'.[50] Furthermore, 'the mode of struggle of 1848 is today obsolete in every respect'.[51] What is this 'mode of struggle'? Engels appears to mean an insurrection-initiated revolution. He does not renounce revolution, but merely restricts the role of violence within it. As he goes on to point out, the proletariat would be foolish to squander the real gains which it can make through non-violent means by carrying out an insurrection. It might lose an insurrection in either of two ways: simply on the grounds of inadequate arms and technique; or because the proletariat as a whole is not involved. The risk is not worth taking where other methods can be as effective, or even more effective.

All revolutions up until then, explains Engels, had been the work of minorities, replacing one ruling class with another. Where the majority took part it was under the tutelage of a minority. Was the proletarian revolution to be like this as well, he asks?

Was there not every prospect then [in 1848] of turning the revolution of the minority into a revolution of the majority? History has proved us, and all who thought like us, wrong.[52]

The reason, he contends, was that economic development was not ripe for eliminating capitalist production. The rule of the working class was impossible both in 1848 and in the 1871 Paris Commune for this very reason.[53] This is not, however, a tacit acceptance by Engels that the strategy which Marx and he advanced in 1848 was Blanquist; it is an admission that the bourgeois revolution could not be turned into a socialist revolution because it lacked the preconditions. After the defeat of the Paris Commune, Engels continues, the German workers' movement began to gain confidence and influence, as revealed by the SPD's electoral returns. The German comrades showed 'how to make use of universal suffrage';[54] it was

transformed by them from a means of deception, which it was before, into an instrument of emancipation.[55]

But had the German comrades removed the constitutional barriers to popular government? Engels avoids the issue.

Universal suffrage, Engels argued, was the key to the changing political situation. It provided the workers with an idea of their strength, 'safeguarding us from untimely timidity as much as from untimely foolhardiness';[56] an assertion which Kautsky and Lenin would later disprove in their opposite ways. But universal suffrage, according to Engels, did more than this. It provided socialists with access to the masses beyond their usual resources, and with a platform in the Reichstag. A new method of political struggle was thus open to the proletariat, whereby it could use the bourgeoisie's own state institutions against the bourgeoisie itself. The bourgeoisie now had more to fear from the legal activities of the workers' party than from its illegal activities.

Rebellion in the old style, street fighting with barricades, which decided the issue everywhere up to 1848, was to a considerable extent obsolete.[57]

Engels questions only rebellion 'in the old style', that is, insurrection; he does not renounce revolution. The reason for Engels' caution is clear: he candidly admits that ultimate victory for any insurrection is rare, simply on military and tactical grounds:

Even in the classic time of street fighting ... the barricade produced more of a moral than a material effect. It was the means of shaking the steadfastness of the military. If it held out until this was attained, victory was won; if not, there was defeat.[58]

Where Engels had gone on to argue that any future street fighting must be undertaken with a clear awareness of its military limitations, the 1895 editors omitted his sentence. Engels' point is that tactically the task of the insurgents had become more difficult, facing as they would bigger and better-equipped armies. 'Does that mean', he asked, 'that in the future street fighting will no longer play any role? Certainly not.'[59] This too was omitted in 1895. It detracts in no way from Engels' conclusion, however:

The time of surprise attacks, of revolutions carried through by small conscious minorities at the head of unconscious masses, is past.[60]

Engels had been impressed by the German Party's electoral successes, and recommended its methods to the other parties of the Second International. He wrote that 'everywhere the *unprepared* launching of an attack has been relegated to the background'.[61] Naturally, Engels continues, we do not thereby renounce the right to revolution.

To keep this growth going without interruption until it of itself goes beyond the control of the prevailing governmental system, not to fritter away this daily increasing shock force in vanguard skirmishes, but to keep it intact until the decisive day, that is our main task.[62]

While the middle of this sentence was edited in 1895 ('not to ... skirmishes'), its thrust is not lost, for Engels contemplates a decisive day. A premature confrontation with the military, he cautions, would be a major setback for the party; when the time is ripe, he later implies,[63] the time for violence may in fact be past. 'We, the "revolutionists", the "overthrowers" – we are thriving far better on legal methods than on illegal methods and overthrow';[64] the bourgeoisie may eventually break its own legality to overcome the advancing proletariat. If the bourgeoisie breaks its own constitutional guarantees, as Engels predicts is likely, he observes that the Social Democrats are likewise freed from legal restraints to retaliate. Engels paints a picture of defensive violence.[65]

Engels' discussion implies that in a democratic republic there is no legal obstacle to the proletariat's assumption of power through universal suffrage. The obstacles will arise through the illegal, undemocratic activities of the bourgeoisie; if so, they must be overcome. In this, his last major piece of work, Engels maintains the revolutionary orientation to which he and Marx had devoted their adult lives. Engels is committed to fundamental social change, to socialism. He implies that this may be a violent change, but argues that the introduction of universal suffrage renders such violence as may be necessary (a) defensive, and (b) short-lived. But his discussion also implies that the revolution for socialism, because it is a revolution of the majority, can only be successful in a democratic republic whose political structure has helped to mature the proletariat. Engels had already said as much in 1891,[66] and in 1884[67] but he had now given his argument a decidedly liberal democratic flavour by pressing for fundamental change within the constitutional framework of a democratic republic (from which category he excluded Germany, though nevertheless recommending the same strategy) and by urging that the role of violence be minimized, and be defensive. The liberal strain in Engels' thought was not new. In 1875 he had written to Bebel of

the first condition of all freedom: that all officials should be responsible for all their official acts to every citizen before the ordinary courts and according to common law.[68]

Had he not also written in 1847, in his *Principles of Communism*, that the socialist revolution would inaugurate a democratic constitution, through which the workers would hold power where they were in a majority? In the nineteenth century, Sartori explains, 'constitution' meant

a fundamenal law, or a fundamental set of principles, and a correlative institutional arrangement, which would restrict arbitrary power and ensure a 'limited government'.[69]

Had Engels changed his opinion on the role of violence in revolution? Earlier, while polemicizing against Dühring in the late 1870s, Engels had underlined the role of force in the transition to socialism:

it is the midwife of every old society which is pregnant with the new … it is the instrument by the aid of which social development forces its way through and shatters the dead, fossilized, political forms.[70]

Had Engels recognized that not all births require a midwife? In his *The Role of Force in History* (1887–8), he identified revolution, force and dictatorship as aspects of the same process. German national unity demanded force;[71] Germany had thus to endure 'seventeen years of Bismarck's dictatorship'.[72] But a dictatorship, as Engels uses the term, could have different forms. In describing the German 'dictatorship' over Alsace, Engels clearly meant the end of freedom of the press, assembly, and association.[73] Yet in Germany itself he describes 'Bismarck's dictatorship in parliamentary forms',[74] in other words, a Reichstag with no decisive power. Engels' idea can be explained if we assume that he employed two conceptions of force: potential force, and actual force. Each is as real as the other, but they involve different methods of rule. Bismarck's home rule, then, rested on a potential force derived from the actual force he was able to deploy outside Germany (e.g., in Alsace). Extending this idea to the role of force in the proletarian revolution, we might say that universal suffrage in a democratic republic encourages a potential working-class force of significant dimension against the bourgeoisie. An actual test of strength, Engels implied, may be avoided – but the potential must be ever ready to become an actual force against a violent challenge from the bourgeoisie. The SPD, among its other errors of judgement, mistook its potential force for the actual force it could muster in a confrontation. Nova maintains that 'Engels did not conceive of revolutions or other forms of coercion as ends in themselves',[75] and the possibility of minimizing violence would have doubtless appealed to him.

If in his more directly political works Engels acknowledged the importance for the socialist revolution of liberal democratic political forms, in his theoretical works on the state he seems to have been heavily influenced, if not by the anarchist attacks on Marxism, then by the anarchist vision of a state-less future. Thus his tendency in works of this type to minimize the importance of state political forms; he did not seem to allow for different forms, or degrees, of oppression. The state was oppressive; it had to be destroyed. The only qualification he made to the anarchist schema was the inclusion of a period in which the state would be the instrument of the workers, a proletarian dictatorship, after which the state would have no further function (for there would be no one to oppress) and would gradually 'wither away'. While his encounters with the anarchists may have caused Marx to be less eager to discuss his ideas on the future communist society, Engels adopted the anarchist standpoint as far as the final goal was concerned. Engels synthesized Marx and the anarchists in this area.

There can be little doubt that Lenin derived his views on the state primarily from those of Engels, and Engels' interpretation of Marx. With its stress on the suppression of one class by another, Engels' theory suited the needs of the Bolsheviks. Engels' use of the expression 'dictatorship of the proletariat' however, limited as it is, does not appear to support entirely its later use by Lenin. However we explain the meaning of this dictatorship, we are still faced with an inadequate exploration of what is to become of opponents to and within the new regime, or indeed, whether there is any difference between such opponents. Engels saw the solution to problems which opponents might cause the dictatorship only in terms of coercion, the repercussions of which view he ignored. Put simply, if Engels recognized the main task of the proletarian dictatorship, in its broadest sense, as the suppression of bourgeois resistance, what was it that constituted 'bourgeois resistance'? Is the very existence of the remains of the displaced bourgeois class a case of resistance? And what will become of working-class opposition? Will it, by disagreeing with the direction or with the specific measures of the dictatorship, pose a new threat to the existence of the dictatorship, or become axiomatically excluded from the proletariat? If certain types of opposition are not explicitly protected, and if the dictatorship of the proletariat increasingly takes on the character of an armed camp, obsessed by real and imaginary enemies of its own making, will the state ever 'wither away'? A transition period, centred on coercion, to a society in which there shall be no coercion, seems to entail overwhelming risks.

Few would maintain that Engels desired a continuing despotism, for he clearly operated with a notion of historical 'ripeness' for socialism which he employed, as we have seen above, to discount the attempts of 1848 and 1871 to achieve socialism. In Russia the Mensheviks retained this notion, and used it against Lenin who had abandoned, or radically modified, it. But the problem that Engels implicitly recognised in his 1895 Introduction, and probably earlier, was that while Marxism had always been strong on the necessity for preconditions for the socialist revolution, it had, and has, never been able precisely to stipulate them. As early as 1850 Engels had written:

The worst thing that can befall the leader of an extreme party is to be compelled to assume power at a time when the movement is not yet ripe for the domination of the class he represents and for the measures this domination implies.[76]

The German Ideology also had been concerned about social and economic preconditions for socialism, lest all the old *Scheisse* reappear. But Marx had no index for these preconditions. Engels highlighted the problem by admitting, in effect, that with such a system one could only know after the event whether the preconditions for the event existed. If a revolution was successful, the preconditions existed; if it failed, the preconditions did not exist. Engels was wise after the event when he re-examined the events of 1848 and 1871. But for Engels, liberal democracy became the required index to eliminate such *ex post facto* determinations. He was understandably cautious at first about liberal democracy, as when he advised that it could only be a gauge of the maturity of the working class. For the establishment of liberal democratic governments in Western Europe was a relatively recent phenomenon, and one with which Social Democrats had not yet properly come to grips. By 1895 Engels had concluded that if sufficient attention were paid to working-class consciousness and to the possibility of bourgeois resistance, liberal democracy was the political system under which the workers could best come to power. He recognized, in fact, that liberal democratic political forms were not a sham, and that here was a more certain method of determining whether the preconditions for socialism existed before the attempt for socialism was made. He killed two problem birds with one stone.

The political maturity of the working class as well as its strength, both revealed through liberal democracy, are factors ensuring that the proletarian dictatorship's offensive, oppressive role will be short-lived — as indeed is the idea of defensive violence which Engels seems to advocate in 1895. To suggest, furthermore, that the democratic republic is the 'specific form' of the proletarian dictatorship implies some commitment to liberal democratic means of resolving conflict and deciding the course of the transition. Like Marx, however, Engels relied far too much upon history than upon institutional or legal devices to act as a safeguard for Marx's project. Add to this their poor expression and inadequate explanation of terms, and their reticence about their earliest works, and it is little surprise that Marx's project was mistaken, and found amenable to the most diverse interpretations. Engels contributed such an example of poor expression in his recollections of the *Neue Rhein-ische Zeitung*:

The editorial constitution was simply the dictatorship of Marx.... More-over, Marx's dictatorship was a matter of course here, was undisputed and willingly recognized by all of us.[77]

This is certainly an unusual choice of terms, for what Engels describes is properly the undisputed or legitimate authority of Marx as editor: that Marx exercised a decisive directing influence over the paper's contents, and that he had not been elected to a position, but had won a role. To Engels' uses of 'dictatorship' as the equivalent of military rule, individual rule, and class rule, irrespective of the political forms of each, we can now add another complication. This terminological imprecision provided a foundation from which the meaning of Marx's 'dictatorship of the proletariat' was difficult to extricate.

What are we to make of Engels? He and Marx were not a composite personality; in fact, he exercised a decisive influence in formulating a Marxism the philosophical aspects of which Marx would probably have rejected. Both were revolutionaries, but Engels' theory of the state owed more to the anarchists and Saint-Simon than to Marx. Consequently, Marx and Engels conceived their goal differently, which affected their respective ideas of the role and structure of the proletarian dictatorship. Engels saw it as the essence of the transition, and as the means to suppress resistance and eliminate classes before withering away. Marx saw the major part of the transition as developing the political, in the sense of universal, nature of man, by 'converting the state from an organ superimposed upon society into one completely subordinate to it'.[78] For Marx believed that 'the human being is in the most literal sense a political animal, not merely a gregarious animal, but an animal which can individuate itself only in the midst of society'.[79] Finally, Engels operated with the concept of 'state' on two levels: theoretical and practical. On the theoretical level he stressed the oppressive, coercive nature of all states, whatever their political form; on the practical level he held that the democratic republic was the culminating political form of capitalism, and the form most suited to the assumption of power by the proletariat.

4

MARXISM AND REVISIONISM

Engels' conception of Marx's project *was* Marxism for the members of the Second International. When Engels said at Marx's graveside that 'just as Darwin discovered the law of development of organic nature, so Marx discovered the law of development of human history',[1] he expected to be, and was, taken seriously. The rest of his life was dedicated to defending Marxism as a positivist social science. Such a Marxism, however, soon came under attack from some of the founders of the academic discipline of sociology: Durkheim, Pareto, Mosca, and Weber. These 'academic critics' rejected the claims of Marxism to scientific status, and questioned whether socialism would be as liberal democratic as capitalism. In the context of this sustained intellectual attack upon Marxism, and of the consolidation of liberal democratic regimes in some of the advanced countries of Western Europe, Eduard Bernstein, a leading theoretician of the SPD and, with Karl Kautsky, Engels' literary executor, sought to provide socialism with a foundation different from Marxism, and to assure the sceptics of socialism's liberal democratic intentions. The position he developed and defended is known as 'Revisionism'. It was based on the contrast between the gradual transformation of existing society through reforms and a violent break in continuity between the existing society and socialism. Bernstein's 'transition period', although he never employed the concept, was the present; but his opponents within the SPD objected that real advances towards socialism could only be made after the socialist revolution. For Bernstein, what was at stake was the existence of liberal democracy under socialism.

The 'academic critics' of Marxism were almost unanimous in rejecting the materialist conception of history as a scientific law of social development, but found it nevertheless to be a highly fruitful hypothesis.[2] But there were more practical criticisms of Marx's project, particularly the charge that it would lead to an undemocratic state of one sort or another. Sometimes it was not the democratic professions of Marxists which were at issue, but the very possibility of democracy. Vilfredo Pareto argued, for example, that

whether universal suffrage prevails or not, it is always an oligarchy that governs, finding ways to give to the 'will of the people' that expression which the few desire.[3]

Yet even before their attempt to establish a democratic society, Pareto perceived among socialists the establishment of a proletarian elite:

The syndicalist [i.e., trade-unionized] workers, while they are socialists, of course, form the 'conscious proletariat'; the non-syndicalist workers, and those who are syndicalists but not socialists, form the 'non-conscious proletariat'. It is necessary to see with what disdain the members of the first speak to those of the second, as if they were their superiors, as if they despised them. . . . *The syndicalist, socialist workers will form the privileged class of the new society.*[4]

Gaetano Mosca was definite about the dangers of Marx's 'collectivist utopia': it would produce a tyranny worse than any under the capitalism which socialists condemned. Communist societies, he argued, will be managed by 'officials' more powerful than today's millionaires. Everyone will have to be subservient and obsequious to these new rulers.

They alone can dispense favour, bread, the joy or sorrow of life. One single crushing, all-embracing, all-engrossing tyranny will weigh upon all.[5]

Mosca's vision was a part of his larger concern for the 'tragic destiny' of all men, who aspire 'ever to pursue and achieve what they think is the good', but 'ever find pretexts for slaughtering and persecuting each other'.[6] Max Weber also believed that the danger of Marxism lay in the dictatorship of the official. In 1908 he declared the 'dictatorship of the proletariat' to be naive.[7]

In general, these critics assumed that a state, either in its present, or more likely in a more oppressive, form would exist under socialism. Bertrand Russell, in 1918, argued that 'there is every reason to fear that under State Socialism the power of officials would be vastly greater than it is at present'.[8] And in 1914, in a published debate between Morris Hillquit and J. A. Ryan, Ryan expressed the fear that the 'Socialist Industrial State' would be a tyranny.[9]

How did socialists respond to such criticisms? Did they offer to guarantee political rights and civil liberties under socialism? Although such a guarantee would have been as easy to give as it would have been to dishonour, none was given. Socialists ignored, or were contemptuous of, their critics. T. G. Masaryk, the Czech philosopher and statesman, who taxed the Marxists on this point, recalled that

the first three issues of the international review *Cosmopolis*, in 1898 published a discussion of the state of the future.... In it Liebknecht [the SPD leader] almost facetiously refuses to depict the future socialist order.... Nor is this the first discussion of its kind. The reader will recall the discussion of the future socialist state in the German Imperial Diet in 1893. At that time critics also asked the socialists to reveal their plans for the future, while the socialist deputies, Liebknecht, Bebel, and others treated the theme lightly.[10]

Nettl notes that in the thirty-two year history of *Neue Zeit*, the theoretical organ of Social Democracy, up to the First World War, there was only one article which dealt with the post-revolutionary society.[11] In 1912, Spargo explained that the socialist state cannot but be democratic, and that any conceptions of an all-powerful socialist state 'belong to the domain of vaudeville'.[12]

The Social Democrats' refusal seriously to examine the outcome of their project and its potential problems was derived in large measure from their confidence in the historical inevitability of socialism, underpinned by Marx's materialist conception of history and his refusal to paint portraits of the future. It was from this that Bernstein dissented, paving the way for his own criticisms of the illiberal consequences of a violent transition to socialism. In many ways, Bernstein paralleled the 'academic critics'; but he remained committed to socialism. The notion of the historical inevitability of socialism was enshrined for Social Democrats in the SPD's major Erfurt Programme of 1891, wherein lies the source of much of the subsequent Revisionism debate.

The Erfurt Programme itself, and Kautsky's elaboration of it, are the classic statements of Marxist political strategy from the period of the Second International. Contemporaries regarded the Programme as a model. Thomas Kirkup, a late-nineteenth-century historian of socialism, believed that it 'may fairly be regarded as the most developed expression of the Social Democratic principles yet put forth'.[13] The Erfurt Programme, like the Gotha Programme of 1875, and the much longer *Communist Manifesto* before it, was divided into two major sections: one dealing with general perspectives, the other with political demands and objectives. The Erfurt and Gotha Programmes are similar almost to the point of identity with regard to basic political demands, such as universal suffrage and direct legislation by the people. The Gotha Programme's pronounced Lassallean vocabulary, including demands for a 'free state' and opposition to the 'iron law of wages', drew Marx's fire in his *Critique of the Gotha Programme*. Not only did such examples reveal the extent of Lassalle's influence in 1875, but Marx believed they revealed sloppy thinking or formulation. The first, general section of the Erfurt Programme, by contrast, reveals the influence of Marx. Yet it seems constructed with a view to compromise: compromise with the German Imperial authorities who retained the power to enforce another Anti-Socialist Law; compromise with Party members who were still committed to Lassalle's views; and compromise between the Party's 'left' and 'right' wings, between revolutionaries and reformists. Such compromises were achieved primarily through omission or vagueness.

What remains in the Erfurt Programme is first of all the commitment to a broadly conceived socialism. Socialism is described as an inevitable historical stage, which will develop from the inevitably increasing division within capitalist society:

Ever greater grows the number of proletarians, ever larger the army of superfluous workmen, ever wider the chasm between exploiters and exploited, ever bitterer the class struggle between *bourgeoisie* and proletariat.[14]

The role of the SPD was 'To shape this struggle of the working class into a conscious and united one, and to point out to it its inevitable goal.'[15] The idea that socialist consciousness must be introduced to the working class from outside, embraced by Lenin, had been formulated earlier by Kautsky, and particularly by Plekhanov.[16] Marx objected to the Gotha Programme's aim of a 'free state' that 'between capitalist and communist society ... the state can be nothing but *the revolutionary dictatorship of the proletariat*'.[17] But the 'dictatorship of the proletariat' was not even mentioned in the Erfurt Programme. As for the 'old democratic litany familiar to all'

93

which Marx criticized in the Gotha Programme, it was contained (with Engels' approval) also in the Erfurt Programme. Furthermore, there was no explicit discussion in the 1891 Programme of the state and its representative political institutions, the relations of Social Democrats towards them, or their role in the achievement of socialism.

The shortcomings of the Erfurt Programme were not much alleviated by Kautsky's commentary upon it. Those sections of Kautsky's work which dealt with the proletariat and parliament, in particular, took as many steps away from clarity as they took toward it. Of the socialist revolution, Kautsky explained: 'It is by no means necessary that it can [*sic*] be accompanied with violence and bloodshed.'[18] But which is the bloodless strategy: through parliament? The state, Kautsky argues, is primarily a class institution. 'This feature is in no wise changed by its assumption of features of general utility.'[19] Nationalization of industry, or the development of a social insurance scheme, for example, do not change the character of the state.

The state will not cease to be a capitalist institution until the proletariat, the working class, has become the ruling class.[20]

But how does the working class become the ruling class: by winning political power? What is the relationship between the Socialist Party and the working class in this process? Kautsky did confront such issues in a discussion of the political struggle, and of the attitude of the SPD towards electoral activities. The political influence of the proletariat, he argued, could be expressed in parliament, although in the struggle for socialism the proletariat must press for 'an increase in the power of parliament', and for 'an increase in their own influence within the parliament':

The power of parliament depends on the energy and courage of the classes behind it and ... on which its will is to be imposed.[21]

For Kautsky, parliament was an important arena of class struggle, although not the only arena. But it was an institution with a rather curious relationship to the 'bourgeois state'. For Kautsky argues only that the bourgeoisie 'manipulates' parliament, not that it is essentially a bourgeois institution. Furthermore:

Whenever the proletariat engages in parliamentary activity as a self-conscious class, parliamentarism begins to change its character. It ceases to be a mere tool in the hands of the bourgeoisie.... It is the most powerful lever that can be utilized to raise the proletariat out of its economic, social and moral degradation.[22]

Clearly, for Kautsky, parliament has a great potential.

The proletariat, Kautsky advises, should exert its energies to increase the power of parliament in relation to 'other departments of government', as well as building its own parliamentary represent-ation. Universal suffrage, he continued, was 'one of the conditions prerequisite to a sound development of the proletariat'.[23] In this discussion, governmental and parliamentary power are not one and the same. What, then, would be the result of an SPD majority in the Reichstag? Would this be the conquering of political power? And how would the Reichstag then stand in relation to the other 'departments of government'? In the face of difficulties, Kautsky resorts to historical necessity:

if the working class did not make use of its mastery over the machinery of government to introduce the socialist system of production, the logic of events would finally call some such system into being....[24]

Would a parliamentary majority represent 'mastery over the machinery of government'? Would a Reichstag majority? And what is the mysterious 'logic of events' that would save the day? The general lack of precision in the use of political terms is aggravated by the omission of a discussion of German conditions, where govern-ment was effectively carried on independently of the Reichstag. The existence of liberal democratic regimes (which did not include Germany) had evidently confused Social Democrats, who formally held to the view of the state as a bourgeois state, while being uncertain of, or undecided in stating their views on, the implications for their strategy of the existence of representative-democratic insti-tutions. Was the state essentially bourgeois, as Marx had held; or was it essentially neutral, only corrupted by bourgeois influence, as Lassalle believed? The Erfurt Programme does not clearly resolve this issue, nor does Kautsky's explanation of it.

The Erfurt Programme, according to Kautsky – its principal drafter – envisaged a period of electoral struggle leading to a parliamentary majority for the SPD (the economic disintegration of capitalism notwithstanding). The SPD's intentions seemed demo-cratic, and it proposed no drastic structural alteration to the state except for the socialization of industry, and presumably the lifting of constitutional limitations on parliament itself. Kautsky addressed himself to objections against his 'Future State' in no more serious a fashion than did his colleagues, resorting once more to 'historical necessity'. He maintained that 'social evolution is a modern science',[25] and that since the 'laws of evolution' were known, no plan of the future was needed. Furthermore, socialism was no longer 'simply desirable, it has become inevitable'.[26] To Kautsky's assertion that socialists had no doubt made their own private inquiries into the details of socialism, the results not being a Party concern, Masaryk replied that 'there is something wrong with asking men to consider the future and at the same time declaring it a private affair'.[27] Critics of socialism, some of whom saw it as a future 'bureaucratic absolutism',[28] were frustrated by the socialists' tactics. Ludwig von Mises pointed out that

Marxists have no occasion to occupy themselves with problems concerned with the political constitution of the socialist community. In this connection they perceive no problems at all which cannot be dismissed by saying nothing about them.[29]

Thus did German Social Democracy venture into the 1890s. It did not care, or was unable, to clarify its political objectives, even though it saw them as inevitable. It seemed uncertain whither its parliamentary strategy would lead. And its analysis of the state showed more deference to Lassalle than to Marx. As Bebel explained: 'like most of us who then became Socialists, I went from Lassalle to Marx. Lassalle's writings were in our hands before we knew anything of Marx and Engels.'[30] But the SPD's complacence about its commitment to Marxism on the one hand, and parliamentary activity on the other, was shattered by the controversy over Revisionism which arose in the late 1890s. The Revisionists wanted the Party to abandon Marxism, on grounds which the 'academic critics' of Marxism had canvassed: if Marxism was a science, it was being falsified by social reality. Tom Bottomore has more recently expressed this view as follows:

Marxist theory, if it constituted an empirical science of society, must clearly be amenable to continuous criticism resulting from new discoveries and new ideas. In that sense 'revisionism' would be the highest virtue rather than the greatest crime.[31]

But Marxism in the SPD, even if it was circumvented by much of the SPD strategy, was dogma; Revisionism was heresy.

Bernstein and Kautsky had shared a close friendship with the aging Engels, and were considered the leading SPD theorists at the beginning of the 1890s. Karl Kautsky was sometimes even known as 'the Pope of Social Democracy'. Both were committed to socialism and democracy. Yet Bernstein took the interpretation of Marxism as a science seriously enough to proclaim himself a Revisionist when he believed that Marxism had failed adequately to analyse a changing capitalism. He summarized his ideas thus, in almost direct contrast with the Erfurt Programme:

> Peasants do not sink; middle class does not disappear; crises do not grow ever larger; misery and serfdom do not increase. There *is* increase in insecurity, dependence, social distance, social character of production, functional superfluity of property owners.[32]

In a series of articles entitled 'Problems of Socialism', published first in Kautsky's theoretical journal, *Neue Zeit*, and then more systematically in book form, Bernstein took the Marxist heritage of the Party to task. The SPD, of course, had no qualms about disavowing Marx or Engels if the occasion saw fit. Engels' polemic against Dühring in the 1870s was almost suppressed by the SPD; it was allowed to continue being published serially only as a literary supplement to *Vorwärts*.[33] Marx's *Critique of the Gotha Programme* (1875), first published in Germany in 1890, was repudiated by the socialist deputies in the Reichstag. Interesting in this context is Bebel's comment on the 1875 Gotha re-unification of German socialists (crudely put, 'Lassalleans' and 'Marxists'):

> it was not an easy matter to satisfy the two old gentlemen in London [i.e., Marx and Engels]. What was really a clever tactical move on our part and the result of prudent calculation they regarded as mere weakness.[34]

But if the Social Democrat deputies were prepared to renounce Marx's dictatorship of the proletariat in 1891,[35] the Party was not yet prepared to disavow 'scientific socialism' some seven or eight years later. For Bernstein went further in his criticisms of Marxism than his epigrammatic note, cited above, suggests; he denied the possibility of a scientific socialism. He explained that,

> to me the chapter [at the end of *Capital*, vol. 1] illustrates a dualism which runs through the whole monumental work of Marx ... a dualism which

consists in this, that the work aims at being a scientific inquiry and also at proving a theory laid down long before its drafting; a formula lies at the basis of it in which the result to which the exposition should lead is fixed beforehand.[36]

Such an objection to Marxism, he argued, was 'quite irrelevant to the strivings of social democracy', which did not depend on Marxism.[37]

Bernstein worked, in effect, to liberate socialism and Social Democracy from their Marxist foundation and to replace it with an explicitly democratic foundation. He explained in a letter to the 1898 Party Congress in Stuttgart that

no one has questioned the necessity for the working class to gain control of the government. The point at issue is between the theory of a social cataclysm and the question whether with the given social development in Germany and the present advanced state of its working class in town and country, a sudden catastrophe would be in the interests of Social Democracy.[38]

Bernstein replied that it would not be in Social Democracy's interests, and appealed to Engels' 1895 Introduction to Marx's *The Class Struggles in France* for support.[39] If his theoretical break with Marxism was not yet complete, it certainly was by May 1901, when Bernstein asked 'How is Scientific Socialism Possible?' and argued that it was not. Bernstein defended an ethical conception of socialism from the prevailing scientific conception of Marx's project. By contrast, Engels had explicitly argued in 1884 that economic crises, not an ethical denunciation of exploitation, would produce socialism. Of the ethical approach, Engels had explained: 'Marx ... never based his communist demands upon this, but upon the inevitable collapse of the capitalist mode of production.'[40] Bernstein first denied that Marx's theory of the necessity of capitalist collapse was accurate; he then denied the possibility of a scientific socialism; and finally, he embraced socialism as an ethically superior system to capitalism.

If he denied that capitalism was prone to ever more disastrous economic, and thus social and political, crises, Bernstein nevertheless maintained that the precondition for socialism was a highly developed capitalism:

we have as the first condition of the general realization of socialism a definite degree of capitalist development, and as the second the exercise of political sovereignty by the class party of the workers, i.e., social democracy. The dictatorship of the proletariat is, according to Marx, the form of the exercise of this power in the transition period.[41]

Marx and Engels, he continued, had the (1789) French Revolution (in its Jacobin phase) in mind as a model for their 'dictatorship'. Yet the working class of today was not homogeneous, nor were the industrial workers a majority of the population.[42] Capitalist development and centralization, he thus believed, had not progressed sufficiently for socialization. Left to its own devices, it would eventually become ripe for socialism. This stress upon the preconditions for socialism was directly related, for Bernstein, to the means of achieving socialism and to the character of the socialist regime. For the proletariat could conquer political power in two ways: by revolution, which was characteristically violent; and by peaceful, parliamentary struggle. If socialism was attempted by revolutionary means, however, the result would be the dictatorship of a small group or an individual.

The charge of Blanquism against Marx of the 1848 period is now a popular one, as we saw in chapter 2; Bernstein was its originator. A violent revolution, the proof for Bernstein that the preconditions for socialism were lacking, would only result

in reckless devastation of productive forces, insane experimentalizing and aimless violence, and the political sovereignty of the working-class would, in fact, only be carried out in the form of a dictatorial, revolutionary, central power, supported by the terrorist dictatorship of revolutionary clubs. As such it hovered before the Blanquists, and as such it is still represented in the *Communist Manifesto* and the publications for which its authors were responsible at that time.[43]

But it was a charge taken up not just by the Revisionists. Jean Jaurès, a popular French Social Democrat, soon echoed Bernstein: 'Marx and Blanqui both believed that the proletariat would seize power by means of a revolution.'[44] If the utopian socialists, Jaurès continues, were distinguished by their lack of reliance on the power of the working class, then the *Communist Manifesto* was a utopian pamphlet. It was not written for a class sure of its power; the *Manifesto*'s propositions

are the Revolutionary expedients of an impatient and feeble class, that wishes to force forward by strategy the progress of events.[45]

Jaurès considered it 'amazing' that Marx believed the proletariat able to utilize the bourgeois revolution for its own ends, yet incapable of establishing communism at the time, 'even in the first flush of victory, and in the most advanced countries'.[46] It was the idea that socialism was the rule of a working class ready to manage its own affairs, on the basis of a highly developed industrial economy, which Bernstein and Jaurès held in common. Georges Sorel, the theorist of anarcho-syndicalism and an opponent of the Social Democrats, also held that Marx had adopted a Blanquist strategy around 1848–51. Even more clearly than Bernstein, Sorel brought out Blanquism's independence from the specific historical and economic prerequisites of socialism:

Blanquism is, in essence, nothing more than the revolt of the poor conducted by a revolutionary General Staff. Such a revolt can occur in any epoch whatsoever. It is independent of the system of production.[47]

But for Sorel, Blanquism was on these very grounds quite distant from Marx's project.

Bernstein believed that socialism was bound up with the extension of democracy into all areas of life, and that it was the 'legitimate heir' to liberalism.[48] But a violent revolution or, in Bernstein's terms, a *revolution*, was generally the work of minorities in situations where the majority was not yet prepared or ready to take power. It is true, he concedes, that revolutions appear to be 'quicker' and 'more radical' than legal and peaceful methods of social change, but this is true only in a superficial sense.

In general, one may say here that the revolutionary way (always in the sense of revolution by violence) does quicker work as far as it deals with the removal of obstacles which a privileged minority places in the path of social progress: that its strength lies on its negative side.[49]

Bernstein abhors violence. On balance, it is counter-productive. Socialism must be a constructive 'social-political work', building upon the achievements of capitalism, not destroying them. Considered from this angle, Bernstein concludes that 'constitutional legislation ... is best adapted to positive social–political work.... Legislation works as a systematic force, revolution as an elementary force.'[50]

But revolutions, for Bernstein, are more than simply destructive, and thus unsuited to building socialism: they are expedients. Given the prerequisites for socialism which were as much a part of the Marxist tradition as the expectation of a revolution, Bernstein asked whether there was any sense in a revolution and its sequel, the dictatorship of the proletariat.

Is there any sense in maintaining the phrase of the 'dictatorship of the proletariat' at a time when in all possible places representatives of social democracy have placed themselves practically in the arena of Parliamentary work, have declared for the proportional representation of the people, and for direct legislation – all of which is inconsistent with dictatorship.[51]

Bernstein took 'dictatorship' in its modern, political sense. He argued that as a political form, it was entirely alien to the spirit of socialism, and should be abandoned. The only way socialism would succeed was if the working class was responsible enough to rule in its own name; experience with democracy and self-government would develop that capacity. The experience would also temper the working class, restraining it from ill-fated experiments in violence:

democracy is a condition of socialism to a much greater degree than is usually assumed, *i.e.*, it is not only the means but also the substance. Without a certain amount of democratic institutions or traditions, the socialist doctrine of the present time would not indeed be possible.[52]

Bernstein's was a theory of economic and political prerequisites, confirmed through the operation of liberal democracy. For a working class which had not the experience of liberal democracy 'will certainly revolt sometimes and join in small conspiracies, but never develop a socialist movement'.[53] Bernstein constantly contrasts liberal democracy and revolution, not simply as means, but as means which have a decisive influence over the desired ends. Without democracy, and its development of the working class, 'the dictatorship of the proletariat means the dictatorship of club orators and writers'.[54] Bernstein does not deny that the political sovereignty of the working class can be represented by the expression 'dictatorship of the proletariat', but he urges that the expression be dropped by Social Democrats because it is ambiguous, and because it is a convenient shelter for Blanquists.

The challenge of Revisionism was a crucial one for German Social Democracy, and for the history of Social Democracy. Bernstein had gone a long way towards 'answering' many of Marxism's and socialism's critics, even if he had conceded a number of important points to them. He had agreed with them that Marxism was not a positivist social science. He consequently abandoned Marxism; but he retained a commitment to socialism which was explicitly democratic. Bernstein shifted the focus of socialism from a particular system of production to a democratic polity. He thus challenged the prevailing conception of socialism as an economic organization, the only problems with which were thought to be organizational and technical. His contribution demanded some response from those who would defend Marxism to questions about the transition to socialism, about the 'dictatorship of the proletariat', and about the political organization of socialism. Bernstein had thrown down the gauntlet; would anyone pick it up? But the response to Bernstein's challenge was primarily dogmatic; some of his most important questions were ignored, while his weaknesses were exploited. Sorel was concerned by this response: *'the triumph of Kautsky would signify the ruination of Marxism'*, he wrote in 1900.[55] Eight years later he concluded that Marx's disciples had become mere popularizers, 'more familiar with the compositional techniques of the liturgists than with modern scientific method'.[56] For the Marxism of the Second International appealed to the model of the natural sciences only for support, not for confirmation. From their now besieged position, the Marxists chose defence by attack.

Bernstein had argued that violence was a method of social change unsuited to the achievement of socialism, and was likely to result in a new form of tyranny. But as Gay notes, 'Bernstein's concentration on Blanquism prevented him from facing fully the crucial question: Was a non-violent revolution possible in Imperial Germany?'[57] Indeed, Bernstein seemed to have over-estimated the possibility for a peaceful transition to socialism in Germany, although he conceded that if workers' action through legal means was frustrated, 'resistance *must* be attempted'.[58] He was certain, however, that electoral alliances with the middle class and their liberal representatives would ensure that legal channels to socialism would not be blocked. But Bernstein was vulnerable on at least two other points. His emphasis on Blanquism, again, had blinded him to the questions: must all revolutions be violent? and, must all violent revolutions be Blanquist?

Kautsky showed little enthusiasm for attacking Bernstein's position, even though he disagreed with it. He maintained the Marxist view, at the SPD's Hanover Conference in 1899, that if capitalism did not economically collapse, there was no necessary, historical cause for socialism. This link was uppermost in the defence of orthodoxy. Kautsky argued that 'the necessity or even only the desirability of socialism is not only not clear in his [Bernstein's] book, but becomes doubtful in the extreme'.[59] Other Party leaders had little enthusiasm for attacking Bernstein because they did not differ greatly from him. Ignaz Auer, for example, wrote to 'Ede' [Eduard] Bernstein:

Do you think it is really possible that a party which has a literature going back fifty years, an organization going back forty years and a still older tradition, can change its direction like this in the twinkling of an eye? For the most influential members of the party to behave as you demand would simply mean splitting the party and throwing decades of work to the winds. My dear Ede, one doesn't formally decide to do what you ask, one doesn't say it, one does it. Our whole activity – even under the shameful anti-Socialist law – was the activity of a Social Democratic reforming party. A party which reckons with the masses simply cannot be anything else.[60]

And Auer was not alone in resisting programmatic change for the sake of Party unity. Victor Adler also resisted such change in the Austrian Social Democratic Party for the same reason.[61] It was, furthermore, useful to maintain a commitment to Marxism as a doctrine which could satisfy both intellectuals and masses, despite its critics and its vulgarization. But the unity of the SPD throughout the Revisionist controversy and after was a unity achieved at the expense of vital clarity over aims and methods. The Party seemed united in spite of itself.

The only serious theoretical defence of Marxism to arise from Bernstein's challenge was made by Rosa Luxemburg, a Polish Marxist, and a young and able SPD theorist, in her *Social Reform or Revolution*. Luxemburg defended Marxism and its revolutionary political strategy, although at that stage she avoided discussing the 'dictatorship of the proletariat'. If the era of capitalist crises was over, if the middle class was not disappearing, and if the workers could improve their lot under capitalism, as Bernstein claimed, then Luxemburg concluded that Social Democracy must not struggle for the 'conquest of political power', but must try to better 'the condition of the working class within the existing order'.[62] Social Democracy must not expect to institute socialism as a result of a political and social crisis, but should build socialism by means of the progressive extension of social control and the gradual application of the principle of co-operation.[63]

But Luxemburg differed fundamentally from Bernstein on all these issues. She denied his claim that capitalism could control its economies so as to exclude crises; she reaffirmed the Marxist claim that socialism was objectively inevitable; and she denied the possibility that the transition to socialism could be peaceful and gradual. It is the last of these which is most significant because it broached those issues which were at the core of Revisionism: the role of reforms under capitalism; their relationship to the socialist revolution in its broadest sense; and the tactics of Social Democrats within the liberal democratic state. It is the most significant, in other words, because it was another contribution to the debate over the proper response of Marxism to the liberal democratic state.

Bernstein, Luxemburg notes, begins his critique of Marxism with a new conception of the objective development of capitalism. In particular, he denies that capitalism must suffer a general economic collapse. Luxemburg reasserts the orthodox view: 'Socialist theory up to now declared that the point of departure for a transformation to socialism would be a general and catastrophic crisis.'[64] Marxism had traditionally expected that the internal contradictions of capitalism would give rise to a situation where the continued functioning of the system was rendered 'impossible'. Indeed, the scientific claims of Marxism rested primarily upon an economic analysis of capitalism. Luxemburg's reply pointed to the increasing anarchy of capitalist production, to the progressive and objective socialization of production, and to a growing consciousness amongst the proletariat. Bernstein had claimed that capitalism could adapt, that it could avoid crises through mechanisms such as the credit system and cartels and trusts. Apart from denying the attenuating effects of these mechanisms, and in fact insisting that they would make capitalist crises even more severe, Luxemburg shifted the discussion by arguing that

if one admits with Bernstein that capitalist development does not move in the direction of its own ruin, then socialism ceases to be objectively necessary.[65]

To this, Bernstein might well have agreed. Yet for Luxemburg, if socialism is not 'objectively necessary' it somehow ceases to be possible. She therefore goes to considerable lengths to maintain the scientific nature of Marxism. She urges that socialism is 'historically necessary', and believes that it is proof enough to show that capitalism will collapse. Bernstein had certainly lost a great deal of support by denying that Marxism was a positive science. Louis Boudin, for example, introducing a work on Marxist economics which bears the scars of the Revisionist controversy, wrote, rather fantastically, that

Marxism is so much *the* scientific doctrine in its sphere (which covers all the life of humanity in organized society, including all its social and intellectual manifestations) that you cannot destroy it without at the same time destroying all scientific knowledge of the subject.[66]

Yet the political, as opposed to the theoretical, leaders of the SPD seemed less attached to the specifics of their scientific heritage. Victor Adler once wrote to Kautsky: 'I understand nothing of the history of surplus value, and, frankly, I don't give a damn.'[67]

If not on 'objective necessity', on what then does Bernstein base his programme for socialism? On ethics. Bernstein, Luxemburg declares, 'is obliged to transform socialism itself from a definite historical phase of social development into an abstract "principle"'.[68] If man's idea of justice is offended by capitalism, she explains, he will be attracted by the justice of socialism:

We return to that lamentable Rosinante on which the Don Quixotes of history have galloped towards the great reform of the earth, always to come home with their eyes blackened.[69]

The notion that Marxist socialism was devoid of all ethical considerations was widespread at that time, not only among Marxists themselves but even among informed commentators.[70] Even though some of the 'academic critics' of Marxism had claimed that Marx's scientific research was directed to confirming preconceived ethical positions, Luxemburg maintained that socialism was a scientifically proven, historically necessary sequel to capitalism and had no need of ethics. By basing socialism on ethical principles, she believed, socialism (as Marxists conceived it) would never be realized. For if capitalist crises could be avoided, she reasoned, socialized production and working-class consciousness would never develop.[71] If Bernstein was correct about capitalism's ability to suppress its crises – a point which Luxemburg would concede only as a debating tactic

– his programme would not lead to the abolition of capitalism, but to the amelioration of its effects.[72]

Extending the supposition that capitalism could adapt, and avoid its economic ruin, what would become of Bernstein's programme? Luxemburg asks. For Bernstein, she recalls, 'trade unions, social reforms and ... the political democratization of the State are the means of the progressive realization of socialism'.[73] But are these realistic or effective means? On the contrary: trade unions, she argues, 'have not ... the power to suppress exploitation'.[74] The capitalist economic law of wages 'is not shattered but applied by trade-union activity'.[75] Trade unions may merely win concessions within the framework marked out for them by capitalist economic relations; they exist within this framework, and do not exist to destroy it. But what of the democratic institutions under capitalism wherein reforms which benefit the working class can be enacted? This is by far the most interesting and important part of Luxemburg's anti-Revisionist polemic. Luxemburg's general position is clear enough, and is a direct parallel to her remarks about trade union activity under capitalism: liberal democratic institutions exist within the framework of a capitalist state; they cannot abolish the framework which gives them life. Reforms are made within the existing framework; revolution abolishes that framework. This is not to say that trade union work and parliamentary struggle are irrelevant to the socialist revolution:

From the viewpoint of a movement for socialism, the trade-union struggle and our parliamentary practice are vastly important insofar as they make socialistic the *awareness*, the consciousness, of the proletariat and help to organize it as a class. But once they are considered as instruments of the direct socialization of capitalist economy, they lose not only their usual effectiveness but cease being means of preparing the working class for the conquest of power.[76]

The means which Bernstein proposes to achieve socialism are, for Luxemburg, merely preparatory to the revolutionary means she advocates. The means which Bernstein proposes should not be judged by their intrinsic results, as Bernstein suggests, but by whether they contribute to revolutionary means. This position of Luxemburg's is, as I have said, clear enough. It is rather her defence of this position which is more interesting and, at times, unclear.

It must be remembered that Luxemburg was committed to the

proposition that the existing state was a capitalist state, despite its liberal democratic institutions or other political forms. Bernstein's argument about the uses to which liberal democracy could be put by the working class was implicitly based on a conception of the state as class-neutral. Because the existing state was a capitalist state, according to Luxemburg, its democratic forms are an obstacle to working-class power. Reforms within the capitalist state are not real conquests for the working class. Capitalist democracy must thus be used as a means for exposing the limitations of reform, and as a means of preparing for the conquest of political power by the working class. Labour legislation, Luxemburg cites by way of example, 'has absolutely nothing to do with ... "supreme ownership"',[77] or 'social control' by the working class. It is, she claims, a protection of capitalist ownership.[78] By Luxemburg's definition, legislation in a capitalist institution, whatever its subject, is capitalist legislation: legislation which is ultimately in the interests of the capitalists. But how does Luxemburg defend her proposition that the state is a capitalist state; and what influence do, or can, representative institutions have upon the class nature of the state? This is the most problematic part of her argument.

'The State became capitalist with the political victory of the bourgeoisie',[79] Luxemburg begins. This political victory was prior to the establishment of liberal democracy. Capitalism, she continues, modified the nature of the state, widening its sphere of action and giving it new functions. 'In this sense, capitalist development prepares little by little the future fusion of the state and society',[80] which will be achieved under socialism. Yet,

The present State is, first of all, an organization of the ruling class.... Labour legislation is enacted as much in the immediate interest of the capitalist class as in the interest of society in general.[81]

The state as it has developed under capitalism, in other words, embodies a central tension: by taking on ever-wider responsibilities, it represents to some extent the 'interest of society in general'; but it also represents the interests of the bourgeoisie. But, Luxemburg argues, this tension exists only up to a certain point. When 'social development' comes into conflict with the bourgeoisie and the state, the state sides with the bourgeoisie: it

loses more and more its character as a representative of the whole of society and is transformed, at the same rate into a pure *class* state. Or, to speak more exactly, these two qualities distinguish themselves more and more from each other and find themselves in a contradictory relation in the very nature of the State.[82]

There is a certain plausibility to Luxemburg's argument that the state, as a class organization, strives to appear as the general representative of society, but that when the interests of the dominant class are under threat (from immediate or long-term historical challenges), this appearance cannot be sustained as it goes to the defence of the bourgeoisie. Yet Luxemburg goes on to claim that this transformation 'into a pure *class* state' is effected by liberal democracy:

the extension of democracy, which Bernstein sees as a means of realizing socialism by degrees, does not contradict but, on the contrary, corresponds perfectly to the transformation realized in the nature of the State.[83]

Luxemburg, rather curiously, implies that the extension of the franchise and of political rights within the general society corresponds to an increasingly particularist policy of the state. How this can be so she does not explain here, but she continues to insist that 'the conflict within the capitalist State, described above, manifests itself even more emphatically in modern parliamentarism'.[84] The democratic form of parliamentarism, she explains, 'serves to express, within the organization of the State, the interests of the whole of society'.[85] The content of parliamentarism, however, reveals it as an instrument of the ruling class. The form and the content of parliamentarism, Luxemburg suggests, are in a constant state of tension. This reasoning leads to the conclusion that parliament is essentially a capitalist institution, and presents no real threat to the rule of the bourgeoisie, even though it appears to be in the general interest. Parliamentarism, Luxemburg declares, is the 'specific form of the bourgeois class State'.[86] It is the political organization of capitalism which, together with 'property relations, that is to say the *juridical* organization of capitalism, become more *capitalist* and not more socialist'[87] with the development of capitalism. They create a rising wall between capitalism and socialism, not a steadily diminishing wall:

Only the hammer blow of revolution, that is to say, the conquest of political power by the proletariat can break down this wall.[88]

This interpretation of parliament as essentially a class institution of the bourgeoisie, as the lynchpin of her argument that parliament must be overthrown for the proletariat's conquest of political power, is leavened, indeed negated, by Luxemburg's assertion that parliament has, or can have, a 'tendency to negate its class character'.[89] Thus when liberal democracy begins to infringe bourgeois interests, she declares, the bourgeoisie will sacrifice democratic forms. Luxemburg wants to have it both ways: that parliament is a bourgeois instrument in essence, and no threat to bourgeois rule; and that parliament can threaten bourgeois rule, but will be suppressed if it dares.

In the later parts of her critique of Revisionism, Luxemburg uses a slightly different approach to the question of liberal democracy, and its potential for socialists. 'No absolute and general relation can be constructed between capitalist development and democracy', she argues.[90] While universal suffrage and liberal democratic institutions may have assisted in the political development of the bourgeoisie, there is no guarantee that they will be preserved. In fact, Luxemburg claims, 'democratic institutions ... have completely exhausted their function as aids in the development of bourgeois society'.[91] The bourgeoisie is only a transient ally of democracy, but 'the fate of democracy is bound with the socialist movement'.[92] That the bourgeoisie would 'desert' democracy was a view held more widely among the socialist opponents of Revisionism than among the Revisionists, and it had been developed by, among others, Engels. But it was also a part of the argument that liberal democracy could present a serious challenge to the bourgeoisie's rule. Socialists, it was maintained, were the only real friends of democracy. But having advanced this type of argument, Luxemburg reverts to its opposite: that democracy can present no real threat to capitalism. For in bourgeois society,

class domination does not rest on 'acquired rights' but on *real economic relations* – the fact that wage labour is not a juridical relation, but purely an economic relation. In our juridical system there is not a single legal formula for the class domination of today.[93]

If democracy cannot touch the real basis of bourgeois society, why should the bourgeoisie ever want to suppress democracy, as Luxemburg suggests above? Furthermore, the very concept of ownership under capitalism is a juridical relation, as well as a 'real economic relation'. One of the standard criticisms of Marx's division of society into 'base' and 'superstructure', and his argument that the former 'determines' the latter, is that the 'base' of economic and production relations cannot be defined except in terms of 'superstructural', that is, legal and political, notions. Luxemburg's attempt to use this base – superstructure division to argue for the superstructural, and hence peripheral, nature of parliament and its decisions, neglects not only the problems which such a division raises, but also the actual legislative effects of parliament upon the bourgeoisie through budgets, social insurance schemes, and even nationalizations. But Luxemburg persists: 'How can wage slavery be suppressed the "legislative way", if wage slavery is not expressed in laws?'[94] Within the framework of bourgeois society, she concludes, parliament is powerless to introduce socialism, for 'no law in the world can give to the proletariat the means of production'.[95] Luxemburg's analysis of the state is at once the most potentially fruitful part of her polemic against Revisionism, but also the least convincing. It held the hope that a Marxist theory of the state would emerge from the confused notions of the state held in the SPD. But while it emphasized the class nature of the state, it was equivocal on the vital question of the socialist potential of liberal democracy. Luxemburg could not decide whether liberal-democratic institutions were mere deceptions, or whether they could become a real challenge to capitalism. She tried to demonstrate that Revisionist hopes in liberal democracy were misplaced either because it could not affect the power of the bourgeoisie, which is extra-legal, or because the bourgeoisie would suppress it if it offered a challenge.

The other important part of Luxemburg's polemic was her evaluation of reform and revolution. Revolutions, she maintained, are 'the pivot and the motive force of human history';[96] they must not be confused with the struggle for reforms. Reforms are carried on, in every historical period, within the framework provided by the last revolution. Of course, Luxemburg does not deny the importance of reforms. As she put it in her 'Introduction' to *Social Reform or Revolution*:

Between social reforms and revolution there exists for the Social-Democracy an indissoluble tie. The struggle for reforms is its means; the social revolution, its aim.[97]

For Luxemburg, socialism is a social transformation which breaks the bounds of bourgeois society before it can be truly in the interests of the working class. Bernstein's hopes for reform, she implies, are based on the idea that the constitutional, legal, and even political framework of capitalism need not be superseded for reform to be manifestly in the interests of the working class. But the difference between them was not just a theoretical one; it had, according to Luxemburg, important practical consequences for the Social Democratic Party. For the consequence of making 'immediate results' the principal aim of the SPD's activity would be

the adoption by the party of a 'policy of compensation', a policy of political trading, and an attitude of diffident, diplomatic conciliation.[98]

Such a policy would reap disillusionment. In 1898, Luxemburg examined a concrete case of this consequence of Revisionism. Attacking a Social Democrat, Comrade Heine, she explained that if one were merely limited to doing what is possible, one might offer to exchange consent to militarism for political concessions or social reforms. The result would be to sacrifice 'the basic principles of the class struggle for momentary advantage',[99] which is based on opportunism.

Opportunism, incidentally, is a political game which can be lost in two ways: not only basic principles but also practical success may be forfeited. The assumption that one can achieve the greatest number of successes by making concessions rests on a complete error.[100]

Chasing after what is possible, and abandoning principles, Luxemburg suggests, is like the hunter who has not only lost his quarry, but his gun as well.

Bernstein, Luxemburg argues, has a different conception of socialism from the one held by Marxists. If capitalism can avoid crises, and if Bernstein's socialism is based on ethical considerations, then Bernstein

renounces the struggle against the *capitalist mode of production* and attempts to direct the socialist movement to struggle against 'capitalist distribution'.[101]

By concentrating on the question of distribution rather than the mode of production, she implies, socialism becomes a matter of just distribution, rather than of an organization of production. This consideration leads Luxemburg to conclude that those who favour legislative reform 'do not really choose a more tranquil, calmer road to the *same* goal, but a *different* goal'.[102] But on these grounds, Luxemburg claims that Bernstein denies working-class interests, and abandons the Social Democratic movement:

He began by abandoning the *final aim* and supposedly keeping the move-ment. But as there can be no socialist movement without a socialist aim, he ends by renouncing the *movement*.[103]

She suggests that Bernstein challenged the *raison d'être* of the SPD. Indeed, by minimizing the class nature of socialism, and of the obstacles to socialism, as they had been conceived in the Marxist tradition, Bernstein had separated Social Democracy and socialism from the proletariat. The SPD, Luxemburg feared, would become just another party of reform if it adopted Revisionism.

Considerable play is often made of Bernstein's statement that it is not the 'ultimate end' which mattered to him, but the 'movement'. Even discounting his own claims of mis-representation, we might conclude from his contribution that in stressing the political and economic prerequisites of his conception of socialism, as well as its links with the liberal democratic tradition, Bernstein was vitally interested in the character of the 'end'. Wistrich declares that Bernstein 'was the first [German socialist] to question the utopian concentration on the final goal of socialism *at the expense* of the means and the methods by which it was to be achieved'.[104] It was Luxemburg who, in reasserting the importance of socialism con-ceived as: (a) a mode of production; and (b) the fulfilment of proletarian interests, missed a first-class opportunity to confound Marxism's critics by being precise about the revolutionary means she defends. She insists only that Social Democrats are not Blanquists:

The Social-Democracy, *does not . . . expect to attain its aim either as a result of the victorious violence of a minority or through the numerical superiority of a majority. It sees socialism come as a result of economic necessity – and the comprehension of that necessity – leading to the suppression of capital-ism by the working masses.*[105]

Her primary point is that liberal democracy can make the proletariat aware of its interests, but it cannot fulfil those interests. An alterna-tive strategy is not presented. It was at least six years later that she developed the strategy of the mass strike, stimulated by the experien-ces of the 1905 Russian Revolution.

Nevertheless, Luxemburg's conception of revolution, such as it is, denies the possibility that the transition to socialism 'can be realized in one happy act'.[106] In this transition, she argues, the proletariat cannot seize power 'in any other way than "prematurely"',[107] and may have to seize power several times before it can *hold* power. Thus,

the objection to the 'premature' conquest of power is at bottom nothing more than a *general opposition to the aspiration of the proletariat to possess itself of State power*.[108]

Bernstein opposed violence (revolution in its narrow sense), not social change (revolution in its broad sense), because he believed that violence was the expedient of a class ill-prepared for power; because he believed that violence fostered Blanquism, the revolutionary substitution of a small group for the proletariat; and because he believed that violence was counter-productive for socialism. But Luxemburg never clarifies the sense in which she uses 'revolution'. By operating on two levels of meaning: (a) revolution as the (rather vague, but presumably violent) conquest of political power by the proletariat; and (b) revolution as socialism itself, she avoids the question of violence and prejudges Bernstein's point at the same time by declaring him opposed to 'revolution'. Above all, Luxemburg did not seriously consider the issue to which this whole debate about Revisionism should have contributed: how can socialism best be introduced in a democratic republic?

Luxemburg's contribution was devoted to the idea that the strength of the workers' movement was based on the depth of its theoretical clarity and commitment. Yet she did not oppose the parliamentary, or trade union, activities of the SPD, which were the breeding-grounds for Revisionists. She attacked the effect, not the cause. She maintained that 'the pivotal point of Bernstein's system is not located in his conception of the practical tasks of Social Democracy',[109] and Nettl comments that she saw the theoretical principles of Marxism as 'a means of keeping tactics revolutionary'.[110] Luxemburg thus did not openly confront the question, upon which Bernstein's theoretical endeavours were predicated, of whether the SPD was a reformist party.

The issue of 'Participationism', the participation of socialists within bourgeois governments, was closely related to the debate over Revisionism. Alexandre Millerand, a French Social Democrat who precipitated the issue by joining the Cabinet of the government of Waldeck-Rousseau in 1899, had ideas similar to Bernstein's. As early as 1896, in his Saint-Mandé Programme, Millerand had argued that immediate reforms bettered the position of the working class, and that in order to begin its emancipation and the socialization of the means of production, 'it is necessary and sufficient for the socialist party to pursue the conquest of public power through universal suffrage'.[111] This is consistent with Revisionism, although Revisionists did not necessarily justify the participation of socialists in bourgeois governments. Yet many of those who abandoned positivistic Marxism with the Revisionists did abandon socialism as well. The reality of this situation was screened by the Social Democratic trend to understate parliamentary manoeuvres as mere tactics. William Liebknecht in 1881, for example, wrote that the idea of a coalition government of socialists and other democratic forces should not be discounted.[112] 'Questions of tactics', he wrote, 'are practical questions and should be absolutely distinguished from questions of principle.'[113] Clarity over this issue was not enhanced by Kautsky's resolution, endorsed by the Paris Congress (1900) of the Second International, which said in part:

The entry of a single socialist into a bourgeois Ministry cannot be regarded as the normal beginning for winning political power; it can never be anything but a temporary and exceptional makeshift in an emergency situation. Whether in any given instance such an emergency situation exists is a question of tactics and not of principle. The Congress does not have to decide that.[114]

Dutt records that his resolution was described as the 'indiarubber resolution'.[115]

Participationism can arise from the Revisionist commitment to parliamentary democracy and the down-playing of class politics. Yet Luxemburg's polemic against Bernstein achieved little by way of clarifying the tasks of Marxists in relation to a democratically elected parliament which itself constituted the government. Instead, as Gay notes, 'her most effective hit was undoubtedly scored by her attack on Revisionist tactics – Bernstein himself was frequently doubtful whether the parliamentary methods he so earnestly advocated could be successfully applied in Germany'.[116] Revisionism in practice, as Luxemburg had predicted, led many socialists to abandon socialism. Conservatives quickly realized that the SPD had 'mellowed'. Orth, for example, considered that

the best school for Socialism has been the school of parliamentary activity. Here the hot-blooded protesters become sober artisans of statecraft.[117]

The controversy over Revisionism succeeded in compelling Karl Kautsky to re-examine and to clarify in the succeeding years his own ideas on revolution, liberal democracy, and the role of violence. The defenders of Revisionism, it will be recalled, had equated the use of violence with minority revolution or insurrection, which they believed was a danger to socialism and to democracy. To the destruction caused by violence, they contrasted the tangible progress of democracy. Jaurès wrote:

Supposing that the democracy is not ready for the Communist movement, will it not annul, instead of extend the effects of the first dictatorial acts of the proletariat instead of carrying them out and extending their scope? But if, on the contrary, the democracy is prepared, if the proletariat can, by legal measures alone, induce it to develop the first revolutionary institutions in a communist direction, we have in the legal conquest of the democracy the sovereign method of Revolution. Every other method, I repeat, is nothing but the expedient ... of a weak and ill-prepared class.[118]

Kautsky too saw in the advance of democracy a great benefit for the proletariat, although he did not limit himself to this method of social change. All socialists, he believed, were committed to social revolution 'in the wider sense',[119] but not to revolution conceived as a particular method of social change. The essential difference between the methods of reform and revolution was the conquest of political power by the proletariat:

The conquest of governmental power by a hitherto oppressed class, in other words, a political revolution, is accordingly the essential characteristic of social revolution in this narrow sense, in contrast with social reform.[120]

Violence is not necessarily a factor in separating reformist from revolutionary; the expression of a class standpoint and the use of political power seem to be the key dividers. For Kautsky, the 'conquest of political power' had a consciously proletarian element. Democracy 'ripens' the proletariat for this conquest, by making them aware of their class interests. The coming revolution, Kautsky predicts, will not be a sudden uprising, but a 'long drawn out *civil war*, if one does not necessarily join to these last words the idea of actual slaughter and battles'.[121] But Kautsky conceives of democracy, liberal democracy, as an essential part of socialism. On the day after the social revolution, he declared, the proletariat – 'the most democratic of all classes' – would 'extend universal suffrage to every individual and establish complete freedom of press and assemblage'.[122]

Kautsky examined the issue of violence in revolution once again in 1903–4 when Krauz, a Polish socialist, questioned Kautsky's assumption that the social revolution would be largely peaceful. Kautsky replied by distinguishing between force and violence, between the availability of force and its use.[123] The socialist revolution in a democratic republic would maximize the force of the proletariat, while minimizing the possibility of its use as violence. It was a position similar to the one Engels had developed between 1890 and 1895. Like Engels, Kautsky does not deny the possibility of peaceful, legal change to socialism; they differed, however, on the question of its possibility, Kautsky believing it to be more likely than Engels. In any case, a separate proletarian standpoint must be developed and maintained, and violence must never be absolutely excluded from consideration. In a democratic republic, it is most likely that the violence needed would be defensive violence against the bourgeoisie's attack on legality. Class consciousness, for Kautsky, was the key to the revolution:

In a highly developed industrial state like Germany or England it (the proletariat) already possesses the strength to capture the power of the state.... But what the proletariat lacks is a consciousness of its own strength.... The Socialist movement does what it can to develop this consciousness.[124]

Democracy assists by insuring against premature attempts at power, and by allowing the parties to gauge their relative strengths. The 'democratic-proletarian' methods may be less spectacular than those of the revolutionary bourgeoisie, Kautsky explains, but they call 'for far fewer sacrifices'.[125] For Germany the prognosis is less sanguine. 'Of what avail is the increase in our influence, and our power in the Reichstag, when the Reichstag itself is without influence and power?' Violent methods will still be necessary, according to Kautsky, to conquer a democratic republic for Germany.

After the death of Marx and before the First World War, European Marxism was subject to some significant changes as well as theoretical and practical challenges. Marxism not only became a *Weltanschauung*, but was endorsed by mass parties such as the SPD. With increasingly successful parliamentary and trade union activities, and in the case of the SPD, with the expectation of a parliamentary majority, these parties became reform-oriented. The controversy over Revisionism was the major part of the SPD's attempt theoretically to come to terms with parliamentary democracy. Bernstein, chief theorist among the Revisionists, argued that socialists could use liberal democracy gradually to introduce socialism, with no major break in political continuity. He was committed to liberal democracy, and believed socialism to be its logical outcome, even though Germany was not a liberal democratic regime. Bernstein's programme was influenced not only by the experiences and expectations of the SPD, but also by the ambiguous theoretical heritage of German Social Democracy. It was a heritage which combined Marx and Lassalle, and which was unclear as to the role of parliament within the state. Bernstein's primary commitment to liberal democracy, to representative majority rule, was in inverse proportion to his commitment to working-class interests. The proletarian interests would predominate when the proletariat became the majority, and exercised its political influence through Social Democracy. Marx's concept of the proletariat as the universal class was lost to the Second International. Yet his revolutionary formulations always justified the rule of the proletariat by virtue of its being a majority class. For Bernstein, the proletariat was a particular interest, competing with other particular interests in the neutral framework of liberal democracy. And as he pointed out, the proletariat was not yet a majority in Germany. Thus, on Bernstein's premises, what was left of socialism was not peculiarly working class: for socialism was in the interests of humanity, something to which all could subscribe; and socialism was ethically superior to capitalism. The working class may have had an especial interest in Bernstein's socialism, but this socialism was classless in its appeal.

Rosa Luxemburg was the most vigorous defender of Marxism against the Revisionists. She pointed out that at stake in this controversy were different conceptions of socialism. Bernstein's conception, she argued, was merely a benign form of capitalism. She defended a conception of socialism, by contrast, which was based on a different mode of production from capitalism, and which represented a complete break with capitalism. The state and its parliament, Luxemburg argued, were class organizations of the bourgeoisie, which ultimately could not be used to implement socialism, the clear expression of working-class interests. But Luxemburg did not properly address the fears over a dictatorial socialism which led Bernstein to oppose violent social change and to embrace liberal democracy as the means and essence of socialism. She did not come to the defence of Marx's 'dictatorship of the proletariat', which Bernstein believed would encourage Blanquism. And her proposed revolutionary strategy was ill-defined.

Kautsky characteristically retained his theoretical pre-eminence by moderating between Bernstein's prosaic socialism and Luxemburg's revolutionary socialism. He stressed the use of liberal democracy to fulfil the proletariat's aims, the class consciousness of the proletariat needed for this task (in other words, the irreconcilable differences between classes), and the defensive violence it must be prepared to employ against bourgeois opposition to the legal implementation of its programme. With this, Kautsky included a commitment on behalf of the proletariat to civil, or 'negative' liberties. But the controversy over Revisionism was unsatisfying and inconclusive. It was ephemeral, and peripheral to the SPD's reformist inertia. And above all, with its tacit divorce of social change from direct proletarian involvement, it emphasized the degree to which Marx's 'proletariat' had failed to fulfil his expectations. As I pointed out above, Plekhanov and Kautsky, not Lenin, were perhaps the first Marxists to declare that socialist consciousness must be brought to the workers from outside the working class.

5

THE RUSSIAN REVOLUTIONARY TRADITION

Any discussion of Marx's project and its influence upon Russia would be incomplete without reference to the Russian revolutionary tradition. For not only do some claim that Lenin was above all a Russian revolutionary, acting according to some longstanding Russian revolutionary imperatives in precipitating the October Revolution and in organizing the Soviet state, but the Russian revolutionary tradition itself was influenced in important ways by Marx and Marxism. This is not to imply that the Russian revolutionary tradition was monolithic; it was quite various. But within its diversity there were characteristic issues arising from a characteristic predicament. It was the predicament of a progressive, intellectual elite removed from, but confronted and challenged by, Russia's social problems. Thus the tradition dates from the Decembrist uprising of 1825, and not from the Pugachev rebellion of 1773–4, distinguished as a peasant war which aimed to return to the customs of pre-Petrine Russia. The Decembrists were, in the main, well-educated army officers who believed that the tsarist autocracy was the major obstacle to further Westernization, of which they themselves were among the first products. The failure of their revolt was due partly to their failure to utilize popular resentment against the Tsar: to their fear that their operation might become a mass uprising. The Decembrists were the first heroes, and martyrs, of the Russian revolutionary tradition. Their revolt embodied two themes which were enduring and basic to that tradition: the relationship between Russia and Western Europe; and the relationship between the revolutionary intelligentsia and the masses to whom the intelligentsia was ultimately dedicated. In other respects, however, the Decembrists differed greatly from the revolutionaries who followed them; they were liberal and republican, positions which never became firmly established in Russia, or its revolutionary tradition.

Throughout the nineteenth century, the two themes mentioned above greatly exercised the radical intelligentsia. The intelligentsia's very existence was a product of the encounter between Russia and Western Europe; members of the intelligentsia were educated in the Western style, and sometimes even in Western Europe. But if they were aliens to Western Europe because of their national identity, they were alienated from Russia by their education and aspirations. The intelligentsia was unenviably 'detached'. From their perspective, members of the intelligentsia wondered whether Russia should follow the path of Western development, whether Russia should anticipate that path and jump ahead of the West to show it the way, or whether Russia should take a different path from the West. Not surprisingly, their isolation from the Russian people led to their preoccupation with ways of overcoming this, and thus implementing their programmes. Berdyaev has written that 'nowhere in the West did there exist so singular a form of the problem "intelligentsia and people" ... for in the West there existed neither intelligentsia nor people in the Russian sense'.[1] Above all else, the Russian revolutionary tradition was possessed by Russia's uniqueness, whether that uniqueness was in its past, its present, or its future. Whether the intelligentsia chose to follow or to overtake the West, or whether it chose a different path, it chose. The principle of the will was written into the foundations of the tradition. The major dissenter from it, Georgi Plekhanov, the 'father of Russian Marxism',[2] enshrined the opposite extreme of a rigid determinism in his theoretical and political works towards the end of the nineteenth century. He is notable not only for his dissent, but for his influence upon Lenin.

Petr Chaadaev, associated in his youth with the Decembrists, but not with their conspiracy, was one of the first intelligents to express the sense of Russia's uniqueness. His *Philosophical Letters*, only the first of which was published in his lifetime in 1836, argued that Russia was neither East nor West, that it had no historical continuity, and thus that it was destined for a special historical mission.

Our memories go no further back than yesterday; we are, as it were, strangers to ourselves. We walk through time so singly that as we advance the past escapes us forever. This is a natural result of a culture based wholly on borrowing and imitation. There is among us no inward development, no natural progress.[3]

In his *Apology of a Madman* (1837), Chaadaev explained that Russia was effectively 'a blank sheet of paper',[4] upon which its special historical mission could be composed. Russia was privileged: it had no traditions which might offer resistance to reforms. Chaadaev's exaggeration, his error, was to confound the intelligentsia with the nation. He attributed to Russia the characteristics of the intelligentsia. But it was a fruitful error, for it gave rise to the debate between the Westernizers and the Slavophiles (though it was not a debate about the error, but a debate based on the error).

From the late 1830s Westernizers and Slavophiles debated the destiny of Russia. The Slavophiles believed that, by avoiding the particular historical development of Western Europe, Russia had become a truly Christian state which was not burdened by the blight of Western individualism. Russians, they believed, were united within the framework of their peasant communes, and were free in the sense that they were free from politics. Slavophiles contrasted this Russian superiority over the West to the demands of the Westernizers, who wanted Russians to follow the path of industry laid down in Western Europe as well as to adopt liberal political forms. Westernizers were accused by the Slavophiles of being without a history because they were alienated from the Russian people; but the Slavophiles themselves, by relying heavily on the work of the German anthropologist Haxthausen in estimating the potential of the *obshchina*, or peasant commune, were almost equally removed from the people and the realities of their lives. Slavophiles condemned the 'rotten West',[5] but Westernizers also felt uneasy about trends in the West, particularly individualism.

Westernism was a loose alliance, which opened into many rifts. Vissarion Belinsky, a literary critic and among the major public antagonists of the Slavophiles, arrived in Paris in 1847 to find a heated discussion on the role of a Russian bourgeoisie among the Westernizers. Aleksandr Herzen and Bakunin opposed a bourgeoisie, and preached a type of socialism based on the peasants and the intelligentsia. Ranged against them was, among others, Vassily Botkin, the son of a merchant, who declared: 'Heaven grant us our own bourgeoisie!'[6] The doubts which many Westernizers shared about the value of Western individualism were paralleled within the emerging French socialist movement. Many Westernizers became converted to socialism. Others, such as Belinsky, became reconciled to the idea of the existence of a Russian bourgeoisie because they believed it to be historically necessary.

Herzen fits rather uncomfortably into the dichotomy of Slavophile and Westernizer, for he combined the idea of a national road, or 'mission', for Russia with a Westernizer's attachment to political freedoms. Herzen's career marks a watershed in the development of Russian revolutionary thought. He gave a sharp form to the idea of Russia's 'privilege of backwardness'. Having become disillusioned with the West, he maintained that

the European, under the influence of his past, cannot free himself from it. For him the contemporary epoch is a many storied house, for us and North America it is an elevated terrace; his attic is our rez-de-chausée. We take up where he leaves off.[7]

Herzen assumed that Russia could assimilate the West's advantages without encountering its obstacles. He believed that the Russian *obshchina* could become the foundation of the new society. In this he was not alone, for, as Martin Malia explains, Herzen probably first heard of the 'socialist' character of the *obshchina* from the Slavophiles defending Russia against European socialism: 'they wished to demonstrate that Russia needed no such revolutionary innovation since the commune already possessed all the virtues which socialism falsely promised'.[8] For Herzen, moreover, the commune had fortunately survived until the advent of Western socialism so that it could fulfil socialism.

Explaining his turn from the West to Russia, Herzen wrote that his distant love of the West had been based on his hatred of tsarist despotism. He had assumed that the 'social question' would be solved in the West, where it had first been formulated. But 'a year of Paris sobered me, for that year was 1848'.[9] He called the Westernizers' attention back to the Russians,

to a people whose way of life incorporated more conditions favourable to an economic revolution than that of the Western peoples which had already set in rigid forms. I called attention to a people which did not have to contend with moral obstacles on which every new social idea was shattered in Europe.[10]

Herzen assumed that Russia did not have to contend with 'rigid forms'. To the Slavophile emphasis on the *obshchina* he added

Chaadaev's view of Russia without a history, as well as the latest Western critique of individualism: socialism. Like the early French socialists, Herzen felt an especial sympathy for the poorest class. But his conception of Russian socialism was essentially different from Western socialism in this respect: 'The man of the future in Russia is the *peasant*, just as in France he is the *worker*.'[11]

Herzen, however, denied historical necessity. His 'Russian socialism' was not inevitable, and he opposed attempts to construct laws of history which might force individuals to conform to a particular society. In his *From the Other Shore* (1850), he argued that history had no goal, and that,

to subordinate the individual to society, nation, humanity, and an abstract ideal is to go on making human sacrifices, to slaughter the lamb in order to placate the Almighty, to crucify the innocent for the guilty.[12]

After the death of Tsar Nicholas I in 1855, Herzen was more willing to compromise with the liberals. In his 1869 *Letters to an Old Comrade*, ostensibly addressed to Bakunin – the other beacon of the 'generation of the forties' who had, like Herzen, served an Hegelian apprenticeship but had remained implacably hostile to the bourgeoisie and the state – Herzen no longer accepted that bourgeois society was in imminent danger of collapse. He also came to adopt a type of historical necessity, based on economic development, but manifest in the historically conditioned will of the masses. Bakunin's project was unacceptable to Herzen, according to Andrzej Walicki,

not because it exaggerated the role of human will and consciousness in history, but on the contrary because it ignored them and attempted to impose the revolutionary's own will on the masses. This 'petrograndism', as Herzen called it, could at best lead to the 'galley slave equality' of Babeauf, or the 'communist serfdom' of Cabet.[13]

With this change in historical perspective, Herzen no longer considered Russia the chosen land of revolution.

Like Herzen, Isaiah Berlin argues, Bakunin placed 'the ideal of individual liberty at the centre of ... [his] thought and action'.[14] But where Bakunin was prepared, according to Herzen's *Letters*, 'to wade through seas of blood'[15] in his struggle for liberty, Herzen opposed all absolute values to which the present must be sacrificed. If Herzen sought to defend and extend the area of personal liberty, Bakunin was dedicated to absolute liberty. Bakunin offered passion, and a love of destruction and adventure, to the Russian revolutionary tradition. He was concerned for people and principles in the abstract, but showed unconcern for individuals and freedoms in the concrete. Herzen opposed violent social change, as his 1860 debate with Chernyshevsky demonstrates. Chernyshevsky declared that 'only by force could human rights be seized by the people from the Tsar's grip, that only those rights are stable which are conquered'.[16] Herzen replied that he differed from Chernyshevsky over the question of means, not ends:

we will not call for the axe as the *ultima ratio*, so long as there remains one vestige of reasonable hope for a solution without the axe. The further I look into the western world, into the chain of events which brought Europe to us Russians, the more there rises in me a disgust for all bloody revolutions.[17]

Was the lack of liberty and of a political tradition under tsarism one of the reasons for the revolutionary tradition's widespread adoption of ideas of absolute liberty? Dostoevski reflected that 'my life long I have never been acquainted with moderation';[18] and in his *Diary* the young Chernyshevsky maintained that 'it would be best if absolutism could retain its rule over us until we are sufficiently permeated with democratic spirit',[19] so that political power could be exercised directly by the masses. Herzen stood almost alone in denouncing the sacrifice of the individual 'to some social concept, some collective noun, some banner or other'.[20]

Zemlia i Volia, or 'Land and Freedom', was the first revolutionary organization to be set up since the Decembrist organizations were destroyed. It was formed in 1861 by, among others, Herzen, Nikolai Ogarev, a friend of Herzen's since their youth whose subsequent political evolution had been similar to Herzen's, and Nikolai Chernyshevsky, a literary critic and a key figure of the 'generation of the sixties'. Arrested in 1862, Chernyshevsky spent some of his imprisonment writing the famous novel *What is to Be Done?*, which made a great impression on Lenin,[21] and which was an idealized portrait of the 'new men', the radicals of the sixties. One of its sections is devoted to the character Rakhmetov, a revolutionary of 'superior nature' devoted to the common good, who knows the people and their hardships. Chernyshevsky believed that revolutionaries could identify, and identify with, the interests of the masses to whom they were devoted. Contributing to

The Contemporary (Sovremennik) from 1855 to 1862, he had led the sons, the generation of the sixties, against the fathers, the generation of the forties. He had been a critic of political liberalism, which led contemporary Russian radical youth to feel, according to Karpovich, 'contempt for political forms in general and constitutionalism in particular'.[22] Yet during his exile he changed this position. Political forms, he argued, could not be a matter of indifference to radicals.

The second *Zemlia i Volia*, founded in 1876, spurned 'politics'. Walicki argues, contrary to the vaguer claims of Karpovich, that

the rejection of the 'political struggle' and the negative attitude towards political freedom became prevalent in the Russian revolutionary movement not earlier than at the beginning of the seventies.[23]

This *Zemlia i Volia* was formed after the experiences of the Populist crusade of 1873–4, when thousands of young, educated, city-dwellers decided to 'go to the people'. Whether they went to enlighten the peasants, as Lavrov had advocated, or to stir them into revolt, as Bakunin had urged, they found a peasantry which turned them in to the police with alacrity. Massive arrests were made; it was a serious setback for Populism. New ideas had to be tried. Members of the second *Zemlia i Volia* were still committed to work among the peasants, but they conceded that the peasants were not ready for immediate revolution. An important role was granted to socialist propaganda, which now had to be less intellectual, and more attuned to the immediate interests of the peasants. With these changes, the *Zemlia i Volia* began to organize along the centralist lines that made it most effective; it became a 'militant centralized organization' which Lenin held up as a model in his own (1902) *What is to Be Done?*[24]

The 1870s were another watershed in the history of the Russian revolutionary tradition. The theorists and organizations of that period constituted 'Populism', if we do not accept under that term all Russian democratic and peasant ideologies which included the belief that Russia could skip the capitalist stage of historical development. Such a broad definition of Populism as this last would encompass, in addition to the contributions of the 1870s, those from Herzen to the Socialist Revolutionaries of the early twentieth century. In the 1870s, Russian revolutionary thought was influenced by three thinkers in particular: Petr Lavrov, Petr Tkachev, and Nikolai Mikhailovsky. Of them, Lavrov and Mikhailovsky helped to inspire the 'go to the people' movement by fostering the myth of 'the people', as well as by compounding the feeling of indebtedness of the intelligentsia to the people. Tkachev was the theorist and practitioner of centralized, conspiratorial, revolutionary organization and of terrorism as a revolutionary means.

Lavrov is perhaps best known for his *Historical Letters*, first published in 1868–9. The *Letters* were not especially radical; they were written before Lavrov's escape from Russia to the West in 1870, and before his conversion to socialism. The *Letters* revealed the profound sense of guilt which the intelligentsia harboured. According to Lavrov, the intelligentsia, the privileged few, owed a debt to the people:

each of the material comforts I enjoy, each thought which I have had the leisure to acquire or to develop, has been bought with the blood, suffering or toil of millions.[25]

This 'cost of progress' could be repaid to the common people by the cultivated minority's striving to 'diminish evil in the present and in the future'. Lavrov's *Letters* were a plea to the intelligentsia. They were, Pomper argues, the 'first systematically developed theory of the origins and role of the Russian intelligentsia'.[26] Lavrov's intelligentsia bore a 'moral responsibility before posterity' for its task of enlightenment and progress.[27] In his eighth letter, Lavrov argued that the intelligentsia must be organized to be effective. Critically minded individuals must unite to form a party which could concentrate and direct their forces. Lavrov recoiled from the terrorist voluntarism of the likes of Nechaev, who in the 1860s had founded a clandestine organization known as 'The People's Vengeance', and was ruthless and unscrupulous. The murder of a colleague by Nechaev brought discredit upon the entire revolutionary movement. Nechaev had, characteristically, confounded his own vengeance with the people's vengeance. Lavrov declared that:

The time for unconscious suffering and dreams has passed; the time for heroes and fanatical martyrs, for the squandering of strength and for futile sacrifices, has also passed. The time has come for cool, conscious workmen, calculated strokes, vigorous thinking, and unswerving, patient action.[28]

Nechaev's conspiratorial techniques had outraged many among the new generation of the seventies, and many turned to Lavrovism as an alternative to Nechaev's amoralism.[29]

Lavrov's conversion to revolutionary socialism came a few years after the *Letters*. From 1873–5, he edited the journal *Forward!* (Vpered!) in Western Europe, gaining an influential role in the revolutionary movement within Russia. Like Lavrov, Mikhailovsky argued that 'we are debtors of the people',[30] but he became more critical as the 'go to the people' movement collapsed:

> Upon my desk stands a bust of Belinsky which is very dear to me, and also a chest with books by which I have spent many nights. If Russian life with all its ordinary practices breaks into my room, destroys my bust of Belinsky, and burns my books, I will not submit to the people from the village; I will fight.[31]

The most serious challenge to Lavrov's and Mikhailovsky's idealization of 'the people' came from Petr Tkachev, a follower of Nechaev, who became the chief theorist of the Jacobin trend in Russian Populism. In reply to Lavrov's *Historical Letters*, Tkachev wrote in 1870 'What is the Party of Progress?' There was, Tkachev maintained, 'an absolute criterion against which to check the validity of ideologies', and thus the possibility of a 'universally valid and obligatory formula of progress'.[32] Needless to say, Tkachev possessed this formula. In contrast to Lavrov's view of progress as the increasing differentiation of individuals, Tkachev proposed a radical levelling. The 'party of progress' had to 'reduce the existing multiplicity of individualities to one common denominator, one common level'.[33] Society's ultimate happiness and the goal of history lay in 'an *organic physiological equality*'.[34] Tkachev promoted the role of a revolutionary vanguard in achieving his revolution, and in the social reorganization and levelling which would follow. Lavrov had conceded that a *coup d'état* would be easier in Russia than perhaps anywhere else in the developed world,[35] but he stressed that a *coup* was not enough to create socialism. He had called upon the intelligentsia to overcome the peculiarites of Russia's historical evolution, not to take advantage of them. Tkachev responded differently: he believed that the people, if left to their own development, 'will build nothing new'.[36] With his emphasis on organizing a revolutionary elite, and his unbounded contempt for the masses, Tkachev gave the traditional problem of the relations between intelligentsia and masses a new direction. If Lavrov and Mikhail-ovsky had looked to the masses for ultimate regeneration, for the source of ultimate truth, Tkachev believed that it was the masses themselves who needed regeneration:

psychological poverty ... monotonous character ... moral immaturity ... a man of the masses is above all else an egotist. ... The result is that the general interest will always be lost sight of, while each behaves strictly according to his own interests. ... The people, so long as they are without leaders, cannot possibily build a new order upon the ruins of the old.[37]

The social Democrat, Akselrod, once recalled that in a debate with a Tkachevist he had asked his opponent whether he would 'force the people to be happy':

'Why, of course!' he answered. 'Since the people themselves do not under-stand their own good, what is truly good for them must be forced upon them'.[38]

Of the revolutionary minority, Tkachev believed that it would impart 'a rational form to the struggle', directing the 'coarse material element', the masses, towards 'predetermined goals'.[39] The masses act as a 'destructive force', never as a 'creative force', in a revolution, and so the task of the revolutionary minority is to direct this destructive force against 'the immediate enemies of the revolution'.[40] Tkachev insisted that the revolutionary minority be highly organized and centralized. The party must be

able to act according to a single, common plan and be subordinated to a single, common leadership – an organization based on centralization of power and decentralization of function.[41]

For Tkachev, politics became technique; leadership was not the ability to persuade or inspire trust, but the ability to command. The revolutionary himself was a professional, with a code of behaviour and a morality of his own. He was a tactician, not a politician; a man of action, not a talker.

It is not the time now for protracted discussion. ... As to the question, 'What is to be done?' let us not preoccupy ourselves with that any longer. That has been settled long ago. Make the revolution. How? However you may, however you are able to. Given a rational organization of forces, no single attempt, no single application of force, can prove useless.[42]

Other than practical questions, such as those about the future social order, must be avoided, since they will lead to division and disunity. Let us concentrate on the present, Tkachev urged, so that we may destroy it. He was concerned primarily with revolutionary means, and consciously distanced himself from discussions about ends. Tkachev stipulated, however, that in the construction of the future society the masses 'are to be given no crucial or determinant role'.[43] Instead, the revolutionary minority, the 'men of the future', would be responsible for making 'the majority of men happy and to invite as many as possible to the banquet of life'[44] – which would be an '*ordered* brotherhood'.[45]

The goal, such as it was, was a distant one. Tkachev employed the idea of a lengthy transition period, a revolutionary dictatorship which embodied strict centralization, unity of purpose, and no opposition. Allowing democracy, Tkachev believed, was to court disaster. It would mean fragmenting the revolutionary minority, who would become subordinate 'to that very majority which is penetrated to the bone with routine traditions' and instinctively yearns for the past.[46]

One can imagine how quickly and successfully we could carry out socialist principles if the programme depended on one-sided local wishes and the capricious arbitrariness of the routine-ridden majority [i.e., on democracy]!

The dream of a state-less future was not entirely cast out by Tkachev, merely postponed. With his insistence on the importance of a transition period, even though 'protracted' was Tkachev's qualifier, not Marx's, Tkachev gave a definite content to what in Marx was a superficially similar but decidedly cautious formulation. Tkachev's transition period was an extension of the pre-eminent, pre-revolutionary role of the radical intelligentsia. It was the product of a concern that the people would halt or reverse the transformation of society. Marx was concerned, on the contrary, that the bourgeoisie would obstruct the transformation of society.

Marx and Engels, from the mid-1870s, had grown increasingly interested in the development of Russian socialism and in the prospects for socialism in Russia. The Russian Populists knew of, and sometimes defended, Marx: particularly his economics. It was an irony which did not escape Marx that the Russians were the first to publish a translation of *Capital*: 'the Russians, whom I have fought for twenty-five years ... have always been my "patrons"'.[47] Walicki maintains that in the 'seventies the Populists were largely responsible for spreading Marxism in Russia'.[48] Many Russian revolutionaries from Lavrov and Mikhailovsky to Bakunin and Tkachev were aware of Marx's work and corresponded, or polemicised, with either him or Engels. The Populist opposition to the development of a capitalist historical stage in Russia was strongly influenced by Marx's description and analysis of capitalism in *Capital*.[49] And where Marx had seen in Russia the bulwark of European reaction, he came to see in it the potential – however equivocal his comments – for a new route to socialism (although only in conjunction with a socialist Europe).

In the 1870s it was generally believed by the Russian intelligentsia that a Marxist approach to the Russian social problem must concede the necessity of an extended capitalist development, and must condemn the intelligentsia to passivity and, by implication, to some guilt in the suffering capitalism would bring. Russian belief in the socialist potential of the *obshchina* was still strong. Because of the emerging capitalist threat to the commune Tkachev, for example, warned that the revolution was a 'now or never' event. The peasants were 'communist by instinct, by tradition'. If the *obshchina* was destroyed, so too were the hopes for Russian socialism:

it is clear that our people, despite their naiveté, stand immeasurably closer to socialism than the peoples of Western Europe.[50]

In response to Tkachev's claim that Russia's lack of a bourgeoisie made the socialist revolution more feasible, Engels declared in 1875:

The bourgeoisie ... is just as necessary a precondition of the socialist revolution as the proletariat itself. Hence a man who will say that this revolution can be more easily carried out in a country, because, *although* it has no proletariat, it has no bourgeoisie *either*, only proves that he has still to learn the ABC of socialism.[51]

Even so, Engels lent some credence to Tkachev's claim that the situation in Russia was 'totally exceptional' by suggesting that the commune might be raised to a higher form of social organization, if a simultaneous socialist revolution was won in the West, and before the commune's complete disintegration.[52]

Engels' 1875 article against Tkachev was an important influence in Plekhanov's intellectual evolution from Populism to Marxism, a process which culminated in *Socialism and the Political Struggle* (1883), the first of his many erudite and influential works which formed the basis for a Russian Marxism. But before we examine Plekhanov's contribution to the Russian revolutionary tradition, the shift in Marx's attitudes towards the Populists must be noted. In the 1870s Mikhailovsky wrote, apropos of Marx and his materialist conception of history:

Your place is not in Russia, but in Europe, and here you are only interfering and fighting with windmills. . . . Our place is in Russia. We not only do not scorn Russia, but we see in its past, and still in its present, much on which one can rely to ward off the falsities of European civilization.[53]

Marx replied, in 1877, protesting that Mikhailovsky

insists on transforming my historical sketch of the genesis of capitalism in Western Europe into an historico-philosophic theory of the general path of development prescribed by fate to all nations, whatever the historical circumstances in which they find themselves. . . . But I beg his pardon. (He is doing me too much honour and at the same time slandering me too much.)[54]

Russia, Marx wrote in the same letter, if she continues on the path followed since 1861, 'will lose the finest chance ever offered by history to a people and undergo all the fatal vicissitudes of the capitalist regime'.[55] In his 1881 letter to Vera Zasulich, Marx wrote of his 'so-called theory' that it expressly limited 'historical inevitability' (Marx's own distancing quotation marks) to the countries of Western Europe.[56] The village commune, he explained to this colleague of Plekhanov's who was seeking to distinguish Marx's programme for Russia from the Populists', is the 'fulcrum of Russia's social revival' if only it can be protected from the onslaughts of capitalism.[57] Marx faced the question squarely in a Preface to the 1882 Russian edition of the *Communist Manifesto*, prepared by Plekhanov. Can the *obshchina*, he asked, be a bridge to communist ownership, or must it dissolve in the face of encroaching capitalism?

If the Russian Revolution becomes the signal for a proletarian revolution in the West, so that both may complement each other, the present Russian common ownership of land may serve as the starting-point for a communist development.[58]

As Bertram Wolfe put it: 'Marx was more than a little seduced by the *narodnik* idealization of the "socialist spirit" of the *obshchina*.'[59] But as Wolfe and others explain, the commune, apart from the fact that its features were the 'product of a comparatively late historical development',[60] was used even after the emancipation of serfs in 1861 to collect taxes and army recruits.[61]

In spite of Plekhanov's attempts to distinguish clearly Russian Marxism from Populism, and to discount the socialist potential of the *obshchina*, Marx and Engels regarded the *obshchina* warmly. They even came close to condoning the terrorist and Blanquist direction taken by the Populists from the late 1870s. In 1881, Marx argued that the actions of the Russian terrorists who were then on trial, these 'sterling people', should not be moralized about.[62] In 1885 Engels, offering some opinions to Vera Zasulich on Plekhanov's recent *Our Differences* (1884), argued that Russia was like a charged powder keg ready for the match: 'if ever Blanquism ... had a certain raison d'être, that is certainly so now in Petersburg'.[63] The essential thing was for the match to be struck and 'the impulse ... given'. Under which flag the revolution was begun, Engels believed, was of little consequence, for the conspirators would be swept away by the revolutionary tide they set loose. This approach towards Populism was softened by the master in the 1890s, and Russian Marxism became 'legitimate'. In 1894 Engels argued that 'the initiative for such an eventual transformation of the Russian community can never come from itself but only from the industrial proletariat of the West'.[64] If the rapidly declining commune was to be salvaged, he explained, 'the first requirement is the overthrow of the tsarist despotism, a revolution in Russia'.[65] It will not be a socialist revolution, however, but it will encourage the labour movement of the West, without which Russia cannot become socialist. In a private letter to Danielson written the year before he wrote these lines, Engels is less optimistic. Of the *obshchina*, he predicts: 'I am afraid that institution is doomed.'[66] Engels had not fundamentally changed his position; he merely concluded that Russia's exceptional chance was lost. Plekhanov, however, never conceded that Russia after 1861 had had that chance.

Marxism was adopted by the most diverse Russian groups in the 1880s and 1890s. Apart from the Emancipation of Labour Group, based in Switzerland around Plekhanov, Zasulich, and Pavel Akselrod, there was 'a brand which might be called "capitalist Marxism"', promoted in the mid-eighties by ... a group of Moscow manufacturers, who used Marxist theory to prove that Russia must go capitalist'.[67] Alexander Gerschenkron adds that

nothing reconciled the Russian intelligentsia more to the advent of capitalism in the country and to the destruction of its old faith in the *mir* and the *artel* than a system of ideas which presented the capitalist industrialization ... as the result of an iron law of historical development.[68]

This helps to explain the power of Marxism during the industrial boom of the 1890s, its ascendancy in the censor-tolerated debates against Populism, and its attraction for a liberal such as Petr Struve, and other talented men of the calibre of Tugan-Baranowsky and Berdyaev. These 'Legal Marxists' turned their attack against 'the decades-old arguments and prejudices against the viability of capitalism in Russia', rather than preaching 'constructive Socialism'.[69] Such Marxists later turned from Marxism, under various influences. Struve, for example, was influenced by Bernstein, and in 1899 he published *Against Orthodoxy*, recommending a 'critical review of the whole of Marx's economic theory'.[70]

The origins of an indigenous Russian Marxism are to be found in the 1870s, and particularly in the evolution of the second *Zemlia i Volia* and its influence on Plekhanov. Towards the end of the 1870s the *Zemlia i Volia* began actively to encourage terrorism; in 1879 it split into the advocates of terrorism, and the advocates of mass propaganda and agitation. The former united in the *Narodnaya Volia*, or 'People's Will', party, which organized the assassination of Tsar Alexander II in 1881. The latter, including Plekhanov, formed the *Cherny Peredel*, or 'Black Repartition', party. In the repression which followed Alexander's assassination the Populist organizations collapsed, although the *Cherny Peredel* had led a meagre existence since Plekhanov's 1880 removal to Geneva. There Plekhanov completed his transition to Marxism, and began to confront the problem of a Marxist programme for Russia. He wondered at first whether there was even a role for a Marxist party in Russia. He found an answer by studying Marx's writings connected with the 1848 Revolution in Germany. Plekhanov concluded that although the coming revolution in Russia was anti-absolutist, and would usher in a period of bourgeois constitutional rule, there was an important role to be played by the workers and by a workers' party. Like Marx, he was sceptical of the liberal commitment of the liberal bourgeoisie, and believed that this commitment must be strengthened by the pressure of the independent proletariat. But the proletariat had to be an independent force so that it could immediately use the political rights it had helped to win to begin its struggle against the bourgeoisie. The proletariat therefore had to have a Social Democratic party. In arriving at this conception of a two-stage revolution, and in finding a role for a Russian Social Democracy, Plekhanov had to overcome the aversion to politics which was a prominent feature of the Russian revolutionary tradition from which he had emerged. The Populists believed that by struggling for political liberties they would be aiding the bourgeoisie, their future oppressors; avoiding politics was part of their strategy to short-circuit history and move directly to socialism. Plekhanov reinstated historical and political drudgery.

Two of Plekhanov's earliest, and most important, Marxist works – *Socialism and the Political Struggle* and *Our Differences* – were written in defence of the political struggle in Russia, and in criticism of the Russian revolutionary movement. They became the foundations of Russian Marxism, including Bolshevism. Plekhanov opposed the view that the struggle against absolutism would be 'sidetracked' by politics. Indeed, by ignoring politics the vital separation of the forces ranged against autocracy would not take place and the working class, in particular, would not be able to assert its own interests. Plekhanov stressed the value of political liberty in the struggle against absolutism, and in the coming struggle against the bourgeoisie. The proletariat, he maintained, must organize itself into a political party. The establishment of a constitutional order was indispensable in the development of the proletariat and in its ambitions for power:

the proletariat demands *direct popular legislation* as the only political form under which its social aspirations can be put into effect.[71]

Consequently, Plekhanov declared, there was no 'early possibility of a socialist government in Russia'.[72]

Plekhanov's abandonment of the belief in Russian exceptionalism sensitized him to the dangers and the folly of socialist attempts prematurely to seize power. He maintained that a political response to their plight depended upon the masses existing in a certain state of economic and social development:

'Hatred of the privileged estates' proves nothing at all; it is often not accompanied by a single ray of political consciousness.[73]

Temporarily victorious conspirators will soon find, he continued, that socialism cannot be built merely upon negative, destructive, social feelings. Socialism may represent a definite organization of production, but it must be based on a politically conscious, and active, population. What if, Plekhanov conjectures, a provisional *Narodnaya Volia* government became a permanent government? If it tried to organize national production, it would face the alternative of proceeding 'in the spirit of modern socialism', and floundering upon Russia's backwardness,

or it will have to seek salvation in the ideals of 'patriarchical and authoritarian communism', only modifying those ideals so that national production is managed not by the Peruvian 'sons of the sun' and their officials but by a socialist caste.[74]

But Plekhanov assured himself that such a scenario was unlikely, since the seizure of power by such a group 'may be considered as absolutely impossible'.[75] It is clear that he sorely underestimated the potential for revolutionary conspiracies in Russia, but his point remains:

the main danger to the *socialist* conspiracy will come not from the existing government, but from the members of the conspiracy itself. . . . [T]here can be no guarantee that they will not wish to use the power they have seized for purposes having nothing in common with the interests of the working class.[76]

Conspiracy, even that of a well-meaning minority, argued Plekhanov, would lead to the aggrandizement of the conspirators themselves: above all, because the peasants would resist the introduction of socialism. Plekhanov greatly discounted the political consciousness and capabilities of the peasantry, and placed his hopes for Russian socialism in the development of a Russian proletariat and a Russian workers' party.

The aims of Russian socialists, according to Plekhanov, must be 'to achieve free political institutions' and to prepare for 'the future *workers' socialist party*'.[77] Thus will conspiracy be avoided, the development of an independent and class-conscious working class assured, and the future of socialism kept intact. The working class was the class of the future; Russian socialists must place their hopes in it. Socialists must struggle for political freedom and prepare the 'working class for its future independent and offensive role'.[78] The overthrow of autocracy and the socialist revolution were two 'fundamentally different matters'; to bind them together *'means to put off the advent of both'*.[79] An appreciation of this difference, and the different tasks it prescribes for each stage, enables socialists 'to *bring* these two elements *closer together'*.[80] This admission by Plekhanov of the human will into the historical process, this subjective influence over what Plekhanov generally conceives as an objective, law-determined process, presents us with another side to Plekhanov. For in stressing the priority of the political struggle in achieving socialism, Plekhanov did not oppose, in principle, the seizure of power by a revolutionary party:

In our opinion that is the last, and what is more, the absolutely inevitable conclusion to be drawn from the political struggle.[81]

But, he explains, 'there is no more difference between heaven and earth than between the dictatorship of a class and that of a group of revolutionary *raznochintsi* [intelligentsia]'.[82] What this difference is, however, he does not explain. And before this 'advanced working class with political experience and education'[83] can take power, it must be educated in socialism by what Plekhanov calls the 'socialist intelligentsia'.[84] The importance of this conception should not be underestimated. In the Marxist tradition it was an innovation. Plekhanov preceded Kautsky in assigning a key role to the socialist intelligentsia. He argued that it 'must become the leader of the working class in the impending emancipation movement, explain to it its political and economic interests'.[85] It is curious indeed that the two major theorists of Marxism who had such a mechanical conception of historical development, Plekhanov and Kautsky, should rely so heavily, and inaugurate the tradition of reliance, upon the intelligentsia, upon what should logically have been seen by them as a kind of *deus ex machina*.

In his *Our Differences*, Plekhanov reviewed the major ideas and strategies of the Russian revolutionary tradition, and examined in detail one of the central questions which had animated the tradition: must Russia go through the 'school' of capitalism? As recently as 1879, Plekhanov relates, he himself had declared that 'history was by no means a monotonous mechanical process' and that the Russian road to socialism would be different from that of the West.[86] He had now reversed his opinion. The task for socialists in Russia was to 'shorten and lessen the birth-pangs' of socialism, not to attempt a jump over capitalism. The *obshchina*, he argued, had lost whatever socialist potential its promoters believed it had. Chernyshevsky's enlistment of Haxthausen to defend the proposition that the village commune was an insurance against the Western diseases of 'pauperism, [and] proletarianism'[87] was of no use after 1861 when the campaign collapsed, according to Plekhanov.

The 'Act of February 19' knocked the village commune out of the stable equilibrium of natural economy and subjected it to all the laws of commodity production and capitalist accumulation.[88]

The revolutionaries who continued to maintain that the *obshchina* was the basis for a socialist transformation of Russia were, Plekhanov argued, faithful only to the letter of Chernyshevsky's work, not to its spirit or method. Indeed, Plekhanov declared against the Populists that capitalism had already become firmly established in Russia, and must ultimately run its course:

It is time for us to have the courage to say that in this field [of manufacturing industry] not only the immediate future but the present of our country, too, belongs to capitalism.[89]

Agriculture was no defence against capitalist development; the village commune had begun to disintegrate, although the Narodniks were blind to it. Plekhanov's insistence on the existence of capitalist Russia led him into a rather sterile debate over the number of workers in Russian industry of all types. He concluded that the number was greater than that allowed by his Populist opponent, Tikhomirov; whether it was significantly greater is dubious. In any case, the question does not seem to be decisive. Plekhanov was adamant that to the question of whether Russia must go through the 'school' of capitalism, the answer was: 'Why should she not finish the school she has *already entered*?'[90]

Plekhanov felt that Russian circumstances were unique only in that socialist ideas had become established with the earliest development of capitalism, not with its maturity. The situation was not as exceptional as he believed, however, for most socialist theories emerged with the abuses suffered by workers during the early stages of capitalism. Russia's uniqueness lay, perhaps, in its pre-capitalist socialism linked with rural utopias, rather than industrial utopias.

The Russian intelligentsia had borrowed from the socialist criticisms of Western capitalism, but had discarded its historical context; Plekhanov reasserted the context. History held for Russia, he believed, the political victory of the bourgeoisie, which would prepare the way for the political and social emancipation of the proletariat. Plekhanov was especially critical of his contemporaries in the *Narodnaya Volia* party, who would not accept this view. They often posed, he argued, as social democrats, proposing to leave the struggle for socialism until after the defeat of absolutism. Yet this was a fraud, a fraud exposed by Populists themselves, such as Tikhomirov, whose views were closely tied with the conspirator Tkachev. Tikhomirov

> tries to substitute his own will for historical development, to replace the initiative of the *class* by that of a *committee* and to change the cause of the whole working population of the country into the cause of a secret organization.[91]

Tikhomirov tries to prove, Plekhanov continued, that the cause of the Executive Committee is the cause of the whole people:

> Forced to admit that *historical development* has so far but little promoted the elaboration of socialist consciousness and *revolutionary* (not merely *rebellious*) tendencies in the Russian people, he endeavours with all the more zeal to convince us of the stability and unshakability of the *prehistoric forms* of the Russian way of life and outlook.[92]

The early Russian Marxists, much more than their Russian revolutionary contemporaries, seem to have appreciated the dangers associated with Blanquism and conspiratorial parties. This may be due to the fact that Plekhanov and his fellow Russian Marxists lived in Western Europe, and were influenced by European thought and conditions. Plekhanov devoted considerable space to such problems in *Our Differences*. But we must not forget that tension in Plekhanov's thought, evident also in *Our Differences*, and which we shall examine shortly, between his determinist view of the history and his voluntaristic view of the role of the Russian intelligentsia.

In his polemic against Blanquism, and its Russian variant, Tkachev-ism, Plekhanov re-examined the 1873–4 polemic between Tkachev and Lavrov. Lavrov had argued that conspirators produce only minority revolutions, which spoil 'even the best people', and cannot introduce happiness by decree. The temporary dictatorship which these conspirators claim to need must be surrounded by force, and will be directed not only against its enemies, but against those 'who simply did not agree with its methods'. Dictatorships spend more time and energy fighting their rivals than carrying out their promises. Lavrov had argued:

dreams of the termination of a dictatorship seized violently by any party can be entertained only before the seizure; in the parties' struggle for power, in the agitation of overt and covert intrigues, every minute brings new necessity for maintaining power and reveals new impossibility of abandoning it.[93]

What would happen, Plekhanov asks, if the present conspirators took power? They would no doubt reply, he claimed, that the provisional government would come to the aid of a popular revolution, and socialism would arise. But for socialism, he objects, there must first be 'the objective economic possibility of the transition to socialism', as well as working-class awareness of that possibility. 'These two conditions are closely connected with one another';[94] they do not yet exist in Russia. Besides, the peasants would merely want the expropriation of landowners, not the socialist organization of agriculture. In the face of such obstacles in Russia, it is a miscalculation to place one's hopes in the European socialist revolution. 'The West European revolution will be mighty, but not almighty'.[95] Plekhanov believed that a socialist seizure of power in Russia would be a fiasco; Russia was not yet ripe for the domination of the working class.

If Plekhanov could argue that the Populists had too much faith in, expected 'social miracles' from, the revolutionary intelligentsia,[96] and if he could argue that the emancipation of the working class 'can be achieved only by its own conscious efforts',[97] he could also argue that the socialist intelligentsia was indispensable to the development of the working class and its revolution. The socialist intelligentsia, the 'thinking proletariat', according to Plekhanov, 'must become the leader of the working class in the impending emancipation movement'.[98] The Russian Social Democrat, a member of this intelligentsia, 'will bring *consciousness* into the working class'.[99] Plekhanov conceded that the normal workings of capitalism would not be sufficient to turn the working class into a revolutionary class; that task would fall to Russian Social Democracy:

As the scattered forces of the workers in individual factories and workshops cannot guarantee the success of such a struggle [against capitalism, the Russian Social-Democrat] ... will have to give it a class character.[100]

The Russians had a rich revolutionary tradition during the nineteenth century. It was a tradition which embraced positions as diverse as constitutionalism and anarchism, as the Russian road to socialism and the Western road. It embraced terror, and denied terror. But its unity consisted in certain characteristic themes: that the programme and impetus for salvation would have to be introduced to the masses from the outside, from the intelligentsia; that whatever path Russia followed in her historical development, the problems raised would be of a different order from that of the west. It was also strongly influenced, from at least the 1860s (although Marx's contact with Bakunin began in the mid–1840s), by Marx and Marxism. Marx's economic work was used by the Populists to highlight the evils of capitalism, in their campaigns to ensure that Russia would avoid capitalism. To these Populists Marx himself gave some succour. Marx's work was also used more systematically by his Russian disciples, chief among which was Plekhanov. Of these disciples, mostly exiled, Marx himself was sometimes contemptuous. The shadow of Marx hung over many of the debates within the Russian revolutionary tradition. For in some ways the Marxist tradition and the Russian revolutionary tradition ran parallel to each other. They both put great emphasis on a philosophy of history; they were both concerned with the transition period to socialism; and they were both concerned with the questions of leadership: its role in the socialist revolution, and its relations with the led. But where Marx was equivocal and enigmatic about these issues, the Russian revolutionary tradition was decided and clear. Plekhanov represents the intersection of these two traditions. To the Russian revolutionary tradition Plekhanov brought Marx's subtlety and breadth of knowledge; to the Marxist tradition he brought the Russian revolutionary's sense of certainty. The resulting historical materialism and two-stage theory of the Russian revolution suited well Engels' attempt to systematize Marxism. The tension in being a Russian revolutionary and a Marxist broke out in Plekhanov in his simultaneous critique of the dictatorship of a revolutionary-socialist minority, and affirmation of the crucial role of the socialist intelligentsia. Having become a pillar of Marxist orthodoxy in the Second International, however, Plekhanov's Russian-revolutionary origins were ignored or discounted; yet within him the two traditions uneasily coexisted. The transformation of Marx's project into a Russian project was the work of Plekhanov. Marx's enduring impact upon Russia was mediated by Plekhanov.

6

LENIN AND THE PARTY

Vladimir Ilyich Lenin, soon after he made his acquaintance with Marxism, became a disciple of Plekhanov. Plekhanov was widely respected, perhaps revered, by many of the generation of the 1890s who increasingly turned to Marxism, and who formed the basis of the Marxist groups which sprang up on Russian soil. Lenin's eventful revolutionary career and his theoretical development and innovations have been the subjects of many histories and interpretations,[1] not all of which sufficiently emphasize his debt to Plekhanov. I propose simply to examine the theoretical work of Lenin in so far as it relates to the question of opposition; a question which arises sharply in the debates over the issue of party organization, around 1902–4, and in the debates over the political organization of the Soviet state after 1917. In both debates, and during both periods, and probably for his entire revolutionary career, Lenin consistently held two positions which coloured his views about everything else. The first position was that he alone, and often with his faction of Russian Social Democracy (although sometimes against it), embodied and represented the true interests of the proletariat. This position was not negotiable. The second was that any and all opposition to Lenin, on almost any matter, was class, that is, non-proletarian or bourgeois, opposition. Lenin adopted, at times, a more flexible approach to his opponents than this position might suggest; but the non-proletarian nature of opposition was implicit in all of Lenin's alliances and tactical manoeuvres.

Lenin inherited directly certain fundamental assumptions of Russian Marxism made by Plekhanov. He accepted that capitalism was advancing rapidly within Russia, and that the future belonged to the proletariat. He also accepted that the proletariat must lead the movement for the democratization of Russia. These assumptions distinguished Russian Marxists from Populists of all shades. P. Akselrod had drawn the correct inference from Plekhanov's two-stage theory of revolution, that

if there is no possibility of assigning to the Russian proletariat an independent, pre-eminent role in the struggle against police-tsarism, autocracy and arbitrariness, then Russian Social Democracy has no historical right to exist.[2]

The Russian Marxists were naturally drawn to Marx's works on the 1848 Revolutions, particularly the German Revolution, for they perceived significant similarities between 1848 Germany and their Russia. Marx's work convinced them that the liberal bourgeoisie was an uncertain ally in the struggle for liberalism. For had not the German, and even French, bourgeoisie in 1848–50 sought refuge from the demands of the proletariat behind the autocracy which it had set out to destroy? In March 1898, the First Congress of Russian Social Democrats delegated Struve to draft a programme in the group's name. The resulting 'Manifesto of the Russian Social Democratic Labour Party' (RSDLP) declared, *inter alia*, that

the further east one goes in Europe, the more cowardly, mean, and politically weak is the bourgeoisie, and the greater are the cultural and political tasks confronting the proletariat. The Russian working class must and will bear on its own sturdy shoulders the cause of winning political freedom. . . .[3]

The Manifesto maintained that it was the proletariat which would 'throw off the yoke of autocracy', and then continue the struggle against the bourgeoisie to attain socialism. This Russian Marxist orthodoxy raised questions of enormous implication. With whom, for example, would the proletariat make alliances in the struggle against absolutism? What would the regime which followed the overthrow of absolutism look like? But while these questions divided Russian Marxists especially after 1905, the immediate task was the organization of a Russian Marxist Party which had not been achieved by the 1898 Congress.

The issue of Party unity and organization proved ironically divisive. It was zealously prosecuted by Lenin, one of the leaders of the new generation of Russian Marxists. Lenin emerged as a prominent figure in debates against the Narodniks. His early works, to about 1899, do not seem particularly exceptional, except perhaps that his major economic *opus*, *The Development of Capitalism in Russia* (1899), was dedicated to the proposition that Russian capitalism had not simply entered its initial phase, but was firmly and irrevocably established, and based on the large-scale enterprises of advanced capitalism. Replete with detailed statistics, this work established Lenin as a formidable Marxist theorist. Furthermore, in an appendix to his 1897 *The Tasks of Russian Social Democrats*, Lenin urged Social Democrats to tighten up their organization, to be more secretive. These ideas on the formation of a Russian Social Democratic Party were developed during Lenin's three-year internal exile (1897–1900), and were begun to be put into effect upon his release as he travelled Russia establishing contacts for his proposed all-Russian, unifying, newspaper. Lenin's efforts were directed, in particular, against the so-called 'Economists'. 'Economism' was a sympathetic response by some Russian Social Democrats to the upsurge in trade union action in the late 1890s, a response which, according to many, including Lenin and Plekhanov, led to a denial of the need for an indepedent working-class party. Kuskova's 'Credo', an extreme statement of the Economist position, would mean, according to its opponents, the participation of Russian Marxists simply in economic struggles of the working class for immediate gains. In effect, they argued, Economism denied the leading role of the working class in the coming democratic revolution; it denied this basic tenet of orthodox Russian Marxism.

In the context of this debate, Lenin determined to use his long-planned, all-Russian newspaper *Iskra* (Spark) to forge a party free from the disorganizing tendencies he saw as the product of Economism. He united with the nucleus of the old Emancipation of Labour Group, Plekhanov, P. Akselrod and Zasulich, to produce his newspaper and to fight Economism. In *Iskra*'s first issue of December 1900, Lenin stressed two crucial ideas: first, that 'isolated from Social-Democracy, the working-class movement ... inevitably becomes bourgeois';[4] and second, that the revolutionaries must 'devote the whole of their lives, not only their spare evenings, to the revolution'.[5] One of the earliest documents on the actual organization of the party which Lenin advocated was his *Where to Begin* (May 1901). From the outset, he argued that the scope of his contribution would be limited to tactical questions of organization, and would not be raising general programmatic questions:

It is not a question of what path we must choose (as was the case in the late eighties and early nineties), but of what practical steps we must take upon the known path and how they shall be taken. It is a question of a system and plan of practical work.[6]

This idea was Lenin's guiding thread in the disputes over the nature of the Party, from his *Where to Begin* (1901), through *What is to Be Done?* (1902), to *One Step Forward, Two Steps Back* (1904). Lenin maintained, in other words, that the political strategy of Russian Social Democracy was fixed and agreed, and that he took up the cudgels on behalf of the organization most suited to achieve that goal. But this was not entirely so, for Economism's challenge to Russian Marxism was primarily on the question of political strategy and aims. No doubt Lenin believed strongly in the merits and appropriateness of his proposed organization, but he used the question of organization to make what were more properly political and strategic points against his opponents.

Lenin consciously modelled his party organization on the experiences of the Russian revolutionary tradition:

the magnificent organisation that the revolutionaries had in the seventies and that should serve us as a model, was not established by the *Narodnaya Volia*, but by the *Zemlia i Volia*.... [N]o revolutionary trend, if it seriously thinks of struggle, can dispense with such an organization.[7]

But the question of organization was a tactical one, not one of principle. Lenin concedes that the model party for all Social Democrats was the SPD; but Russia was not Germany, and such an organization was impossible. Plekhanov himself, in *Our Differences*, had taken account of the lessons of the Russian revolutionary tradition on the question of organization. He, however, had recommended the 'absolutely necessary and highly useful organisation' of the *Narodnaya Volia*.[8] But Lenin went one step further. If questions of organization were merely tactical, differences over these questions revealed 'a deplorable ideological instability and vacillation'.[9] Differences over tactics are surreptitiously linked, by Lenin, to differences of principle. Similarly, when Lenin discusses the vital role that an all-Russian newspaper would play, he introduces the question of principle. A newspaper, Lenin declared, 'is not only a collective propagandist and a collective agitator, it is also a collective organiser'.[10] The 'network of agents' required to distribute the paper would form the 'skeleton' of the organization.[11] But this merely tactical device would somehow 'render impossible unprincipled and opportunist deviations from revolutionary Marxism ... which must inevitably lead to the conversion of the labour movement into an instrument of bourgeois democracy'.[12] Lenin took the proposition, widely accepted among Russian Marxists, that the working class left to its own devices would not develop socialist consciousness, and transformed it into the proposition that the working class, without the organizational recipe of the *Iskra*-ites, would not develop socialist consciousness. He transformed a general proposition about the role of Social Democracy, however arguable, into a particular proposition aimed against his opponents within Russian Social Democracy. Lenin's innovation is not on the question of the role of Social Democracy in bringing consciousness to the working class, but the unwarranted link between views on organization opposed to his and the failure to introduce socialist consciousness into the working class.

Lenin's best-known and most influential statement of his organization views is his *What is to Be Done?*,[13] directed against his Economist, terrorist, and federationist opponents within Russian Social Democracy. There are two fundamental trends in international Social Democracy, Lenin begins. There is revolutionary Marxism, and the 'new', 'critical' trend, which 'has been clearly enough *presented* by Bernstein and *demonstrated* by Millerand'.[14] Lenin places all Social Democratic disputes within these two categories. He considered that Economism represented Revisionist opportunism in the Russian context. The Economists differed from Lenin over their appreciation of workers' struggles and the proper Social Democratic reaction to them. The strikes of the 1890s, Lenin argues, merely 'represented the class struggle in embryo'.[15] They were not yet Social Democratic struggles; the workers had not yet realized their irreconcilable antagonism towards capitalism:

We have said that *there could not have been* Social-Democratic consciousness among the workers. It would have to be brought to them from without. The history of all countries shows that the working class, exclusively by its own effort, is able to develop only trade-union consciousness. ... The theory of socialism, however, grew out of the ... theories elaborated by educated representatives of the propertied classes, by intellectuals.[16]

Economism is characterized, he argues, by a '*slavish cringing before spontaneity*'.[17] But it is a mistake to believe that the labour movement will spontaneously discover socialism. In fact, Lenin believed that the '*spontaneous* development of the working-class movement leads to its subordination to bourgeois ideology',[18] since bourgeois ideology is older than socialist ideology, more fully developed, and is disseminated by innumerable means. Social Democrats must not confine themselves to the economic struggle; 'We must take up actively the political education of the working class and the development of its political consciousness.'[19] Even if economic struggles bring workers into conflict with the government, Lenin contends that they remain at the level of 'trade-unionist politics':

Working-class consciousness cannot be a genuine political consciousness unless the workers are trained to respond to *all* cases of tyranny, oppression, violence, and abuse, no matter *what class* is affected – unless they are trained, moreover, to respond from a Social-Democratic point of view and no other.[20]

Socialist consciousness was quite different from working-class consciousness. Socialist consciousness was in the possession of Social Democrats who were not opportunists; and opportunists were beginning to be defined by Lenin as those who did not share his organizational views. The Social Democrat must aim to be a 'tribune of the people',[21] agitating among all strata of the population. Social Democrats are to be drawn from all classes. The task, as Lenin saw it, was to lead the forces for the democratic revolution. So to what extent did Lenin's conception of the Russian revolution need the working class at all, except as a beast of burden? After all, Social Democratic consciousness was possessed by the party, it was not a peculiarly working-class attainment; indeed, the working class was at a distinct disadvantage in acquiring it.

The two ideas on which Lenin hinges his argument were, for Russian Social Democrats, generally unexceptionable. The first was the idea that the workers themselves could not achieve a socialist consciousness, which would have to be brought to them by Social Democracy. The second was that left to their own economic devices, the workers would invariably come under the sway of bourgeois ideology. In 1898, for example, Akselrod had argued in his *Present Tasks and Tactics* that Western experience demonstrated that economic struggle did not automatically lead to the growth of political consciousness among the workers, and that the political strivings of the workers usually fell under the sway of the bourgeoisie.[22] Plekhanov, since 1883, had urged a role for the socialist intelligentsia in introducing socialist consciousness to the workers. His Preface to the *'Vademecum' for the Editorial Board of Rabochee Delo* (1900), directed against the Economists, also spoke of the workers' lag of consciousness.[23] But Lenin used directly the argument of Karl Kautsky which declared that socialist consciousness was something which came easily to intellectuals, who have the time to ponder and reflect, that

socialist consciousness is something introduced into the proletarian class struggle from without and not something that arose within it spontaneously.[24]

Though these ideas were, as I have said, generally unexceptionable at the time, there was some opposition to them (from the Economist Vladimir Akimov, among others). They were not, in any case, Lenin's innovation. His innovation was to link his organizational views with revolutionary Marxism, and those of his opponents with opportunism.

Under Russian conditions, Lenin argued with some justification, Social Democracy could not be organized like a trade union. It must be organized by professional revolutionaries, and its organization 'must perforce not be very extensive and must be as secret as possible'.[25] It would thus be able to maintain itself as against the political police, and be able to attract members from all social classes. The movement, Lenin claimed, would not survive without this type of organization.[26] *What is to be Done?* is no practical manual, but it does exclude democracy because it contradicts the prime imperative of the organization: secrecy. Democracy 'in Party organization, amidst the gloom of the autocracy and the domination of the gendarmerie, is nothing more than a *useless and harmful toy*'.[27] With secrecy, Lenin argues, strong bonds can be formed between the party and workers. And 'something even more than "democratism" would be guaranteed to us, namely, complete, comradely, mutual confidence among revolutionaries'.[28] Secrecy and complete confidence, however, are rarely found together. In summary of *What is to Be Done?*, Lenin writes:

All without exception now talk of the importance of unity, of the necessity for 'gathering and organising', but in the majority of cases what is lacking is a definite idea of where to begin and how to bring about this unity.[29]

But Lenin's entire discussion is a substitute for addressing the major political differences which were beginning to emerge among the Russian Social Democrats. These problems are merely alluded to as a background to the organizational debate. Nevertheless, Lenin tries to place his opponents on the organizational question outside revolutionary Marxism, and trusts through his organizational proposals to place them effectively outside the yet-to-be formed RSDLP.

In September 1902, in his 'Letter to a Comrade on Our Organizational Tasks', Lenin conceded that in a secret organization an 'incapable' person may concentrate great power into his hands, but this

cannot be obviated by the elective principle and decentralization, the application of which is absolutely impermissible to any wide degree.[30]

If the elective principle cannot 'obviate' such events, however, it can at least 'correct' them. Yet Lenin continued to stress centralization and secrecy.

Armed with Lenin's views on organization, the *Iskra* group came to the Second Congress of the RSDLP in 1903 determined to form a party. Major division occurred, rather unexpectedly, over the first Article of the proposed 'Organizational Rules of the RSDLP'. The formulation eventually adopted was modelled on the membership article of the SDP, and read:

A member of the Russian Social Democratic Labour Party is one who accepts its Programme, supports it financially, and extends it regular personal assistance under the guidance of one of its organizations.[31]

This paragraph was at the centre of an important debate during that part of the Congress held in London, which helped to dash the hopes for unity. The so-called Third Party Congress, convened by Lenin in April 1905 and consisting exclusively of Bolsheviks,[32] revised the membership article to read:

A member of the party is one who accepts its Programme, supports the party financially, and participates through personal work in one of its organizations.[33]

This was the alternative debated in 1903 and, ironically, it was accepted by the Menshevik-dominated Fourth (or Unity) Congress of the RSDLP in 1906. Why did the Party split if, as it seemed, there was no question of principle at stake? Many European Social

Democrats asked the same question. The issues dividing Russian Social Democrats were not at all clear to most of their European colleagues. Even the split itself came not explicitly over the question of professional revolutionaries, but over Lenin's plan for a three-man editorial board of *Iskra* and a three-man Central Committee. Furthermore, the split took place largely among the *Iskra*-ites. Both sides appealed to their European colleagues for support, but most of the latter, including Kautsky, refused to take sides. Kautsky explained:

I do not see any difference in principle between proletarian and intellectual tendencies, nor between 'democracy' and 'dictatorship'; it [the question or organization] is simply a question of expediency.[34]

In some ways Kautsky even favoured Lenin's Bolsheviks. Adolf Braun (an editor of the SPD's *Der Kampf*) probably best summed up the European feeling of puzzlement and helplessness when he wrote to Akselrod in 1911 that differences 'of all dimensions' seemed to be the prime concern of the Russian émigrés, who squandered their energies on struggle between comrades. 'For those of us who do not know Russian this is an extraordinarily painful experience.'[35] Only in 1914 did the International Socialist Bureau of the Second International declare of the factions of the RSDLP that 'there are no tactical disagreements between them which are sufficiently important to justify a split',[36] but war intervened before unity could be attempted, or imposed.

What was the cause of the split at the Second Congress? And why was there such vehemence over the question of Party membership? After all, Lenin's *What is to Be Done?* did not represent a departure from orthodoxy on the issue of socialist consciousness, as Plekhanov and the other *Iskra* editors realized when they supported Lenin's views on it. It was when Lenin proposed that Zasulich and Akselrod should be dropped from the editorial board of *Iskra* that the *Iskra*-ites split, with Zasulich, Akselrod, and the young leader Martov declaring their opposition to Lenin (and Plekhanov). The Congress revealed a great deal of bitter enmity towards Lenin, not just, or even primarily, towards his views on Party organization. As Neil Harding argues:

Lenin's views of the Party as presented in his writings from 1899 to 1902 are not to be regarded as extraordinary, innovatory, perverse, essentially

Jacobin or unorthodox. On the contrary, they had long been canvassed in *Iskra* and accepted by Lenin's co-editors who were the only ones who could reasonably be described as having a claim to expressing the orthodoxy of Russian Marxism.[37]

Thus Plekhanov broke with Lenin only after the Second Congress, and the *Iskra*-ites supported Lenin's formulation on Party membership. The Mensheviks themselves adopted Lenin's formulation at the Fourth Congress in 1906.

The 'organizational question' has been given unwarranted significance in the split between Bolsheviks and Mensheviks. Underlying the personal antagonisms, and whatever organizational differences there were, or came to be, were differences over political strategy and the objectives of the democratic revolution which emerged fully only in 1905 and 1906. The emergence of these differences suited Lenin's consistent attempts to turn the question of organization into a question of principle, either directly or by association. And while the Mensheviks split away from the Bolsheviks, it was only Lenin who took the organizational question seriously enough to make a split. Lenin's ends were achieved, and his hands were still clean – even if they were grubbied later by the affairs of the Schmidt inheritance and the Caucasus 'expropriations'.

The attempt to translate organizational differences into differences of principle was made once again in Lenin's next major statement on the question, published in May 1904 after the Second Congress. His *One Step Forward, Two Steps Back (The Crisis in Our Party)* reviewed the dispute and the resulting division. By 1904, Lenin claims, the 'central and fundamental points at issue' had emerged.[38] They concerned, according to him, primarily organizational questions (not those of programme or strategy), and his opponents were accused of 'opportunism in matters of organization'. But are these matters of principle? Taken by itself, Lenin explained, the debate over paragraph one at the Second Congress revealed 'shades of principle', yet it was not a matter of 'life or death'.[39] Lenin equivocates over whether the question of organization is a matter of principle. He first moves to link the differences with the swing towards mistaken views:

Every *little* difference may assume *tremendous* importance if it serves as the starting-point for a *swing* towards definite mistaken views.[40]

Differences over organizational questions, he implies, may lead to mistaken political views. But little differences do not necessarily lead to major differences, and we have no reliable method of determining the relationship between the two. Nevertheless, Lenin insists that the debate over paragraph one 'started the swing towards the opportunist profundities and anarchistic phrase-mongering of the minority'.[41]

Lenin soon overcame his hesitation, and assigned to types of organization a class character in a formulation as ingenuous as it is unfounded:

In words, Martov's formulation [of paragraph one, adopted at the Second Congress] defends the interests of the broad strata of the proletariat, but *in fact* it serves the interests of the *bourgeois intellectuals*, who fight shy of proletarian discipline and organisation.[42]

Perhaps for the first time in this, or any debate, 'discipline and organisation' were assigned a class character. Lenin's organizational views were proletarian; Martov's were bourgeois. Whether or not Lenin was right to see intellectuals as dilettantes who wish to avoid disciplined activity is beside the point. How did Lenin ascertain the class character of a type of organization, or even of an actual organization? By its organization, by its composition, or by its programme? It is not so much Lenin's type of organization which is objectionable and bound to lead to authoritarianism, for the character of the political system is more important than the character of the parties which compose it, but his insistence on ascribing to organization a class character and on ascribing to his organization a proletarian character.

The question of organization was naturally connected to the political tasks of Russian Social Democrats. If the goal was to lead the overthrow of tsarism, and to seize power under conditions imposed by the autocracy, then the type of organization Lenin advocated had considerable justification. If it had to lead liberals and other anti-autocratic forces against tsarism, then again it had some justification. But what would take the place of tsarism? Even Lenin did not believe, until at least 1914, that socialism was on the agenda for Russia. But the precise character of the new regime was a point of contention among Russian Social Democrats from about 1905. Lenin, however, on the basis of his organizational views, held that the Party minority was opportunist, and represented a continuation of the international division of Social Democracy into revolutionary and opportunist wings.[43] Lenin even argued that a revolutionary Social Democrat was defined by his relationship to organization:

Who is it that insists that the worker is not afraid of organisation, that the proletarian has no sympathy for anarchy, that he values the incentive to organise? ... *The Jacobins of Social-Democracy.*[44]

Lenin took no offence at being called a Jacobin; he considered it to be a compliment. He continued to focus on the charge of opportunism when the only explicit difference between him and the Mensheviks was over questions of organization:

opportunism in programme is naturally connected with opportunism in tactics and opportunism in organisation.[45]

Yet the Mensheviks accepted the same programme as Lenin did at the Second Congress. Lenin remained undeterred; in the debate over party organization he established the principle by which all later disagreement with him would be judged: opposition was opportunism, which was class opposition. Even though Lenin maintained that party organization was a tactical matter, to be decided by prevailing conditions (and thus changing his views about the openness of the Party in 1905 and 1917), he connected opposing organizational views with deviations from Marxism.

His organizational views did not go unchallenged. As members of the *Iskra* group fell out with Lenin they cast about for arguments to use against him. But the arguments generally lacked conviction, for they were arguments against positions which the *Iskra* group had shared. It was also generally unclear how far the Mensheviks differed from the Bolsheviks; 'democratic centralism', after all, was an expression coined by the Mensheviks.[46] Two of the most interesting and substantial critiques of Lenin's views came from Russian Marxists not directly connected with either of the factions: Vladimir Akimov and Leon Trotsky. Akimov, an Economist delegate to the Second Congress, was ridiculed by the united *Iskra*-ists, so he published his comments after the Congress. Not being party to the split over the organizational question, which he considered subsidiary, Akimov turned his attention to the *Iskra*-ite Programme, drawn up largely by Plekhanov. Akimov claimed that compared with the Erfurt Programme, the *Iskra*-ite Programme was a 'remarkably complete expression' of a 'sharply divergent' philosophy.[47] Where the former had set down both material and spiritual pre-conditions for the proletariat's emancipation, the Russian pro-gramme included only the material conditions. The proletariat was regarded by the *Iskra*-ites, he declared, merely as instruments of revolution. What of the class consciousness of the proletariat, he asked? How could a Social Democratic programme not 'find it necessary to note the conscious, revolutionary, and class character of the proletarian struggle?'[48] Lenin regarded the proletariat as a 'passive medium in which the bacillus of socialism, introduced from without, can develop'.[49] Akimov, however, insists that Social Democracy has no need to divert the proletariat from what Lenin considers a false path:

Consciousness within the movement of the proletariat is the *essential precondition* of social revolution, and this must be stated in our programme. As long as only 'professional revolutionaries' approach the struggle consciously, we shall see repetitions of the sad events of 1848.[50]

Akimov may have recalled Engels' interpretation of 1848 as a 'revolution carried through by small conscious minorities at the head of unconscious masses'.[51] That time, Engels had argued, had passed.

Akimov also reviewed the concept of the 'dictatorship of the proletariat'. He complained that since it was not included in any other Social Democratic programme,[52] its inclusion in the Russian programme required some justification which was not forthcoming. This is a more interesting observation than Akimov realized, as he was not likely to have seen Lenin's 'Notes on Plekhanov's First Draft Programme' for the Second Congress. In fiery language, Plekhanov had concluded that the 'dictatorship of the proletariat is an essential political condition of the social revolution'.[53] Lenin noted alongside this passage:

Page 9. 'Master of the situation', 'ruthlessly to smash', 'dictatorship'??? (The social revolution is enough for us.)[54]

Curiously, when Lenin presented his own draft programme a few weeks later, the formulation about the 'dictatorship of the pro-letariat' remained the same as Plekhanov's, and only the phrase 'ruthlessly to smash' was removed.[55] However, when criticizing

Plekhanov's second draft programme, Lenin indicted the absence of the dictatorship concept:

the concept of 'dictatorship' is incompatible with *positive* recognition of outside support for the proletariat. If we really knew positively that the petty bourgeoisie will support the proletariat in the accomplishment of its, the proletariat's, revolution it would be pointless to speak of a 'dictatorship', for we would then be fully guaranteed so overwhelming a majority that we could get on very well without a dictatorship.... The recognition of the necessity for the *dictatorship* of the proletariat is *most closely and inseparably* bound up with the thesis of the *Communist Manifesto* that the proletariat *alone* is a really revolutionary class.[56]

Lenin's remarks indicate not only that he conceived of the dictatorship of the proletariat as a coercive political form for an embattled and minority proletariat, a position he would maintain hereafter, but that he regarded such a dictatorship as being possible in Russia. It was no doubt this coercive and minority conception of dictatorship which prompted Vera Zasulich, in the 1901–2 discussions among *Iskra* editors, to make light of Lenin's threats of force: 'On millions! Just try! You'll have to take the trouble to persuade them and that's all there is to it.'[57]

Akimov explains that 'the word "dictatorship" denotes a special form of government'.[58] Even if we assume that the proletariat elects this government, 'it would be a dictatorship of the revolutionary government over the proletariat'.[59] Was the Second Congress aware of these implications of the dictatorship concept? Akimov criticized the concept as inappropriate on two grounds: (i) it expresses an idea that cannot be realized, that is, the direct rule of an entire class over another; or (ii) it expresses a Blanquist idea of the investment of absolute, unlimited power in a provisional revolutionary government. If, Akimov writes, the *Iskra*-ites intended to use 'dictatorship' to mean class rule, or the political power of the proletariat, there was no need to use dictatorship with all its ambiguities.[60] Besides, the dictatorship concept harbours distinct dangers for post-revolutionary society. Plekhanov had written that

the dictatorship of a given class is ... the rule of this class which enables it to wield the organized force of society in order to defend its own interests and to suppress all social movements which directly or indirectly threaten these interests.[61]

What are we to make of the idea of suppressing movements which 'indirectly' threaten proletarian interests? Akimov warned that such an interpretation of dictatorship could only bring disaster to the proletariat. The most 'dangerous' movements, he added, might well be formed among the proletariat itself. 'They will then be branded "not truly proletarian", "not conscious", and so on, and to them will be opposed the "enlightened despotism" of the revolutionary government.'[62] Akimov had perceptively exposed the implications and limitations of Lenin's view that class interests, consciousness, and even class membership depend upon an ideological position rather than an economic, or material, position. For Akimov, the heterogeneity of the proletariat is a guarantee of democratic socialism:

The proletariat needs a broadly democratic organization of power and a guarantee of non-intervention by this power into the sphere of individual and social freedom. It needs what is embraced by a single term – democracy.[63]

If the *Iskra*-ites attempted to smuggle in a non-democratic conception of proletarian rule, they must be reproached, according to Akimov, for advocating in essence a conspiratorial seizure of power, a non-Marxist, Blanquist idea.[64] The major thrust of his analysis of the Second Congress was not concerned with the debate over membership, in itself merely a symptom, but with an as yet unarticulated difference between Bolsheviks and Mensheviks over programme. Such a difference should have been apparent from just one highly significant exchange at the Congress. Pasadovskii, Akimov relates, declared that 'there are no democratic principles that we should not subordinate to the *interests of our Party*'.[65] Plekhanov took the floor in support:

If the success of the revolution should demand temporary curtailment of this or that democratic principle, it would be criminal to stop short of such curtailment.... [E]ven the principle of universal suffrage ought to be approached from the point of view of the basic principle of democracy I have indicated – *Salus populi suprema lex est*. The revolutionary proletariat can restrict the political rights of the upper classes as the upper classes once restricted its political rights.[66]

Akimov argued that such a principle led to 'Nechaevism'. Lenin, moreover, 'is a Blanquist, and nothing Blanquist is alien to him'.[67]

For Akimov, the incongruous feature of the Second Congress was that the Mensheviks agreed to an essentially Blanquist programme, but then refused to accept the Blanquist organizational principles which complemented it. The Mensheviks
sense that this is wrong, that it should not be so. And yet, instead of re-evaluating the premises underlying the conclusion, they declare the premises correct. They accept the programme and declare that it is not they who deviate from it, but Lenin.[68]

Subsequent reactions to the results of the Second Congress were neither immediate nor precise, nor did they take Akimov's route and criticize the Party programme. The result was a rather lame response to Lenin's supposed organizational deviations, which, for example, were dubbed 'bureaucratic centralism' in P. Akselrod's 1903 pamphlet 'The Unification of Russian Social Democracy and its Tasks'. Akselrod saw Lenin as a 'fetishist of centralization';[69] he later claimed that the Leninist party would never lead to the maturation of the proletariat as a class. According to Akselrod, the choice was between the intelligentsia using the labour movement as an instrument of revolution – a conspiratorial party of superior technique – and a working-class party basing its strength on the political maturity and initiative of the proletariat.[70] Martov, who had also formerly agreed with Lenin's *What is to Be Done?*, now criticized the 'state of siege' that had beset the Party.[71] Many former Economists now joined with the Mensheviks, basing their union partly on a shared enmity towards Lenin and his views of the nature and consequent organization of the Party.

To this nebulous opposition to Lenin among the Mensheviks were introduced Trotsky's reflections on the Second Congress and on the organizational question. Some of Trotsky's earliest political works, Baruch Knei-Paz reminds us, concerned the question of organization.[72] In his 'Report of the Siberian Delegation' (1903) on the Second Congress, and in *Our Political Tasks* (August 1904), Trotsky 'emerged as a supporter of centralism, but a centralism governed by scrupulous democratic arrangements';[73] he opposed the idea of an organization becoming the master, instead of a servant, that is, a leadership becoming separated from the movement and outside its control. Trotsky, too, condemned Lenin's 'state of siege' mentality, which bred 'organized mistrust'.[74] He considered that Lenin's drive for power was not personal ambition, but the logical outcome of his whole system. Lenin's 'ego-centrism', Trotsky feared, would devour independent thinking, since independent thinking might lead to opposition. Lenin's planned Central Committee would be 'an all-mighty Committee of Public Safety so that he may play the role of an "incorrupt" Robespierre',[75] and maintain internal control. Trotsky was concerned that this 'caricature Robespierre' would destroy the Party when his inevitable downfall came.

Our Political Tasks was even more strident in its anti-Leninism. Trotsky claimed that Leninism would lead to conspiracy, unjustifiably claiming to represent working-class interests. Lenin's organization would 'make it far more difficult for workers to join the party than for the intellectuals'.[76] Thus it was not just organization, but the character of the entire movement that was at stake. Trotsky dubbed as 'substitutionism' the relationship which would obtain between Lenin's Party and the proletariat, the class whom he felt Lenin had abandoned:

In one case, we have a system of *thinking* for the proletariat, of the political *substitution* of the proletariat; in the other, a system of *educating* politically the proletariat, *mobilizing* it, so that it may exercise effective pressure on the will of all groups and parties. These two systems produce political results which are, objectively, totally different.[77]

The Party did not exist to call upon the workers to recognize their objective interests when the Party deemed the time ripe for revolution. The Party existed, Trotsky considered, to develop the proletariat's interests from an objective fact into a subjective reality so that the proletariat could emancipate itself. Substitutionism, however, was a short-cut to revolution. As Plekhanov had said many years earlier,[78] so Trotsky now concurred, if the Social Democratic movement was to succeed, it would succeed as a movement of the working class. The pervasive logic of substitutionism prevented this:

In inner-party politics, these methods [of Lenin] lead, as we shall yet see, to this: the party organization substitutes itself for the party, the Central Committee substitutes itself for the organization and, finally, a 'dictator' substitutes himself for the Central Committee.[79]

Although this is one of Trotsky's best-known statements (which he later repudiated), and deserves more than most others to be considered prophetic, it expressed an idea which was familiar at the time. The internal life of the Party seemed in grave danger. Could it tolerate a regime of 'terror', led by a 'dictator'? Surely this would result in a 'dictatorship *over* the proletariat'.[80] Trotsky was complacent, however, believing that Leninism would inevitably disintegrate.

Plekhanov, after co-operating with Lenin as co-editor of *Iskra* for some months after the Second Congress, joined the Mensheviks. Considering Party unity close at hand, he argued that to split over mere organizational differences would be 'a heinous *political crime*'.[81] But when Lenin left the *Iskra* editorial board, and Plekhanov had recalled those former editors who had been excluded from the board by the Congress or by their own choice, Plekhanov's criticisms of 'Lenin's' organizing principles followed the Menshevik pattern. Even Rosa Luxemburg contributed to the debate against Lenin, arguing that his was an 'ultra-centralist' solution, and that Lenin was a Blanquist centralist.[82] Yet as Nettl relates, Luxemburg herself was no model democratic leader within her own Party.[83]

Lenin had an inclination for turning peripheral questions into questions of principle, of class division. Any aspect of life, from philosophy to literature and art, could become a question of principle for Lenin when he so chose. Four years after his collaboration with the philosopher Bogdanov had begun, for example, Lenin decided to campaign against the philosophical trend of 'empiriocriticism' which he knew had been held by Bogdanov from the start.[84] In 1908 he published his *Materialism and Empirio-Criticism*, a (prolix) restatement of the philosophical views of Engels and Plekhanov. Without philosophical significance (except in so far as it dominated Soviet epistemology until the late 1950s, when Lenin's *Philosophical Notebooks* supplanted it), this work is a monument not just to Lenin's relentless pursuit of 'error', but to his skill at turning all questions into questions of principle. He declared:

behind the epistemological scholasticism of empirio-criticism one must not fail to see the struggle of parties in philosophy, a struggle which in the last analysis reflects the tendencies and ideology of the antagonistic classes in modern society.[85]

Bogdanov had been placed outside of Lenin's 'proletariat' at a stroke.

Social Democrats, both Menshevik and Bolshevik agreed, must lead the struggle against Russian absolutism. But what would become of the Party after the revolution? Before 1914 Lenin stopped short of advocating socialism. 'Marxists', he wrote in 1905, 'are absolutely convinced of the bourgeois character of the Russian revolution.'[86] The revolution must open the way for a rapid development of capitalism and of the working class. It must not 'overstep the bounds of bourgeois social and economic relationships',[87] but their political forms should be stretched to the limit. Lenin saw the task of Social Democracy as establishing a revolutionary-democratic dictatorship of the proletariat and peasantry. It was a strategy based on the commonly held, Social Democratic belief in the 'treachery of the [Russian] democratic bourgeoisie',[88] but also on Lenin's particular evaluation of the peasant contribution to revolutionary struggle which he observed in 1905. Lenin's rather curious formula of the 'revolutionary-democratic dictatorship' was meant to suggest the victory over tsarism carried out by the 'revolutionary people – the proletariat and the peasantry',[89] although the bourgeoisie would become the new 'ruling class'.[90] This outcome was not quite according to the European model of capitalism, Lenin conceded,[91] but it was not socialism: 'if Social-Democracy sought to make the socialist revolution its immediate aim, it would assuredly discredit itself'.[92]

Nevertheless, Lenin had firmly established a unique Bolshevik political strategy, based on the potential of the peasant rebellion. 'The agrarian question is the basis of the bourgeois revolution in Russia',[93] he argued, but because of the peasants' conditions of work, their narrowness and disunity, a *peasant* revolution ... is possible only under the leadership of the proletariat [i.e., Social Democracy]'.[94] For Lenin, the lesson of the 1905 Revolution was that:

The tactics of Social-Democracy in the Russian bourgeois revolution are determined not by the task of supporting the liberal bourgeoisie, as the opportunists think, but by the task of supporting the fighting peasantry.[95]

Lenin's strategy fell somewhere between Plekhanov's 'two-stage revolution', and Trotsky's and Parvus' 'permanent revolution' strategies, which respectively separated and telescoped the bourgeois and socialist stages of the revolution. More than either of its competitors, Lenin's strategy relied upon two features of the Russian revolutionary tradition: a centralized party of professional revolutionaries, and a keen appreciation of the peasantry as the decisive material factor of the revolution. These ideas were crucial to Lenin's success, and to the character and later development of the Soviet state. But we should not be too quick to make these suggestive parallels definite links between Lenin and figures of the Russian revolutionary tradition. Such a move has spawned the 'guilt by association' school which has linked Lenin variously with Nechaev,[96] Tkachev,[97] and Ogarev.[98] Soviet historiography itself during the 1920s stressed the link between Bolshevism and the Russian revolutionary heritage. In 1926, for example, Steklov proclaimed Bakunin 'the founder of the concept of Soviet power, the political form of the dictatorship of the proletariat'.[99] Of course, Lenin himself openly acknowledged his debt to Chernyshevsky (whose novel *What Is To Be Done? 'completely transformed my outlook'*),[100] and to the party organization of *Zemlia i Volia*. But there is little evidence to suggest that Lenin was primarily or directly influenced by the Russian Jacobins.

Rather, it was Plekhanov and Plekhanov's interpretation of Marxism which decisively influenced Lenin. The assumptions which Plekhanov brought to Marxism, and the tasks of Social Democracy as he conceived them, represent the influences of the Russian revolutionary tradition. Lenin, it might be said, experienced that tradition vicariously through Plekhanov. The 'father of Russian Marxism' was father to both Bolshevism and Menshevism; the author of the programme of 'unified' Social Democracy left a divided legacy.[101] If he recognized the need for political freedoms for the development of the working class, and if he recognized the dangers of revolutionary coups, Plekhanov could also be authoritarian in his conception of the role of the Party and of the socialist revolution and its transition period. Voden wrote the following after a meeting with Engels in 1893:

Engels inquired about Plekhanov's personal attitude to the question of the dictatorship of the proletariat. I [Voden] had to confess that G. V. Plekhanov had often told me he was convinced that, of course once 'we' had come to power, 'we' would grant freedom to no one else but 'ourselves'. . . . In response to my question of whom one should understand more precisely as enjoying the right to this monopoly of freedom, Plekhanov replied: the working class, led by comrades who correctly understand the teaching of Marx and draw from it the correct conclusions.[102]

Plekhanov does not seem to have elaborated upon who should decide what was the 'correct' understanding of Marx, but the authoritarian implications are obvious. Plekhanov had also, as we noted above, stressed the intelligentsia's role in bringing socialism to the workers. Harding argues that Plekhanov sometimes adopted 'a positively instrumental view of *intelligentsia* designs';[103] and Baron has seen clearly what we only glimpsed above: that Plekhanov's work 'bristled' with expression such as 'dictatorship of the proletariat', and 'seizure of power'.[104] With his mechanistic conception of historical development, and his attachment to the methods of West European Social Democracy, Plekhanov combined a Jacobin and cynical element. Up to 1900, Lenin held a great respect for Plekhanov,[105] whose influence over him seems to have been decisive. Certain of Plekhanov's attitudes remained with him, as Valentinov indirectly attests:

Plekhanov once said to me about a critic of Marxism ... 'First, let's stick the convict's badge on him, and then after that we'll examine his case.'[106]

The organizational dispute and split at the Second Congress was symptomatic of a much deeper ambivalence in Russian Marxism which was embodied in Plekhanov's works.

7

LENIN AND THE DICTATORSHIP

Between Lenin's 'revolutionary-democratic dictatorship of the proletariat and peasantry' and the 'proletarian revolution' of October 1917, the theory of imperialism came to play a major role in Lenin's strategy. Although the concept of imperialism was first elaborated systematically by 'bourgeois' economists, such as J. A. Hobson, and then was taken up by Marxists, such as Luxemburg, Rudolph Hilferding, Nikolai Bukharin and Kautsky, Lenin used his version of imperialism to explain why proletarian revolutions had not yet occurred in the West as predicted, and ultimately to justify the attempt at socialist revolution in Russia. Under imperialism, Lenin explained, 'the division of nations into oppressor and oppressed ... [is] basic, significant and inevitable'.[1] Class analysis of capitalist societies was thus transformed into a global classification of 'haves' and 'have-nots', imperialist and colony, oppressor and oppressed. The strategic significance of such a theory lay in its proposition that, in the oppressed nations at least, the working class must use the dynamic of the anti-imperialist struggle – in which it was by no means the largest force – to advance the socialist revolution:

The main thing *today* is to stand against the united, aligned front of the imperialist powers, the imperialist bourgeoisie and the social-imperialists, and *for* the utilisation of *all* national movements against imperialism for the purposes of the socialist revolution.[2]

Lenin's concept of imperialism, and his pamphlet of the same name, suggested not only that conditions were objectively favourable for revolution in the oppressed nations (among which Lenin included Russia), but that conditions for revolution had deteriorated in the imperialist countries. It was not simply that 'imperialist ideology ... penetrates the working class',[3] but that the leaders of the working class, those inculcators of socialist consciousness, had become 'social-imperialists', 'socialists in words and imperialists in deeds'.[4] In the 1920 Preface to his pamphlet *Imperialism*, Lenin maintained that the imperialists' huge profits had bribed many labour leaders, who had become *'agents of the bourgeoisie in the working-class'*,[5] although he also believed that entire working classes had been bribed by higher wages. But in turning the focus of socialist revolution towards the East, Lenin's theories and the Bolshevik coup divided forever two major groups of Marxists: Communists and Social Democrats. Their differences are epitomized in the post-October debate between Kautsky, who stressed the liberal heritage of Marxism, and Lenin, who stressed its revolutionary content.

Kautsky fired the opening salvo against the Soviet regime, soon after the October Revolution, in his *Dictatorship of the Proletariat*. He based his argument against Lenin's seizure of power on two propositions, one of them a general proposition about socialism, the other a particular proposition about the 'dictatorship of the proletariat'. Kautsky believed that what was at stake between his position and Lenin's was a clash 'of two fundamentally distinct methods, that of democracy and that of dictatorship'.[6] He believed that socialism must be achieved democratically (in the liberal sense), and that Lenin's 'dictatorship of the proletariat' was neither democratic nor the transition to socialism. If socialism is conceived as a particular organization of production, he argues, then that alone 'is not our goal'.[7] If democracy is conceived as simply a means to socialism, then that too is opposed by Kautsky. The goal, he argues, 'is the abolition of every kind of exploitation and oppression';[8] it is neither a narrowly technical goal, nor a narrowly procedural goal: it is a human goal. Democracy and the socialist organization of production 'are means to the same end',[9] the liberation of man. If the socialist organization of production cannot achieve this aim it should be abandoned. But democracy and socialist production (by which Kautsky seems to mean state-controlled production) are not necessarily connected; they must be connected by socialists.

Kautsky thus makes a general plea for the notion of active participation in the transition to and the constitution of socialism. In this conception pre-socialist democracy is of the utmost importance for inculcating the habits, responsibilities, and consciousness needed by the proletariat to achieve human liberation. Pre-socialist democracy is here a prerequisite of socialism. Kautsky also operates with a notion of historical 'ripeness' for socialism. A country is ripe for socialism when it possesses a highly developed capitalism (although he conceded that this is 'not a condition which lends itself to statistical calculation'),[10] as well as conditions such as the 'Will to Socialism', the strength to realize it, and the maturity of the proletariat. Such maturity, he argues, can only be gained in the struggle for democracy and in its working. Thus Kautsky implies that the prerequisite for socialism is a democratic capitalist republic. Once a country is 'ripe' in this general sense, the decisive factor becomes 'personal'. The question then becomes whether the proletariat is 'strong and intelligent enough to take in hand the regulation of society'.[11]

Universal suffrage, according to Kautsky, matures the proletariat through the progressive recognition that the proletariat's class interest coincides with the collective interest of society.[12] Democracy could not remove class antagonisms, nor prevent the overthrow of capitalism, but 'it can avoid many reckless and premature attempts at revolution'.[13] Democracy made the proletarian revolution a less dramatic affair; it ensured against the premature provocation of the proletariat, and made the proletariat's victory easier to maintain.[14] What role does the dictatorship of the proletariat play in Kautsky's scheme?

Between these two stages, the preparation for Socialism and its realization which both require democracy, there is the transition stage when the proletariat has conquered political power, but has not yet brought about Socialism in an economic sense.[15]

Kautsky regrets that Marx had not specified what he meant by the 'dictatorship'. 'Taken literally', he observes, 'the word signifies the suspension of democracy. But taken literally it also means the sovereignty of a single person, who is bound by no laws.'[16] But the dictatorship of a class is a different matter; for Kautsky it proves that Marx did not intend 'dictatorship in the literal sense'.[17] What then did Marx intend? He did not mean a 'form of government', Kautsky argues, but a 'condition which must everywhere arise when the proletariat has conquered political power'.[18] To support his claim that the dictatorship is not a form of government, Kautsky cites the Paris Commune as a dictatorship in Marx's sense, although Marx never did.

The idea of 'dictatorship' as a form of government, implying the suppression of opposition, the suspension of freedom of the press, and association and the denial of franchise to opponents, is a basic source of the dispute between communists and Social Democrats. The question, according to Kautsky, is

whether the victorious proletariat needs to employ these measures, and whether Socialism is only or most easily realizable with their aid.[19]

Moreover, if dictatorship is a form of government, it cannot represent the dictatorship of a class, for 'a class can only rule, not govern'.[20] For Kautsky, the 'dictatorship of the proletariat' means simply that the proletariat is the ruling class; the concept has no directly political connotations. He implies that the best way for the proletariat to rule is through a government based on universal suffrage. For even the political dictatorship of a working-class party does not represent properly the dictatorship of the proletariat.

The social revolution, Kautsky explains, is a 'profound transformation of the entire social structure',[21] a process which may take decades. Generally, it is inaugurated by a political revolution, 'a sudden alteration in the relative strength of classes in the State'.[22] The political revolution may be peaceful or violent; a peaceful revolution is the best guarantee against the rule of a Cromwell or a Napoleon.[23] 'By the dictatorship of the proletariat', Kautsky argues, 'we are unable to understand anything else than its rule on the basis of democracy.'[24] But because the Bolsheviks had placed their hopes in a European revolution which did not occur, they now faced insoluble problems: 'it became inevitable that they should put dictatorship in the place of democracy'.[25] The Constituent Assembly, Kautsky believed, was the real test of the Bolsheviks' popular support, not the soviets (workers', peasants', and soldiers' councils) on which Lenin based his test. But Lenin had wanted it both ways. He had waited until the Bolsheviks had lost the Assembly elections before he reasserted his claims that the Assembly was undemocratic and that, in any case, the soviets were a 'higher form of democracy'. There is no doubt that Lenin based his views to some extent on Marx's evaluation of the Paris Commune, but as Kautsky comments:

It is only a pity that this knowledge was arrived at after one had been left in a minority in the Constituent Assembly.[26]

But, Kautsky asks, do the soviets really represent a 'higher type' of democracy? 'Hitherto democracy has connoted equal rights for all citizens',[27] but the Soviets deprive those who are not represented within them of political rights. It was not at all difficult, he continues, to be 'labelled a capitalist, and to lose the vote'.[28] Arbitrariness was a grave danger because 'a juridicial definition of the proletariat, which shall be distinct and precise, is not to be had'.[29] In reality, the Bolsheviks had excluded all opposition to them from the soviets under cover of labelling all opponents as capitalists. Because the 'material and moral prerequisites for Socialism' did not exist in Russia, the Bolshevik Revolution was 'the last of the middle class, and not the first of the Socialist Revolutions'.[30]

For Kautsky, the so-called 'dictatorship of the proletariat' in Russia was really the dictatorship of a party. It was a rule of desperation born of lack of support. The proletariat's real interest was with democracy:

Where the proletariat represents the majority, democracy will be the machinery of its rule. Where it is in the minority, democracy constitutes its most suitable fighting arena in which to assert itself, win concessions, and develop.[31]

Kautsky acknowledged that the Bolsheviks were the only Russian socialists consistently to advocate the 'dictatorship of the proletariat', but their current methods had little in common with Marx's project. Why did they not explain their methods on the grounds of exceptional circumstances, which 'left no choice but dictatorship or abdication'? They chose, instead, to formulate a new theory, 'for which they claimed universal application'.[32] Lenin had so changed Marx's meaning that he had claimed that 'no essential contradiction can exist between the Soviet, that is, the Socialist democracy, and the exercise of dictatorial power by a single person'.[33] The Bolshevik experiment, Kautsky warned, would lead to disaster for other socialist parties. Imagine socialists struggling for the extension of democracy under capitalism saying:

that which we demand for the protection of minorities, the opposition, we only want so long as we ourselves are in the opposition.... As soon as we have become the majority, and gained the power of government, our first act will be to abolish as far as you are concerned all that we formerly demanded for ourselves.[34]

This would compromise the very idea of socialism, if socialists who offer opposition are banned in Soviet Russia and dubbed 'Social Traitors', and if the Bolsheviks persist in identifying themselves with the proletariat. The question of the right to opposition is at the heart of Kautsky's criticisms of the Bolsheviks, of the soviets and of Lenin's concept of the 'dictatorship of the proletariat'.

Lenin replied to Kautsky in a short article in *Pravda* (11 October 1918) entitled 'The Proletarian Revolution and the Renegade Kautsky', the two central themes of which were soon incorporated into a lengthy polemic of the same title. Lenin does a certain justice to Kautsky's position, in the first of these themes, which he represents as follows:

what Marx meant by 'revolutionary dictatorship of the proletariat' was not a '*form of governing*' that precludes democracy, but a *state*, namely, 'a state of rule'. And the rule of the proletariat, as the majority of the population, is possible with the strictest observance of democracy.[35]

Lenin counter-claims that the dictatorship of the proletariat is rather a '*state of a different type*' which gives 'the working people *genuine democracy*'.[36] The second major theme of Lenin's argument confirms to some extent Kautsky's point that any opposition to Bolshevik rule is ruled out of court as bourgeois. Kautsky's position, according to Lenin, 'is a complete renunciation of the proletarian revolution'.[37]

As Lenin expands these themes, he explains that the dictatorship of the proletariat is the 'very essence', the 'key problem' of the proletarian revolution.[38] Yet Kautsky's contribution does not add much to its elucidation: it 'is such an awful theoretical muddle, such a complete renunciation of Marxism, that Kautsky, it must be confessed, has far excelled Bernstein'.[39] Nevertheless, Lenin is prepared to combat the misconceptions Kautsky has spread. The dictatorship of the proletariat, he repeats, is the 'very *essence* of Marx's doctrine',[40] and is clearly explained in the *Critique of the Gotha Programme*. Marx and Engels, Lenin erroneously claims, '*repeatedly* spoke about the dictatorship of the proletariat'.[41] He also claims that they provided 'quite a number of the most detailed indications' of the dictatorship's form, although he fails to specify them. The dictatorship, he explains, is the 'historically concrete ... formulation of the proletariat's task of "smashing" the bourgeois state machine'.[42]

Like Kautsky, but for different reasons, Lenin claims that the *'form of government* has absolutely nothing to do with' the dictatorship of the proletariat.[43] They are agreed on this point, Kautsky because he believed that the proletariat had no need to rule dictatorially, or despotically, but Lenin because he argued that all class rule is dictatorial. Lenin, however, shared little of Kautsky's concern for the political form of the dictatorship of the proletariat. Lenin refers to the bourgeois state: of course, monarchy and republic are different forms of government, but

> *both* these forms of government, like all transitional 'forms of government' under capitalism, are only variations of the *bourgeois state*, that is, of the dictatorship of the bourgeoisie.[44]

For Lenin, political forms are contingent; they are not necessary to the definition of the 'dictatorship'. Thus dictatorship does not necessarily 'mean the abolition of democracy for the class that exercises' it,

> but it does mean the abolition ... of democracy for the class over which, or against which, the dictatorship is exercised.[45]

But does a 'dictatorship of the bourgeoisie' signify, in its republican and liberal democratic phase, a democracy among the bourgeoisie and an absence of democracy for the working class? Is universal suffrage a 'very material restriction' of democracy? Two ideas seem conflated in Lenin's argument: the scope of democracy, the extent to which democratically decided policies control society; and the extent of democracy, the basis of political institutions (i.e., franchise, political rights) no matter what their particular scope or powers. Because an institution such as parliament may have a limited scope within bourgeois society, it does not necessarily mean that it is not democratically constituted. Lenin, nevertheless, describes dictatorship as 'rule based directly upon force and unrestricted by any laws'.[46] To counter such 'bourgeois dictatorships', Lenin proposes the revolutionary dictatorship of the proletariat, 'rule won and maintained by the use of violence by the proletariat against the bourgeoisie, rule that is unrestricted by any laws'.[47]

For Lenin the Soviet republic was a 'proletarian democracy', which 'has brought a development and expansion of democracy unprecedented in the world, for the vast majority of the population, for the exploited and the working people'.[48] Lenin uses proletarian democracy and proletarian dictatorship synonymously, yet neither refers to a concrete political form – they are both a (higher) type of state. It is in the state's 'structure' that Lenin perceives its class nature:

> The Soviet government is the *first* in the world ... to *enlist* the people, specifically the *exploited* people, in the work of administration.[49]

Lenin argues, in effect, that the character of the state is determined not by its representative institutions, but by its 'machine', the people who work in it, and the interests it serves. Real democracy is thus to be found in the 'structure of the state', not in its political forms. Of what purpose, then, are the soviets, and is their political form of no consequence? Lenin explains that the soviets 'are the direct organization of the working and exploited people themselves, which *helps* them to organise and administer their own state in every possible way'.[50] This implies that the soviets are not essential in guaranteeing the state's proletarian (and thus democratic) character. Lenin claims that 'proletarian democracy is a *million times* more democratic than ... the most democratic bourgeois republic'.[51] But this only obfuscates the point. Proletarian democracy is a type of state; its 'democracy' does not consist in its electoral arrangements or its protection of opposition or minority rights, but in the claim that the state represents the interests of the majority. The claim is quite simple, once the convenient confusion about 'democracy' is overcome. The proof that the state represents the interests of the majority, however – especially in the absence of liberal democratic political procedures – is beyond calculation, and lies in the realms of conviction and dogma. Using Lenin's logic, we find that a capitalist state is an undemocratic, bourgeois dictatorship, and a workers' state is a democratic, proletarian dictatorship, irrespective of the political forms in either. Lenin's almost interchangeable use of the terms 'state', 'dictatorship', and 'democracy' in relation to the Soviet republic seems intended to deceive.

Even though Lenin fully expected the prolonged resistance of the exploiters to the Soviet republic, and even though they had advantages which might help them to regain power, he argues that the withdrawal of the right to vote for the exploiters 'is a *purely Russian* question, and not a question of the dictatorship of the proletariat in general'.[52] This reinforces Lenin's idea that the proletarian state is democratic not because of its electoral arrangements, which can vary from proletarian state to proletarian state. 'Proletarian democracy' is really not a question of democracy at all, in the way Kautsky and most Westerners conceive of democracy, as a liberal political form. Lenin believed that the restriction of the franchise 'is not an *indispensable* characteristic of the logical concept "dictatorship"'.[53] On the contrary, the indispensable characteristic of the proletarian dictatorship 'is the *forcible* suppression of the exploiters as a *class*'.[54]

Lenin emphasizes the coercive nature of the state to reduce the significance of its political institutions in determining its class nature, and its 'democracy', and to emphasize the task facing the Soviet dictatorship as being primarily the suppression of (bourgeois) opposition. How the state actually represented the proletariat's interests, and how they can be determined, irrespective of its political forms, is the crucial question which Lenin avoids. To confuse the issue even more, Lenin adds that

the proletariat cannot achieve victory *without ... forcibly suppressing its adversaries*, and that, where there is 'forcible suppression', where there is no 'freedom', *there is, of course, no democracy.*[55]

Having accused Kautsky of using 'pure' categories, Lenin himself indulges in 'pure' categories. Lenin has already claimed that the proletarian democracy is a million times more democratic than a bourgeois democracy but now, because it is still a state, and thus coercive, he claims that there is no democracy. Lenin uses 'democracy' in two different, but self-contradictory, ways (for democracy as a political form, in Lenin's terms, is only conceivable within the framework of a state, yet the existence of a state means that democracy is inconceivable), to justify the lack of political democracy in 'the most democratic state in the world'.

As for the soviets they are, as Lenin explains, 'the Russian form of the proletarian dictatorship'.[56] Kautsky had urged that they should not become state organs, but should give way to the decisions of the Constituent Assembly. Here, argues Lenin, is the contrast between 'proletarian' and 'bourgeois' democracy.[57] Lenin justifiably points to his advocacy of a government of soviets as early as the *April Theses* of April 1917, as a new and superior type of state, based on his understanding of the Paris Commune.[58] But he does not explain why the Bolsheviks allowed the elections to the Assembly to proceed, and why he resurrected his arguments on the state of a new type only after the Bolsheviks were left in a minority. Kautsky's belief in the democratic superiority of the Assembly is, according to Lenin, a 'formal democratic' view.[59] Lenin, by contrast, is neither 'formal' nor 'democratic', since anything that obstructs what he perceives as the proletariat's interests is immediately suppressed, and branded 'bourgeois'. The clash between 'bourgeois democracy' and 'proletarian democracy' is, in reality, the clash between political democracy (how the majority see their interests) and the proletarian state (how Lenin and the Bolsheviks see the majority's, or rather the proletariat's, interests).

Lenin attempted to appropriate all the legitimacy which the term 'democracy' can signify, while applying a test of democracy, even a conception of democracy, that was quite different from that in the Western tradition. Yet, at times, he seems determined to beat Kautsky on more traditional ground. He claims, for example, that the soviets are more democratic and more representative than the Constituent Assembly could ever be.[60] But Lenin's ultimate test is based on his conception of proletarian interests. Because universal suffrage 'sometimes produces petty-bourgeois, sometimes reactionary and counter-revolutionary parliaments',[61] it is not to be trusted as a method of representing the proletariat's interests. Thus in Russia, universal suffrage was aborted in the majority's (or rather in the proletariat's) interests. Even though the Assembly elections returned an overwhelming majority of socialist deputies, it remained a bourgeois institution, since non-Bolshevik socialists were agents of imperialism, 'social-imperialists', the concept which Lenin had developed at the beginning of the First World War. Furthermore, the very idea of giving rights to opposition, allowing its legal existence, 'belongs to the peaceful and only to the parliamentary struggle', which corresponds 'to an absence of revolution'.[62] There can be no doubt that to deny Lenin the right to suppress bourgeois opposition would cripple any socialist attempt to transform society. The danger of Lenin's approach, and the source of the authoritarianism of the new Soviet republic, was the idea that not only did the Bolshevik Party represent the proletariat's interests, but that the Bolshevik Party alone represented the proletariat's interests. Thus any opposition to Bolshevik rule would, according to this conception, need to be suppressed; all opposition to the Bolsheviks was conceived as bourgeois opposition. Opposition from other socialists, opposition from within the working class, was regarded as bourgeois opposition.

Lenin did not develop these ideas on dictatorship and democracy directly he read Kautsky's attack on the Soviet regime. They can be traced back at least to his *The State and Revolution* (1917). Marian Sawer maintains that this work represented a theoretical leap in Lenin's views because of his discovery (under the stimulus of Bukharin) of Marx's views on the 'smashing' of the bourgeois state machine,[63] and was thus the basis for his claims that the soviets were a 'new form' of state. It was a product, in other words, of Lenin's attempt to take seriously Marx's evaluation of the Paris Commune, even though Hannah Arendt considered that Lenin failed properly to assess the council form.[64] Neither did Lenin analyse the post-revolutionary role of the vanguard party; it is mentioned only once, indirectly. In *The State and Revolution*, Lenin represents the state as primarily a coercive instrument of the ruling class. The role of parliament is almost dismissed; there is no room for consensus among people in Lenin's view of the state. The proletariat must overcome the military and the bureaucracy if it is to take state power. It then needs this power, 'a centralized organisation of force, an organisation of violence' to 'crush the resistance of the exploiters' and to organize a socialist economy.[65] But the proletariat only needs the state power temporarily, until classes have disappeared, or pose no threat to the proletariat. The continued existence of the state is an indication of a condition of class war, in which 'formal' democracy has no place.

Lenin notes that Marx did 'not set out to *discover* the political *forms*' of the 'proletariat organised as the ruling class'.[66] Engels, however, had written that the 'democratic republic ... is even the specific form for the dictatorship of the proletariat'.[67] Lenin remarks, with little justification:

Engels repeated here ... the fundamental idea which runs through all of Marx's works, namely, that the democratic republic is the *nearest approach* to the dictatorship of the proletariat.[68]

Engels also wrote of the 'withering away' of the state, and argued that the proletariat needed state power only to hold down its adversaries once it had conquered power. How then will the state be used to organize the socialist economy, as Lenin suggests? Will non-coercive state institutions be used? Lenin is not clear. The dictatorship of the proletariat, he declares, is 'the organisation of the vanguard of the oppressed as the ruling class',[69] yet it results in 'an immense expansion of democracy' for the poor and exploited, and a corresponding restriction of freedom for the erstwhile exploiters. Consequently, Lenin argues, 'there is no freedom and no democracy where there is suppression and ... violence'.[70] On the one hand, the proletarian dictatorship represents an immense expansion of democracy; on the other hand, it represents no democracy. As in his later reply to Kautsky, Lenin uses two conceptions of democracy: one relative, where democracy for the exploited is increased; the other absolute, where there is no democracy. But what does the increase in 'relative' democracy mean: will workers' decisions direct the dictatorship?

Lenin also develops an argument about the economic tasks of the transition to support his proposition that a state must continue to exist in some form. The transition, he explains, corresponds to Marx's notion of the period of 'bourgeois right', prior to this boundary being crossed and the principle of society being 'From each according to his ability, to each according to his needs!'[71] Lenin argues that the state exists to enforce this bourgeois right. Bourgeois right will be overcome, he maintains, when 'labour has become so productive that they [i.e., people] will voluntarily work *according to their ability*'.[72] The state is necessary, it seems, to compel people to work in the first phase of communism. This may be consistent with Lenin's notion of the state as direct class violence,[73] but now directed against the workers themselves. Furthermore, Lenin suggested that the proletarian dictatorship was unfettered by any laws; the dictatorship rested on force, not laws. Lapenna comments on this notion that, 'in Lenin's opinion, the dictatorship of the proletariat is not bound even by its own laws'.[74] Soviet experience bears out this interpretation. The legal profession was treated with contempt after the October Revolution. Article 3 of the People's Court Act of 1918 instructed courts to act according to their 'socialist (legal) consciousness'.[75] Judgements were thus not based on a body of written law, but could at any moment be determined or changed by decision of the supreme Party authorities. Lapenna describes this political understanding of legality as 'legalized arbitrariness'.[76] It lent itself to the unchallengeability of Bolshevik rule. Lenin's attitude towards the Extraordinary Commission, the *Cheka*, exemplifies this approach. In a note of 1 March 1922,[77] Lenin wrote that the *Cheka* should come to an agreement with the Commissar of Justice to give the Commissariat instructions. The secret police, that is to say, should instruct the courts on what sentences should be passed.

This arbitrary, violent conception of dictatorship was not entirely new for Lenin, even in 1917. As early as 1905, in his *Two Tactics of Social-Democracy*, he had described the dictatorship as 'the forcible suppression of resistance by force and the arming of the revolutionary classes of the people'.[78] Lenin suggested that a revolutionary government was a dictatorship because of the manner in which it acts: the major questions of what tasks it must perform, and who shall decide them, are subordinated to the question of how those tasks will be performed. This is evident in 1918 also, when Lenin argued that 'it would be extremely stupid ... to assume that the transition from capitalism to socialism is possible without coercion and without dictatorship'.[79] This might even require (i.e., it does not logically exclude for Lenin) the dictatorship of individuals – in which context, 'dictatorship' has its more usual connotations. For Lenin, socialist democracy and socialist dictatorship have very little to do with actual political forms, but much more to do with an argument about the class nature of the state and whose interests it serves. Lenin uses the term 'democracy' primarily to bask in its prestige. His argument about Soviet democracy is, at best, doubtful, and at worst, sophistical. Lenin never makes his real meaning clear, as he shifts from one meaning of 'democracy' to another, from conventional use to his own use. Moreover, he never explicitly defends his underlying proposition: that the Bolshevik Party is the only legitimate representative of the interests of the proletariat, and the Russian exploited in general. Consequently, he writes that the proletarian dictatorship is exercised by working people through individuals, that the dictatorship is democratic because it represents the interests of the working people as well as suppressing their exploiters. Yet only their 'representatives' are to have any say in defining the interests of the workers and to make the crucial decisions of the transition.

Rosa Luxemburg contributed to this debate by criticizing both sides. Lenin, she argued, had missed the fundamental point of the proletarian dictatorship: that its 'life element' was the 'political training and education of the entire mass of the people'.[80] This process had stopped in Russia because freedom had been stifled. Freedom, she noted, 'is always and exclusively freedom for the one who thinks differently'.[81] Restricting public control of government, as in Soviet Russia, only promoted corruption; its remedy was 'the broadest democracy and public opinion'.[82] The suppression of all opposition gave life only to the bureaucracy. If political life completely dies out, she warned, there will be a dictatorship, 'not the dictatorship of the proletariat, however, but only the dictatorship of a handful of politicians, that is a dictatorship in the bourgeois [i.e., established, usual] sense'.[83]

The basic error of the Lenin–Kautsky dispute, according to Luxemburg, was that 'democracy' and 'dictatorship' were being counterposed. Kautsky, she charged, upheld bourgeois democracy, while Lenin and Trotsky upheld the dictatorship of a handful, a bourgeois 'dictatorship'. 'Socialist democracy', she counters, 'is not something which begins only in the promised land after the foundations of socialist economy are created.'[84] Socialist democracy is 'the same thing as the dictatorship of the proletariat'.[85] Lenin had reconciled democracy and dictatorship by removing the discussion to the nature of the state. Any state was a dictatorship, by definition, but the proletarian state – because it served the interests of the proletariat, the majority – was also democratic. Any proletarian state, whatever its political or representative forms, was a democracy. Thus the proletarian dictatorship was, by definition, democratic. Kautsky, on the other hand, contrasted dictatorship as a political form with democracy as a political form. He believed that it was in its representative institutions that the character of the proletarian state must be sought; it worked in the interests of the proletariat because it was responsive and accountable to them through liberal democratic institutions. Luxemburg's position in this debate is difficult to define accurately. She is attached to democratic political forms, but also to Marx's 'dictatorship of the proletariat'. 'Dictatorship', she explains enigmatically, 'consists in the *manner of applying democracy*, not in its elimination.'[86] The mistake of both Lenin and Kautsky, she argues, is that 'they make a virtue of necessity and want to freeze into a complete theoretical

system all the tactics forced upon them by these fatal circumstances'.[87] Luxemburg believed that the Bolshevik experiment was
doomed for lack of international support, but that it was a brave and
daring venture. The Bolsheviks' 'immortal historical service' lay in
their seizure of power in the name of socialism, posing the problem
of socialism in an immediate and practical way. 'In Russia the
problem could only be posed. It could not be solved in Russia.'[88] For
this purpose European revolutions were required.

Kautsky responded to Lenin's *The Proletarian Revolution* with
Terrorism or Communism, a detailed historical examination of the
concept of 'dictatorship'. He contradicts his earlier position by
finally rejecting Marx's terminology:

the type of dictatorship as a form of government lies in *personal* dictatorship. Class-dictatorship is pure nonsense. Class-rule without laws and
regulations is unthinkable.[89]

Dictatorship, Kautsky concedes, can only be a form of government.
But by abandoning his earlier distinction, Kautsky is hard pressed to
explain what Marx meant by the 'dictatorship of the bourgeoisie'.
As in his earlier work on the Soviet regime, Kautsky cites the Paris
Commune to demonstrate that the role of violence should be
reduced in a proletarian revolution, and to demonstrate the necessity
for democracy in the socialist revolution. Terrorism, Kautsky
claims, was regarded by Marx as a feature of 'the revolution of the
"higher classes"', as compared with the proletarian revolution'.[90] If
Marx had agreed with Engels that the Paris Commune was a
proletarian dictatorship, as both Lenin and Kautsky believed, then
Kautsky's argument stands: that Marx and Engels 'in no way
understood the withholding of universal and equal suffrage or the
suppression of democracy'[91] by the concept 'dictatorship'. But
having been carried away by the 'mass psychology' and made their
coup, the Bolsheviks now used the expression 'dictatorship of the
proletariat' 'to gain absolution from all sins against the spirit of
Marxism'.[92] Kautsky abandoned 'dictatorship' because he recognised that it was a weak base from which to defend Marxism, and
that popular sentiment identified it too closely with the practices of
Bolshevism. Kautsky decided to cut his losses, and to reject the term
entirely.

Kautsky then set out to demonstrate how the Soviet regime was undemocratic, contrary to Lenin's claims, and how it lent itself to authoritarianism. The soviets, he argues, are particularly liable to manipulation, since the eligibility of their voters is not secure. If only a worker can get the vote, what constitutes a worker? The demarcation of the middle from the working class 'can never be accurately drawn':

There will always be something arbitrary in such endeavour, which fact makes the council idea peculiarly liable to become a foundation for a purely dictatorial and arbitrary rule.[93]

This is also the case with 'the bourgeoisie'. Having been dispossessed and forced to labour, Kautsky explains, they are then denied the right to vote because they do not work. A 'bourgeois' is so defined because of his position before the Revolution. 'The bourgeoisie in this respect appears in the Soviet Republic as a special human species, whose characteristics are ineradicable.'[94] Kautsky believed that this displayed a 'thirst for vengeance' not at all appropriate to the transition to socialism. The abolition of democracy is only justified on the unjustifiable assumption 'that there really exists an absolute truth, and that the Communists alone are in possession of that truth'.[95]

If, as Lenin claims, there is no contradiction between Soviet democracy and the rule of an individual dictator, then Kautsky draws out the implication that any and 'every form of compulsion which might be applied with a view to introducing Socialism is compatible with democracy'.[96] And if for Lenin Socialist Democracy is the same as the dictatorship, Kautsky replies:

that may be; but it would only show that Soviet democracy is a very peculiar structure, which one could employ to uphold any form of arbitrary domination, provided one merely gave it the name Socialism.[97]

But Bolshevik rule, he declares, has not collapsed because it has abandoned the aim of socialism in favour of retaining its own power. The result is a 'new class of governors ... formed under the leadership of the old Communist idealists and fighters'.[98] Conditions in Russia were not ripe for the abolition of capitalism, thus 'industrial capitalism ... has now become a State capitalism'.[99] The catastrophe of the Bolsheviks is a moral one: 'The Regiment of Terror ... became the inevitable result of Communist methods.'[100]

Bolshevik methods produce an ever-widening spiral of terror; the Bolsheviks are prepared to compromise on anything, except democracy, for they know themselves to be 'in a minority among the people'.[101]

Trotsky's reply to Kautsky's latest attack, similarly entitled *Terrorism and Communism*, was less vehement than Lenin's *Proletarian Revolution* partly because it sought to win over to the newly formed Third International those wavering elements in the socialist parties of Europe. Trotsky justified the October Revolution by arguing that 'the development of the technical command of men over nature has *long ago* grown ripe for the Socialization of economic life'.[102] In this situation, revolutionary parties such as the Bolshevik Party could play a decisive role. The Russian dictatorship of the proletariat required, as Trotsky put it, 'an exceptional regime – a regime in which the [working] class is guided, not by general principles calculated for a prolonged period, but by considerations of revolutionary policy'.[103] Trotsky seems to mean 'considerations of revolutionary *expediency*', but his point is that the Soviet regime can be justified in part because it will be short-lived. Since 'only force can be the deciding factor' in the struggle between bourgeoisie and proletariat,[104] consideration of political forms must be subordinate to force. Trotsky believed that if socialist policy was subordinated to democracy 'in countries where formal democracy prevails, there is no place at all for the revolutionary struggle'.[105] The Bolsheviks are akin to the Blanquists only in so far as they 'understood the meaning of a revolutionary government, but did not make the question of seizing it depend on the formal signs of democracy'.[106] Impatient with the 'superficial balance of forces in parliament', Trotsky appeals to historical necessity, 'the immanent requirements of history',[107] to justify the Revolution. A revolution need not have majority support to begin with, although Trotsky considers a socialist parliamentary majority 'not an absolute impossibility'.[108] The point at issue between Kautsky and the Bolsheviks here is an epistemological one: the Bolsheviks stress *praxis* as the road to consciousness, while Kautsky stressed patient propaganda by means of the printed word and electioneering, rather than the deed.

As for the January 1918 dissolution of the Constituent Assembly, Trotsky explains that the Assembly placed itself across the path of the revolutionary movement, and was swept aside. The opportunist majority in the Constituent Assembly represented ... the mental confusion and indecision which reigned amidst the middle classes ... and amidst the more backward elements of the proletariat.[109]

But the election of an overwhelming majority of Socialist-Revolutionary deputies would seem to indicate quite the opposite of a confusion of mind. In reality, it was not mass confusion on which the Bolsheviks based the Assembly's dissolution, but the 'opportunism' of the Socialist Revolutionaries. For the Bolsheviks, the Assembly had become an obstacle to the realization of the masses' interests. The Bolsheviks, according to Trotsky, supported the Constituent Assembly idea during 1917 in contrast to the power of Kerensky, not in contrast to the power of the soviets. If this is so, if the Bolsheviks consistently recognized the superior authority of the soviets, then their stated position on the Assembly was merely a deception. The Assembly, Trotsky continues, was 'the out-of-date reflection of an epoch through which the revolution had already passed'.[110] After its dissolution the Bolsheviks saw 'no need' to summon a new Assembly. Throughout his argument, Trotsky maintains the supreme right of the Bolsheviks to seize power, irrespective of their popular support. Yet he feels constrained to construct an argument from democracy, to demonstrate that the Bolshevik regime was indeed democratic. First, he denigrates traditional parliamentary forms: determining national opinion through a parliament, he declares, is a 'rather crude method':

The Soviet regime, which is more closely, straightly, honestly bound up with the toiling majority of the people, does achieve meaning, not in statically reflecting a majority, but in dynamically creating it. ... Such democracy goes a little deeper down than parliamentarism.[111]

Trotsky may have a point that the soviets were, at that stage, a more effective means of determining the relative support of political groups. But he cannot have it both ways: either he maintains the historical right of Bolshevik power, irrespective of democracy; or he subordinates Bolshevik power to the soviets. Trotsky's defence of democracy is disingenuous, however he re-defines democracy, for he is not prepared to countenance any sort of challenge to Bolshevik power, as the suppression of the Kronstadt soviet was to show.

Trotsky soon concedes, in effect, that his description of the soviets as 'democratic' was too generous. Their heterogeneity was the reason 'why the Communists could and had to become the guiding party in the Soviets'.[112] The soviets had become the tools of the Bolsheviks. No important decision could be taken in them without Party authorization, as Trotsky himself reveals: the Party 'has the final word in all fundamental questions'.[113] Such a system required the 'unquestioned authority' of the Party. What role was left for democracy?

The question is of the dictatorship of a class. In the composition of that class there enter various elements, heterogeneous moods, different levels of development. Yet the dictatorship pre-supposes unity of will, unity of direction, unity of action. By what other path then can it be attained? The revolutionary supremacy of the proletariat pre-supposes within the pro-letariat itself the political supremacy of a party, with a clear programme of action and faultless internal discipline.[114]

Trotsky not only verifies Kautsky's argument that the dictatorship of a class is impossible, but implies that democracy is not able to provide the unity needed for the transition to socialism. He goes so far as to say that the dictatorship can only be maintained by single-party rule: 'the policy of coalitions contradicts internally the regime of the revolutionary dictatorship'.[115] Such a position suggests a fundamental distrust of the maturity and capacity of the pro-letariat. Furthermore, Trotsky does not examine this idea of 'unity'. Marx's concept of the transition suggests that unity was required to overcome the enemies of the revolution, but that diversity within the working class was required for the development of a socialist policy.

Trotsky is more direct than Lenin. He admits that the 'dictator-ship of the Soviets became possible only by means of the dictatorship of the party'. Perhaps recalling his own fears of 'substitutionism' seventeen years earlier, Trotsky argues that there is no substitution at all, for: 'The Communists express the fundamental interests of the working class.'[116] Of what use, then, are the soviets, and of what use is the device of deriving from them the claim of democratic legit-imacy? The debate over Soviet democracy is a debate about how representative Soviet institutions are of the Russian people. And if no government is perfectly representative, liberal democratic governments are at least accountable and subject to periodic chal-lenge by their opponents who form a potential government. The Bolshevik claim to democracy, however, rests solely on its claim to represent the interests of the proletariat; a claim which cannot be 'tested' practically in the liberal democratic sense, and which does not admit of 'testing' in the theoretical sense, because the Bolsheviks could not conceive that there might be any other representatives of the workers' interests.

Trotsky argued that because the Bolshevik Party was the workers' party, the Soviet state was a workers' state. This was the basis of his proposal to 'militarize' labour, since it had become a question of the workers simply subordinating themselves to their own state:

No social organization except the army has ever considered itself justified in subordinating citizens to itself in such a measure ... as the State of the proletarian dictatorship considers itself justified in doing, and does.[117]

By this logic, the decision to 'militarize' labour will have been taken by the 'will of the workers themselves'.[118] The essence of Trotsky's position, seen most clearly here, accords with Lenin's view that the Bolshevik Party is the only true representative of the proletariat. Thus any Bolshevik government, no matter how constituted, would be 'democratic'. The important question of the proletarian dictatorship, Trotsky declares, is 'Who is in power? In Russia, he is convinced, the working class holds power.[119] But even if we allow the identity of the workers' interests and the Bolshevik Party, can the workers be identified with the state in which the Bolsheviks hold power? Trotsky's assumption that they can, and thus a fundamental defence of the notion that the Soviet dictatorship was the proletarian dictatorship, was criticized by Lenin himself at the end of 1920. Trotsky had argued that in a workers' state trade unions were no longer needed to protect the interests of labour. Lenin demurred:

That is a mistake. Comrade Trotsky speaks of a 'workers' state'. May I say that this is an abstraction. It was natural for us to write about a workers' state in 1917: but it is now a patent error to say: 'since this is a workers' state without any bourgeoisie, against whom then is the working class to be protected, and for what purpose?' The whole point is that it is not quite a workers' state.... For one thing, ours is not actually a workers' state but a workers' and peasants' state.... But that is not all. Our Party Programme ... shows that ours is a workers' state *with a bureaucratic twist to it.*[120]

But would Lenin have conceded the right to opposition parties, on the grounds of protecting the workers, if he believed that the Bolshevik Party had a 'bureaucratic twist' to it? Lenin may have perceived dangers within his own Party before he died in 1924, but he was prevented from acting by his illness, and by his reluctance to turn the incipient struggle between Stalin and Trotsky into a class struggle. In a Party where all opposition was conceived in class terms, Lenin alone was axiomatically 'proletarian' – although, as his wife Krupskaya hinted, Lenin's death occurred before he might have been hoist with his own petard. As his successors quickly realized, their proletarian credentials had to be established either by associating themselves with Lenin's works or Lenin's wishes, or by gaining real organizational control over the Party.

Bukharin also contributed to the theoretical defence of the Soviet republic, and to the attempt to undermine Kautsky's reputation among socialists. In his 'The Theory of the Dictatorship of the Proletariat' (1919), Bukharin recognized that one of the major tasks of the transition period was the defeat of bourgeois opposition, which could assume numerous forms:

having smashed the state organization of the bourgeoisie, the proletariat is obliged to reckon with its continued resistance in various forms. And precisely in order to overcome this resistance, there must be a strong, firm, comprehensive and, therefore, *state* organization of the working class.[121]

The bourgeoisie will resist for a whole period, using civil war and sabotage, as well as the aid of foreign intervention. The dictatorship of the proletariat is thus essential to the survival of the transition. But the dictatorship is also, for Bukharin, a new and distinctive type of state, where 'the proletariat is the *ruling class* which, before it disappears as a class, must crush all its enemies, re-educate the bourgeois and remake the world in its own image'.[122] Bukharin, however, by stressing the manifold forms of bourgeois resistance, and arguing that the proletarian dictatorship must exist until the proletariat's victory is world wide, justifies the authoritarian character of the Soviet republic. He does not explain how the opposition is to be determined as bourgeois; in fact, he rejects all opposition. The rights of the minority, he argues, are really the rights of the counter-revolution. Furthermore, he does not explain how the proletarian dictatorship is a 'proletarian' dictatorship. He is concerned primarily with its repressive nature, not with its class nature.

The merit of Bukharin's contributions to this debate is their unashamed, and to some extent quite justifiable, defence of the repressive nature of the transition to socialism. The transition's positive tasks of economic and political re-construction and reorganization are less satisfactorily dealt with. Bukharin places great emphasis on the economic tasks. The transition needs

to *break the old relations of production and to organize new relations in the sphere of social economics.* . . . The fundamental purpose of the dictatorship of the proletariat lies in the fact that it is a means of *economic* revolution.[123]

How it was to achieve these tasks he explained at greater length in his 1920 'The Economics of the Transition Period'. But it is Bukharin's defence of the political organization of the dictatorship which is of more interest here. Bukharin relies upon the soviet, or council, form which sprang up in revolutionary Russia in 1917 as in 1905. The soviets, he argues, 'are a direct class organization'.[124] The soviet form of government is thus 'the *self-government of the masses*'.[125] Indeed, the soviets '*are the perfect form of proletarian dictatorship discovered by the Russian revolution*'.[126] Comparing the soviets favourably with the 'talking shop' of parliament, and decrying the division of powers and the obstructions caused by a state bureaucracy to parliamentary policy in bourgeois states, Bukharin does not concede that there might be different, or even related, dangers in the Soviet system. In particular, he does not clarify the relations between the Bolshevik Party and the soviets. Bukharin shies away from any prolonged discussion of the role of the Party during the transition.

Bukharin's position on opposition to the dictatorship of the proletariat is similar to Lenin's and Trotsky's, if more cautiously expressed. The dictatorship's coercion must not only be directed against the bourgeois forms of resistance, but is 'also carried over to the workers themselves and to the ruling class itself'.[127] Bukharin explains this by declaring that since the working class is not homogeneous, the proletarian dictatorship is not simply concerned with inter-class mechanics, but also with intra-class mechanics:

The proletariat comes to power as a class. But this does not signify the cohesive nature of the class where every one of its members represents some ideal mean. The proletarian vanguard actively leads the others behind it. . . . [T]he proletarian vanguard grows and expands numerically as it absorbs the ever-growing strata of the class, which more and more becomes a 'class for itself'.[128]

Clearly, Bukharin assumes that the majority of the working class becomes class conscious only under the proletarian dictatorship. He also assumes that the 'vanguard' embodies class consciousness, which does not admit of any divergence. But Bukharin also justifies the view that working-class opposition to Bolshevism (or to 'Soviet power') is really bourgeois opposition which must be suppressed: 'even comparatively broad sections of the working class bear the stamp of the capitalist commodity world. Hence, *compulsory discipline* is absolutely inevitable.'[129] Yet wherever this compulsion is carried out, it is (by definition) the 'self-coercion of the working class'.[130] The working class is suppressed in its own interest, if not by itself. Bukharin's indiscriminate treatment of the concept of 'opposition' under the proletarian dictatorship distinguishes him from neither Lenin nor Trotsky, and provides a further justification for Soviet authoritarianism.

Lenin's defence of the Soviet republic as the most democratic in the world, despite his conflicting assertion that since the Soviet regime was a state there could be no democracy, rested on the claim that the Bolshevik Party represented the true interests of the Russian working-class and exploited: the majority. It was a claim, however, which was not allowed to be tested by the usual methods, that is, by formal democracy. But it was a claim which, in some senses, could not be tested; for it was axiomatic, rather than contingent. The defenders of the Soviet regime did their best to question the validity of the usual means for determining the representation of interests by drawing attention to the (sometimes genuine) limitations of formal liberal democracy. They sometimes drew a rather dubious distinction between formal and real democracy, real democracy always taking precedence. In 1919 Lenin wrote: 'We recognise no freedom, no equality, no labour democracy if it conflicts with the cause of emancipating labour from the yoke of capital.'[131] Whether or not the new Soviet regime was a 'democracy', in any of its many senses, is not my real concern. Nor do I merely want to suggest the distance between rhetoric and reality. What was vital for the character of the new regime was Lenin's conception of, and attitude towards, opposition. The discussion about Soviet democracy, its vaunted merits over liberal democracy, and how they might be proved, is a diversion from the more important discussion of the proletarian dictatorship and opposition. The character of Lenin's Bolshevik Party, its 'democratic centralism', is not the source of Soviet authoritarianism, even though it increasingly influenced Soviet authoritarianism's specific character, with its stress upon the leader. My purpose in examining the early debate among Russian Marxists over the party was not to highlight the dangers of a particular organizational formula, but to observe Lenin's response to his Russian Marxist opponents. Lenin responded by promoting the question of organization from a tactical to a principled question, and by declaring his opponents to have placed themselves outside the working class.

It became a characteristic position, and ploy, of Lenin to declare that those who did not accept socialist consciousness, as he defined it, were advocating bourgeois ideology. Applying this conception consistently to the Soviet regime, Lenin believed that any opposition to the Bolsheviks was bourgeois opposition. This was so even within the Bolshevik Party, where opposition to the working-class interest was translated into opposition to Lenin:

Whoever brings about even the slightest weakening of the iron discipline of the party of the proletariat (especially during its dictatorship), is actually aiding the bourgeoisie against the proletariat.[132]

Lenin's conception of opposition was even more important during the 'dictatorship of the proletariat' because of the dictatorship's task of suppressing bourgeois opposition. Lenin not only made this task the most important of the transition, thus distorting the significance of the 'dictatorship' within Marx's project, but by suppressing all opposition as a danger to the continued existence of the socialist revolution he made impossible the transition he sought to protect. Lenin's position also raised the more traditional problem of *quis custodiet custodes?* as well as providing the basis for the internecine intra-Party struggle which followed his death when it was found that only Lenin *custodiet custodes*.

Lenin's stress upon the dictatorship of the proletariat was in marked contrast with its neglect, and in some cases its abandonment, among European Social Democrats; it added to Lenin's belief in his legitimate succession from Marx. But Lenin's interpretation of the dictatorship was peculiarly his own, deriving more from his general view of 'opposition' than from fidelity to Marx. While the problem of bourgeois opposition to the socialist project had been widely acknowledged and debated among Social Democrats, being linked closely with the problem of the character of the socialist revolution, only Lenin resolved the problem by declaring all opposition bourgeois, and by outlawing all opposition. The Western liberal heritage, by which Marx also had been influenced, was confronted by Lenin's dictum: 'Who is not with us, is against us.' Lenin's embattled outlook so coloured his conception of the transition to socialism that the defence of the Revolution against enemies real or imagined became his overriding concern. Marx's formula for the defence of the socialist revolution was transformed by Lenin, under circumstances quite different from those Marx had anticipated, into a recipe for unbounded authoritarianism.

8

CONCLUSION

This study has sought to contribute to a larger debate, begun just after the October Revolution, concerning the relationship between Marx's project and Soviet society. Is the Soviet system a necessary part of the fulfilment of Marx's project, or a travesty of that project? The study has focused, however, only on the directly political aspects of the matter by examining whether early Soviet authoritarianism was the necessary and logical outcome of Marx's attitudes and beliefs. Since Lenin's practice and Lenin's theory, which I have taken to be two sides of the one coin, largely determined and justified the early political character of the new Soviet state, the examination has been confined to the theoretical links between Leninism and Marx. How far is Marx causally responsible for Leninism, and thus for Soviet authoritarianism?

While Leninism was not the only causal factor, it was certainly the chief cause of the origins of Soviet authoritarianism. Some other factors were the existence of fierce bourgeois and foreign military resistance to the Bolshevik coup, and the destruction visited upon Russia during the First World War. These other factors, however, were not decisive in the formation and subsequent development of Soviet authoritarianism. They may have provided opportunities for Lenin to consolidate Bolshevik rule, and they have since been cited to justify the nature of that rule, but they were subsidiary causes.

Which characteristics of Leninism produced Soviet authoritarianism? Uppermost among them was Lenin's attitude towards, and conception of, opposition. The prime force for Soviet authoritarianism came from Lenin's unshakeable belief that he, and through him the Bolshevik Party, was the only true representative of the historical working-class interest. Lenin's fundamental hostility toward opposition, which flowed from this belief, was the basis for Soviet illiberalism. Indeed, Lenin's conception of opposition is basic to the character of Leninism. The early dispute within Russian Marxism over the type of organization appropriate for revolutionary work in tsarist Russia, in which Lenin's plan had much to recommend it, was nevertheless an occasion for Lenin to brand his opponents as enemies of the working class. He was perhaps the first Marxist to describe other Marxists as 'agents of the bourgeoisie' – even when, as in 1903, the two factions agreed on the same (Marxist) programme for Russia. All opponents of Lenin's Party, of the Soviet regime, or of Lenin himself, whatever form their opposition took, whoever they were, were for Lenin bourgeois opponents. If the bourgeoisie was the opposition, then any opposition was bourgeois. This standpoint was later 'refined' with the introduction of a pernicious twist to the distinction between reality and appearance: one could be vilified as 'objectively bourgeois' for making a proposal that was meant, subjectively and in good faith, to benefit the working class.

It might well be argued against my account that some opposition to the Bolsheviks and to Lenin was tolerated after 1917. The Mensheviks and the left Socialist Revolutionaries, for example, continued to exist as legal parties for varying lengths of time, even though their activities were severely limited. Certain oppositions within the Bolshevik Party itself, those that Robert Daniels has called the 'conscience of the Revolution', were tolerated until 1921. But in this 'golden age' of the new Soviet regime, as I described it in chapter 1, such oppositions had only a tenuous hold on political freedoms and the Bolsheviks certainly held no respect for these freedoms. Ironically, Lenin himself tolerated, in this period, somewhat more opposition than his colleagues would have. For if he defined and condemned opposition as 'bourgeois' *tout court*, he could also take a certain amount of opposition because of his position of authority within the Party and, through it, the regime. Lenin had created for himself, and in some respects had earned, a position which was increasingly unchallengeable within his Party and within Russia. Such a situation applied to no other Bolshevik leader, actual or potential. They, to gain legitimacy and authority, had to invoke close association with Lenin himself or membership of the pre-1917 Bolshevik Party. The new regime scrambled to establish traditions in terms of which its rule could be made legitimate in the eyes of its subjects by stressing, in particular and at first, the national foundations of Bolshevism and later, the national mission of Soviet communism. Similarly the Party, rejuvenated and remade during 1917, set about creating traditions designed to integrate new members, to keep internal order, and partly in order to keep Trotsky from succeeding Lenin. Thus the proclaimed enemies of Tradition became staunch traditionalists. However, as long as the question of Lenin's successor could not be raised by a Party member, save perhaps for Lenin, some opposition within the new regime was tolerated. The rights of opposition and the right to opposition were in no way guaranteed, nor even tolerated. Opposition, despite its limits, lived by the grace and the authority of Lenin; it disappeared soon after his demise. The existence of some post-1917 opposition had no significant impact upon the basic features or the direction of the new Soviet regime.

Lenin built and defended the Soviet republic as an example of Marx's dictatorship of the proletariat. The vital feature of Leninism, its hostility toward opposition, found its consummate expression in Lenin's interpretation of Marx's dictatorship of the proletariat. For Lenin, the dictatorship was proletarian (or party) rule based on force and unrestricted by laws. The notion of opposition, he declared, belonged only to the absence of revolution. For Lenin, the vanguard party alone – under his direction – was sufficient guarantee of the democratic character of the dictatorship, of its proletarian character and of its commitment to socialism. Lenin justified the authoritarian nature of the transition to socialism on the grounds of the continued existence of bourgeois opposition. The defenders of the Soviet dictatorship stressed, with a justice which was tempered by great cynicism, the international and subversive aspects of bourgeois opposition, and from this argued for the extended nature of the transition and the need for repression. But what relationship does Lenin's interpretation and application of the dictatorship of the proletariat have to Marx's own conception of the transition to socialism? Did Marx himself reject, or is there a theoretical basis in Marx's works for rejecting, all opposition during this period of transition? To answer this question properly, I have in effect made a distinction between Marx's works and Marx's legacy to his early disciples. For what Marx wrote about the transition to socialism only partly accounts for the debates within the Marxist tradition, from Marx to Lenin, concerning the dictatorship of the proletariat, and for the success in Russia and among communists of Lenin's claims to be the faithful interpreter of Marx.

Marx never asked directly, let alone answered, whether all opposition must be suppressed in the period of the transition to socialism. He was generally reluctant to provide any detail of future social or political organization. Early socialism had derived part of its impetus from the construction of detailed plans for the future society, some of them fantastic, all of them highly structured. Marx realized that these utopias would become the curios of socialism; he had no wish to exemplify, as their authors had done, the historically limited nature of man's vision of the future. But he had a more substantial objection to these utopias: they presented an external framework for conducting human relations, and were thus simply forms of mechanical solidarity. Marx did not believe that having to button a tunic down the back, thus needing the assistance of another to dress, for example, was a step in the direction of a truly human society. Marx held that human beings were naturally connected with one another even though these connections were mediated in class-divided society; the task was to remove these mediations to allow truly human relations to assert themselves and take their own forms. Yet Marx's considered reasons for disapproving of blueprints are not sufficient excuse for failing to provide concrete guidance on the immediate political objectives of the proletariat.

Along with Marx's reluctance, however, there seem to be deeper reasons why he failed to be precise about the political organization of the transition to socialism. Marx's conception of the transition embodies a central tension derived from the competing tasks which it must undertake. I have described the transition as Janus-faced. The transitional power must look backward, to the society whence it came, to protect itself from those who would drive it back; and it must look forward, to the society which it strives to become, so that it will not stagnate but progress, so that it shall be truly a transition. The transitional power must protect the proletariat's gains from destruction by the dispossessed bourgeoisie, and it must prepare for the new society in which fundamental social division is overcome and unalienated politics is the expression of man's social unity. This tension is evident in Marx's conflicting statements about whether the state power must be perfected or must be destroyed after the socialist revolution. Marx was deeply influenced by the ferocity of bourgeois opposition to the workers who, in the 1848 Revolutions, tried to assert their interests. Every revolution, he concluded, required a dictatorship to consolidate its success. But if the use of concentrated state power against its enemies was commended by Marx to the revolutionary proletariat, he also (after 1848, but particularly in 1871) commended to it the destruction of the old state apparatus and the state itself. Because of its decentralization and its potential to bring politics back to man, Marx described the Paris Commune as 'the political form at last discovered under which to work out the economic emancipation of labour'.

This tension between the transition as a state and as a non-state was blurred by Marx's inconsistent use of the expression 'dictatorship of the proletariat'. Marx originally developed the 'dictatorship' concept to denote only the defensive aspect of the transition, but he also used it to denote the entire transition period. This conflation of the tasks of the transition under the heading 'dictatorship', the organization of which was nowhere clearly described by Marx, suggested that the political form of the transition should be subordinated to its defence. It blurred the central question which Marx's conception of the socialist transition raised: how can opposition to the transition be distinguished from opposition within the transition? A discriminating study on opposition and the socialist revolution is not to be found in Marx's works. Bourgeois opposition to the revolution must be suppressed; this much is evident from Marx's works. But the development of the transition seems logically to require the flowering of working-class, or at least non-bourgeois, opposition. Marx gives us grounds for believing this by his concern over the political form of the pre-transition, or pre-revolutionary, period, and by his concern that the transition will be the development of an unalienated politics. Marx's goal was eminently political, and politics, even non-class and non-state politics, requires opposition. Marx's use of the concept of the dictatorship of the proletariat was misleading; devised to describe one aspect of the transition, it was sometimes used to encompass all aspects. It thereby blurred the line between the legitimate defence of the socialist revolution and illegitimate oppression, a boundary vital to the success of Marx's project.

I do not mean to suggest that Marx was a misunderstood liberal democrat. Marx's journalism for the *Rheinische Zeitung* reveals that, at the time, he was a liberal; from at least the time of his first Hegel critique in 1843, Marx was a democrat. But Marx was never a liberal democrat. In 1842, Marx believed that the concept of the state was the 'realisation of rational freedom'. By contrast with 'pseudo-liberalism', that is, Lockean liberalism, which saw the estates and estate representation as protectors of freedom, Marx urged the state to assert itself, and thus the general interest, against the ineradicably particular interests of the estates. He thought that estate representation, as in the Rhine Province Assembly whose debates he reported upon, polluted the nature of the state. In 1843, having abandoned the notion that there could be a separate sphere of universality, Marx argued that democracy constantly brought the constitution 'back to its real basis': the people. Only democracy, the self-determination of the people, was the true unity of general and particular. Marx's liberalism and his elevation of democracy were but aspects of his quest for the correct expression and programme for universality, for a society in which man could properly express his human nature. The complexity of Marx's conception of universality, or communism, invoking as it did the competing strains of autonomy, solidarity and rationality, was the source of wider tensions within Marx's works. This complexity was also, along with the early unavailability of some of the most important of those works, an important source of the diverse interpretations of his thought made by his disciples.

Marxism, from the time of Engels' canonical interpretation of Marx's project, has been bothered by 'the state': what it is; what its relation to class society and particular classes is; what the proletariat has to do to and with it; and what its future is. In particular, Marxists have always been uneasy about liberal democratic states: about their potential for use by the proletariat, and about the tasks of Marxists within them. More recent, and now more intellectually persuasive, Marxists seem to derive much of their persuasiveness from making the rather obvious point that 'the state' is a more complex and subtle institution than Marx believed. Be this as it may, the evident stability of liberal democratic states in Western Europe posed a major challenge for Social Democrats by the end of the nineteenth century. Engels, late in life, had assured them that a liberal democratic republic provided the best means for the proletariat to take power and transform society. Yet elsewhere he argued that the state would exist after the revolution only so that the proletariat could suppress its enemies, and would then disappear in an anarchist utopia. On the maximalist reading of Engels, the proletariat uses the state to suppress its enemies, who are not defined further. However, if we interpret Engels as maintaining that liberal democracy can become the transition to socialism, the notion of opposition is quite clear and limited: opponents are those who challenge liberal democracy itself, and the right of the proletariat (or rather, its representatives) constitutionally to rule under it. This theory of 'defensive violence' was widely accepted by Social Democrats, even though its warmest supporters embraced only its commitment to liberal democratic means of taking power, not its warning about bourgeois resistance.

The question raised by Marx's project, 'Which opposition must be suppressed during the transition period?', became for Social Democrats the question: 'What opposition will there be to be suppressed during the transition?' From this central question developed the twin answers, the twin conceptions, of Revisionism and Leninism. The Revisionists believed that bourgeois opposition to the democratic assumption of power by the working-class party in a liberal democratic republic was unlikely. Revisionism developed within the spirit and traditions of Western liberal democracy, and was committed to it. But some aspects of Revisionism were just as preconceived as the Marxism which it criticized. For if there *was* opposition to the implementation of socialism in a liberal democratic republic, Revisionists merely considered that the time for socialism was not yet ripe. When the time was ripe, there would be no opposition. It was a position born of their conception of socialism as a class-independent ideal. Revisionists actively discouraged the use of Marx's expression 'dictatorship of the proletariat', arguing that with its undoubted illiberal connotations it would be a minority and embattled regime, built on the unstable foundations of an unprepared proletariat. The dictatorship, they argued, was an expedient; it would not be needed when the time for socialism had come. But while Revisionists doubted the very existence of bourgeois opposition to the ambitions of a mature working class, Lenin widened the concept of bourgeois opposition to include all those who opposed, practically or theoretically, his Party or his views.

Conclusion

Lenin's interpretation of Marx's project was essentially illiberal. Revisionism was perhaps the first serious response among Marxists to the crisis of Marxism at the turn of this century: to its failure to come to terms with a changing social reality (or a social reality that never quite confirmed Marx's analysis) and with basic methodological criticisms, and to the recognition that the proletariat had not, and would not, fulfil Marx's expectations. Leninism was the second. But while Revisionism conceded the truth of many of the criticisms of Marx's project, Leninism became insular and dogmatic in defence of it. Revisionism abandoned or diluted Marxism; Leninism would not.

Leninism and Revisionism are the progeny of Marxism. They were attempts by Marxists, under the influence of diverse traditions, to revivify what they believed was worth saving in Marx's project. Leninism, however, is generally accepted as the genuine interpretation of Marx's project, as the authentic Marxism. This is not simply because Lenin insisted it was so, and because Bernstein renounced Marxism. Nor is it simply because of Lenin's success in Russia. Rather it is because there was no serious or lasting Marxist challenge to Lenin, particularly to his interpretation of the idea of the dictatorship of the proletariat. Most non-Leninist Marxists conceded the field of 'Marxism' to Leninists, and new historical disputes within 'Marxism', where they arose, tended to share the common ground of 'Marxism–Leninism'. Non-Leninist Marxists, such as there were, did not rise to the challenge of constructing a theory of opposition: its methods, class position, dangers and benefits – a theory which could help to resolve the problem of the transition period, namely 'who must be suppressed?' Instead, they ceded the field to Lenin's *kto-kovo?* Their challenge to Lenin's claim that the dictatorship of the proletariat was the keystone of revolutionary Marxism was half-hearted. Lenin's illiberal interpretation of the *dictatorship* was tacitly conceded by non-Leninist Marxists, even by those who disputed the Marxist credentials of the Soviet regime. Furthermore, there was wide acceptance of the notion that the dictatorship represented the entire transition. As a result, non-Leninist Marxists, except for a few stalwarts, eventually abandoned Marxism itself. In the heyday of the Second International, the illiberal interpretation of Marx's transition stage was predominant. Non-Leninist Social Democrats, if they acknowledged the liberal strain in Marx's work, nevertheless found liberal democracy more congenial and less demanding. Indeed, the very notion of a 'transition period' had begun to lose its relevance for them.

Lenin's Marxism was largely a product of the debates and disputes of Social Democracy, and of the Russian revolutionary tradition whose chief representative for him was Plekhanov. Leninism was not simply a strategy 'of its time', although time and place had a major impact upon it. The various sources of Lenin's illiberalism are not at issue. What is of concern here is that Lenin took the illiberal aspects of Marx's transition period, those aspects which made the very notion of transition distasteful to many Social Democrats, and elevated them to a position of dominance in the transition. Marx's project is unarguably one of Leninism's sources, but it is not the sole source; nor on the question of the political characteristics of the transition period, is it the major source. Lenin's feat was to remain within the Marxist tradition, to introduce to it important elements of a different tradition, and to make himself accepted as Marxism's only legitimate interpreter.

To the objection that Marx's project can only ever be implemented in an authoritarian manner, not because it is explicitly authoritarian but because it is basically flawed and unrealistic, I can only reply that a crucial question has been avoided: can Marx's project be said to be successful if it is authoritarian? Lenin's interpretation of Marx's work was based on a number of things, but not on its lack of realism; his illiberalism was apparent long before his attempt to implement it. But even if we accept the basis of this objection, Revisionism itself could be justified as a legitimate interpretation of Marx's project, for did not Revisionism make something 'realistic' of it? Leninism, of course, claimed to be based on Marx; Revisionism did not. Must we take them at their word? This study is based on the belief that we need not, perhaps should not.

Marx was a gifted thinker whose complex ideas have suffered more at the hands of his friends than of his enemies. While there may be no precedent for an entirely coherent political tradition, the Marxist tradition seems distinguished by the degree of internal conflict over basic issues bequeathed to it by its reluctant founder. The Marxist tradition is held together by a framework of inherited problems, rather than by a series of unambiguous solutions. The interpretation of Marx is therefore the first task of every thinking

Marxist. And, just as some choose nowadays to defend, as the 'true' Marx, the 'young' Marx against the 'old' Marx, or vice versa, there have always been Marxists who would choose this or that aspect of Marx's project which best suited their taste or purpose. The conflicting strains of Marx's project led to the collapse of classical Marxism, and its fragmentation into conflicting strategies under various other influences. Part of this transformation has been documented in these pages. To Marx's ambiguities Lenin undoubtedly contributed illiberal solutions. To Marx's ill-explained notion of the transition to socialism Lenin brought only an understanding of the imperatives of the dictatorship of the proletariat, a concept he revived and exploited masterfully in his debates against other Marxists. Marx's was a sin of omission, not commission. Lenin supplied the theoretical foundations for Soviet authoritarianism; Marx's contribution to them was not decisive. While there are many cogent reasons for rejecting Marx's project as a panacea for society's ills, the project's direct and necessary association with Soviet illiberalism is not one of them.

NOTES

Full title, publisher, place and date of publication are given when a work is cited for the first time in these notes. Subsequent references to it, where they do not follow directly, are covered by the author's surname and the title, or an abbreviation of the title. Commonly used abbreviations follow:

LCW   V. I. Lenin, *Collected Works*, 45 volumes, Progress Publishers, Moscow, 1960–70.

MECW   K. Marx and F. Engels, *Collected Works* (in preparation, 17 volumes available) Progress and Lawrence and Wishart, Moscow and London, 1975–82.

MESW   K. Marx and F. Engels, *Selected Works*, 3 volumes, Progress, Moscow, 1976.

I. INTRODUCTION

1   G. Urban, 'Introduction', G. Urban (ed.), *Eurocommunism, Its Roots and Future in Italy and Elsewhere* (Temple Smith, London, 1978), p. 12.

2   M. Azcárate, 'What is Eurocommunism?', Urban (ed.), *Eurocommunism*, p. 14.

3   J.-F. Revel, *The Totalitarian Temptation* (Secker and Warburg, London, 1977).

4   Urban, 'Introduction', Urban (ed.), *Eurocommunism*, p. 8.

5   Ibid.

6   A. Amalrik, 'Russia and the Perplexing Prospects of Liberty', Urban (ed.), ibid., p. 252.

7   N. McInnes, *Euro-Communism* (The Washington Papers, vol. IV, Sage Publications, Beverley Hills, 1976), p. 17.

8   J. Elleinstein, *The Stalin Phenomenon* (Lawrence and Wishart, London, 1976), p. 17.

9   J. Elleinstein, 'The Skein of History Unrolled Backwards', Urban (ed.), *Eurocommunism*, p. 78. The title is a quote from Trotsky which Elleinstein uses.

10   Ibid., p. 85.

11 Elleinstein, *The Stalin Phenomenon*, p. 207.

12 Ibid., p. 218.

13 Elleinstein, 'The Skein of History', p. 75.

14 Ibid., p. 92.

15 S. Carrillo, *'Eurocommunism' and the State* (Lawrence and Wishart, London, 1977), p. 13.

16 V. I. Lenin, *The State and Revolution*, LCW, vol. 25, p. 479.

17 Carrillo, *'Eurocommunism' and the State*, p. 89.

18 Ibid., p. 95.

19 Ibid., p. 140.

20 Ibid., p. 149.

21 Ibid., p. 151.

22 I am not prepared to suggest, as Avineri does, that 'the whole course of Soviet history was determined by Lenin's policies on land tenure, nationalization of industry, and relations with Germany' (S. Avineri, Comments on M. Rubel, 'The Relationship of Bolshevism to Marxism', R. Pipes (ed.), *Revolutionary Russia* (Harvard University Press, Massachusetts, 1968), p. 329). Yet in the area of liberal democracy the early decisions were crucial, as even the Bolsheviks seemed aware. On 17 November 1917, a number of People's Commissars resigned their posts, arguing that terror was the only means by which a purely Bolshevik government could survive (L. Schapiro, *The Origins of the Communist Autocracy, Political Opposition in the Soviet State, First Phase 1917–1922* (Macmillan, London, 1977), p. 77). These same fears had led Kamenev and Zinoviev publicly to dissociate themselves from Bolshevik plans for the October coup.

23 The terms 'Leninist' and 'Leninism' used throughout refer to the theory and practice of Lenin, not the post-Lenin manipulation of theory.

24 B. Russell, *The Practice and Theory of Bolshevism* (Allen and Unwin, London, 1969), p. 87.

25 H. Arendt, 'Thoughts on Politics and Revolution, a Commentary', *Crises of the Republic* (Harcourt Brace Jovanovich, NY, 1969), p. 206.

26 Lenin, *The Tasks of the Proletariat in the Present Revolution (April Theses)*, 7 April 1917, LCW, vol. 24, pp. 21–6; Lenin, *The Bolsheviks Must Assume Power, A Letter to the Central Committee and the Petrograd and Moscow Committees of the R.S.D.L.P.(B)*, 25–7 September 1917, LCW, vol. 26, pp. 19–21.

27 L. Trotsky (entry of 25 March 1935), *Trotsky's Diary in Exile, 1935* (Atheneum, NY, 1974), p. 46.

28 G. Plekhanov, *On the Question of the Individual's Role in History*,

Selected Philosophical Works, vol. 2. (Progress, Moscow, 1976), pp. 306–7.

29 M. Liebman, *Leninism under Lenin* (Cape, London, 1975), p. 232.
30 L. Fischer, *The Life of Lenin* (Weidenfeld and Nicolson, London, 1965), p. 150.
31 Ibid., p. 123.
32 As have: W. Gurian, *Bolshevism: Theory and Practice* (AMS Press, NY, 1969), p. 191; S. W. Page, 'Prophet of Eastern Revolution', S. W. Page (ed.), *Lenin, Dedicated Marxist or Revolutionary Pragmatist?* (Heath, Massachusetts, 1970), p. 43; and E. V. Wolfenstein, *The Revolutionary Personality: Lenin, Trotsky, Gandhi* (Princeton University Press, NJ, 1967), especially p. 307. Such constructions, or reconstructions, of Lenin's personality and psychological drives must face the claims of conflicting psycho-analytic theories as well as the objection that they are based upon no personal interviews. Perhaps they tell us more about their authors than about their subjects.
33 D. Childs, *Marx and the Marxists: An Outline of Theory and Practice* (Benn, London, 1973), p. 71.
34 B. D. Wolfe, 'Leninism', M. M. Drachkovitch (ed.), *Marxism in the Modern World* (Stanford University Press, California, 1965), p. 48.
35 P. Akselrod, 1910, cited B. D. Wolfe, *Three Who Made a Revolution, A Biographical History* (Dell, NY, 1964), p. 249.
36 L. Kolakowski, 'Marxist Roots of Stalinism', R. C. Tucker (ed.), *Stalinism, Essays in Historical Interpretation* (W. W. Norton, NY, 1977), p. 297.
37 J. Walkin, *The Rise of Democracy in Pre-Revolutionary Russia, Political and Social Institutions under the last Three Czars* (Thames and Hudson, London, 1963), p. 245. A similar position is held by N. S. Timasheff, *The Great Retreat, the Growth and Decline of Communism in Russia* (Dutton, NY, 1946), p. 16.
38 E. Halévy, *The Era of Tyrannies, Essays on Socialism and War* (NY University Press, NY, 1966), pp. 266–7.
39 M. Fainsod, *How Russia is Ruled* (Harvard University Press, Massachusetts, 1963), p. 59.
40 For example, W. Laqueur, *The Fate of the Revolution: Interpretations of Soviet History* (Weidenfeld and Nicolson, London, 1967); J. H. Billington, 'Six Views of the Russian Revolution', *World Politics*, vol. 18, no. 3, 1966, pp. 452–73; D. Joravsky, 'Introduction', R. Medvedev, *Let History Judge, The Origins and Consequences of Stalinism* (Macmillan, London, 1972); D. Bell, 'Ten Views in Search of Reality', *The End of Ideology, On the Exhaustion of Political Ideas in the Fifties* (Free Press, NY, 1967), pp. 316–53.

41 R. N. Carew Hunt, *Marxism, Past and Present* (Bles, London, 1954), p. 3.

42 Ibid., p. 171.

43 R. W. Postgate, *The Bolshevik Theory* (Richards, London, 1920), p. 26.

44 Carew Hunt, *Marxism, Past and Present*, p. 3.

45 R. G. Wesson, *Communism and Communist Systems* (Prentice-Hall, NJ, 1978), p. 64; see also R. G. Wesson, *Why Marxism? The Continuing Success of a Failed Theory* (Temple Smith, London, 1976), p. 217, and G. Leff, *The Tyranny of Concepts: A Critique of Marxism* (Merlin, London, 1961), p. 15.

46 D. Shub, *Lenin: A Biography* (Penguin, Harmondsworth, 1966), p. 10.

47 Ibid., p. 73.

48 B. Souvarine, *Stalin, A Critical Survey of Bolshevism* (Longmans, Green and Co., NY, 1939), p. 357.

49 S. Possony, *Lenin, the Compulsive Revolutionary* (Allen and Unwin, London, 1966), p. 88.

50 Lucio Lombardo Radice, 'Communism With an Italian Face?', Urban (ed.), *Eurocommunism*, p. 50.

51 J. H. Kautsky, *Communism and the Politics of Development, Persistent Myths and Changing Behaviour* (Wiley and Sons, NY, 1968), p. 42.

52 Rubel, 'The Relationship of Bolshevism to Marxism', p. 311.

53 T. H. Von Laue, *Why Lenin? Why Stalin? A reappraisal of the Russian Revolution, 1900–1930* (Lippincott, NY, 1971), p. 89.

54 N. Berdyaev, *The Origin of Russian Comunism* (University of Michigan Press, Ann Arbor, 1972), p. 7.

55 Ibid., p. 187.

56 R. Fülöp-Miller, *Lenin and Gandhi* (Books for Libraries Press, NY, 1972), p. 104.

57 R. V. Daniels, 'What the Russians Mean', H. Swearer and R. Longaker (eds.), *Contemporary Communism: Theory and Practice* (Wadsworth, California, 1963), p. 50.

58 R. V. Daniels, *The Conscience of the Revolution, Communist Opposition in Soviet Russia* (Simon and Schuster, NY, 1969), p. 7.

59 R. V. Daniels, 'Lenin and the Russian Revolutionary Tradition', *Harvard Slavic Studies*, IV, p. 339.

60 Ibid., p. 340.

61 A. Gray, *The Socialist Tradition; Moses to Lenin* (Harper and Row, NY, 1968), p. 461.

62 A. B. Ulam, *Lenin and the Bolsheviks, the Intellectual and Political History of the Triumph of Communism in Russia* (Fontana, London, 1973), p. 232; see also A. B. Ulam, *The Unfinished Revolution: An*

Essay on the Sources and Influence of Marxism and Communism (Vintage, NY, 1960), p. 196.

63 C. Wright Mills, *The Marxists* (Penguin, Harmondsworth, 1971), p. 100.

64 S. Hook, *Marx and the Marxists: The Ambiguous Legacy* (Van Nostrand, Princeton, 1955), p. 85.

65 M. M. Drachkovitch, 'Introduction', Drachkovitch (ed.), *Marxism in the Modern World*, p. xiii.

66 R. Aron, 'The Impact of Marxism in the Twentieth Century', Drachkovitch (ed.), ibid., p. 8.

67 Ibid., p. 43.

68 G. Lukács, 'What is Orthodox Marxism?', *History and Class Consciousness. Studies in Marxist Dialectics* (Merlin, London, 1971).

69 L. Kolakowski, 'Permanent vs. Transitory Aspects of Marxism', *Marxism and Beyond. On Historical Understanding and Individual Responsibility* (Paladin, London, 1971).

70 L. Kolakowski, *Main Currents of Marxism, its Rise, Growth and Dissolution* (Clarendon Press, Oxford, 1978), vol. I, pp. 408–9.

71 Ibid., p. 420.

72 Kolakowski, 'Marxist Roots of Stalinism', p. 284.

73 Ibid., p. 284.

74 Acton, cited F. A. Hayek, *The Road to Serfdom* (University of Chicago Press, Chicago, 1950), p. 101.

75 J. L. Talmon, *Political Messianism, The Romantic Phase* (Praeger, NY, 1960), p. 20.

76 J. L. Talmon, *The Origins of Totalitarian Democracy* (Praeger, NY, 1960), p. 252.

77 K. R. Popper, 'Utopia and Violence', *Conjectures and Refutations: The Growth of Scientific Knowledge* (Routledge and Kegan Paul, London, 1974), pp. 358–9.

78 Ibid., p. 360.

79 Hayek, *The Road to Serfdom*, p. 70; L. Von Mises, *Socialism, An Economic and Sociological Analysis* (Yale University Press, New Haven, 1962).

80 A position also implied by M. Djilas, *The New Class* (Unwin, London, 1966), p. 148.

81 Marx, 'Debates on Freedom of the Press', *MECW*, vol. I, p. 164.

82 See A. Gilbert, *Marx's Politics, Communists and Citizens* (Martin Robertson, Oxford, 1981).

83 B. Moore Jr., 'Some Readjustments in Communist Theory', *Journal of the History of Ideas*, vol. 6, 1945, p. 482; see also B. Moore Jr., *Soviet*

Politics – Dilemmas of Power, The Role of Ideas in Social Change (Harper and Row, NY, 1965), p. 4, for a similar formulation.
84 J. Dunn, *Western Political Theory in the Face of the Future* (CUP, Cambridge, 1979), p. 11.
85 S. Stojanovic, *Between Ideals and Reality. A Critique of Socialism and its Future* (OUP, NY, 1973), p. 108.
86 J. A. Schumpeter, *Capitalism, Socialism and Democracy* (Harper, NY, 1950), p. 236.
87 Schapiro, *Origins of the Communist Autocracy*, p. vi.

2. MARX AND THE TRANSITION TO SOCIALISM

1 Marx, *Capital, A Critique of Political Economy* (Lawrence and Wishart, London, 1959), vol. I, p. 17.
2 M. Bakunin, cited J. Hampden Jackson, *Marx, Proudhon and European Socialism* (English Universities Press, London, 1958), p. 159.
3 Bakunin, cited A. Masters, *Bakunin, the Father of Anarchism* (Sedgwick and Jackson, London, 1974), p. 182.
4 Marx to Engels, 30 October 1869, Marx, *On the First International* (McGraw-Hill, NY, 1973), p. 478; see also Marx to Engels, 17 December 1869, ibid., p. 486, and Marx to Engels, 27 July 1869, ibid., p. 475.
5 Cited E. Topitsch, 'How Enlightened is "Dialectical Reason"?', *Encounter*, vol. LVIII, no. 5, May 1982, p. 54.
6 Cited ibid., p. 54.
7 Marx, *Herr Vogt* (1860), Marx and Engels, *Werke*, vol. 14 (Dietz Verlag, Berlin, 1964), pp. 381–686.
8 Marx to Engels, 9 April 1863, Marx and Engels, *Selected Correspondence* (Progress, Moscow, 1975), p. 130.
9 Cited D. Footman, *Ferdinand Lassalle, Romantic Revolutionary* (Greenwood, NY, 1969), p. 178.
10 Cited ibid., p. 179.
11 Cited ibid., pp. 195–6.
12 F. Lassalle, *The Open Answer*, cited ibid., pp. 167–8.
13 Bakunin, *God and State* (Dover, NY, 1970), p. 30.
14 Ibid., p. 55.
15 Cited G. Lichtheim, *The Origins of Socialism* (Praeger, NY, 1969), p. 92.
16 Marx to Proudhon, 5 May 1846, cited B. Nicolaevsky and O. Maenchen-Helfen, *Karl Marx, Man and Fighter* (Penguin, Harmondsworth, 1976), pp. 122–3. For an example of the work of the Brussels

Communist Correspondence Committee see 'Letter to G. A. Köttgen', *MECW*, vol. 6, pp. 54ff.

17 P.-J. Proudhon, 'Proudhon to Marx', *Selected Writings of Pierre-Joseph Proudhon* (Macmillan, NY, 1969), pp. 150–1.

18 Bakunin, G. P. Maximoff (ed.), *The Political Philosophy of Bakunin: Scientific Anarchism* (Free Press, NY, 1964), p. 321.

19 Cited Marx, *Fictitious Splits in the International*, *MESW*, vol. 2, p. 269.

20 Marx to F. Bolte, 23 November 1871, *Marx on the First International*, p. 545.

21 Marx, confidential communication to L. Kugelmann, 28 March 1870, ibid., p. 168; see also Marx to P. Lafargue, 21 March 1872, Marx and Engels, *Selected Corresondence*, p. 262.

22 Marx to A. Ruge, 1843, *MECW*, vol. 3, p. 144.

23 Marx, *Poverty of Philosophy*, *MECW*, vol. 6, p. 177.

24 G. D. H. Cole, *A History of Socialist Thought*, vol. 2 (Macmillan, London, 1954), p. 256.

25 Marx, *Poverty of Philosophy*, p. 212.

26 Except perhaps for Marx's letter to P. V. Annenkov, 28 December 1846, in K. Marx, F. Engels, V. Lenin, *On Historical Materialism* (Progress, Moscow, 1974), pp. 273–83.

27 Marx, *Poverty of Philosophy*, p. 211.

28 Ibid., p. 177.

29 Ibid., p. 212.

30 Marx, *Manifesto of the Communist Party*, *MECW*, vol. 6, p. 505.

31 Ibid., p. 497; the words in brackets were added by Engels in the English edition of 1888.

32 Ibid., p. 498.

33 Ibid., p. 504.

34 See ibid., p. 505.

35 Ibid., p. 495.

36 Engels, *Principles of Communism*, 1847, *MECW*, vol. 6, p. 350.

37 Engels, 'The Communists and Karl Heinzen', October 1847, *MECW*, vol. 6, p. 295.

38 Ibid., p. 299.

39 Ibid., p. 299. Similar formulations may be found in Engels, 'The Civil War in Switzerland', November 1847, *MECW*, vol. 6, p. 368, and in Engels, 'The "Satisfied" Majority', January 1848, ibid., p. 440.

40 Marx and Engels, *The German Ideology*, *MECW*, vol. 5, pp. 46–7. The paragraph from which this quotation is taken was probably written by Engels.

41 E.g. S. Avineri, *The Social and Political Thought of Karl Marx* (CUP, Cambridge, 1972), p. 204.

42 R. Miliband, *Marxism and Politics* (OUP, Oxford, 1977), p. 138.

43 H. Draper, 'Marx and the Dictatorship of the Proletariat', *New Politics*, vol. 1, no. 4, 1962, and H. Draper, 'Marx and the Dictatorship of the Proletariat', *Cahiers de l'ISEA, Etudes de Marxologie*, vol. 6, 1962.

44 B. D. Wolfe, *Marxism, One Hundred Years in the Life of a Doctrine* (Chapman and Hall, London, 1967), pp. 168–77.

45 R. N. Hunt, *The Political Ideas of Marx and Engels*, vol. I, *Marxism and Totalitarian Democracy, 1818–1850* (University of Pittsburgh Press, Pittsburgh, 1974).

46 Draper, 'Marx and the Dictatorship', *New Politics*, p. 95.

47 Wolfe, *Marxism*, p. 169.

48 Draper, 'Marx and the Dictatorship', *New Politics*, p. 91.

49 H. Arendt, *On Revolution* (Penguin, Harmondsworth, 1973), p. 121.

50 Wolfe, *Marxism*, p. 169.

51 Marx, 'The Crisis and the Counter-revolution', September 1848, *MECW*, vol. 7, p. 431.

52 Engels, 'Military Dictatorship in Austria', March 1849, *MECW*, vol. 8, p. 102; Marx, 'The New Martial-Law Charter', May 1849, ibid., pp. 40–5.

53 Engels, 'The 24th of June', June 1848, *MECW*, vol. 7, p. 135.

54 Marx, *The Class Struggles in France*, *MECW*, vol. 10, p. 127.

55 Marx, *Manifesto of the Communist Party*, section III, 'Socialist and Communist Literature', pp. 507–17.

56 Draper, 'Marx and the Dictatorship', *New Politics*, p. 92; R. N. Hunt, *The Political Ideas of Marx and Engels*, vol. I, p. 298. It is not clear whether Blanqui ever used the expression.

57 See Hunt, *The Political Ideas of Marx and Engels*, vol. I, p. 236, who claims that Marx never personally supported his own general manifestoes in the 1848 period which Hunt concedes were influenced by Blanquism.

58 Marx, *The Class Struggles in France*, p. 69.

59 Ibid., p. 72.

60 Ibid., p. 76.

61 *MECW*, vol. 10, p. 614.

62 *MECW*, vol. 10, p. 387.

63 Ibid., pp. 387–8.

64 Marx to J. Weydemeyer, *MESW*, vol. 1, p. 528.

65 Hunt, *The Political Ideas of Marx and Engels*, vol. I, p. 304. Weydemeyer's article was essentially a summary of the *Communist Manifesto*.

66 Marx, 'Speech on the Seventh Anniversary of the International', Marx, *The First International and After* (Penguin, Harmondsworth, 1974), p. 272.

67 *MESW*, vol. 3, p. 26.
68 Engels to C. Schmidt, 27 October 1890, *Selected Correspondence*, p. 402.
69 Engels, 1891 'Introduction', Marx, *Civil War in France*, *MESW*, vol. 2, p. 189.
70 Engels, *A Critique of the Draft Social-Democratic Programme of 1891*, *MESW*, vol. 3, p. 436.
71 Engels, *Principles of Communism*, p. 350.
72 G. Sartori, *Democratic Theory* (Greenwood Press, Connecticut, 1973), p. 418.
73 Engels, *Programme of the Blanquist Commune Emigrants*, *MESW*, vol. 2, p. 381; see also Draper, 'Marx and the Dictatorship', *New Politics*, p. 96, and Wolfe, *Marxism*, p. 177.
74 Engels, *MESW*, vol. 3, p. 181; see also Marx to W. Blos, 10 November 1877, *Selected Correspondence*, p. 291.
75 *MECW*, vol. 11, pp. 448–9.
76 Marx and Engels, 'Review of *Les Conspirateurs*', *MECW*, vol. 10, p. 318.
77 Ibid., p. 318.
78 Marx at the Meeting of the Central Authority, 15 September 1850, *MECW*, vol. 10, p. 626.
79 Kolakowski, 'Marxist Roots of Stalinism', p. 294.
80 Hunt, *The Political Ideas of Marx and Engels*, vol. 1, p. 314.
81 D. McLellan, *The Thought of Karl Marx, An Introduction* (Macmillan, London, 1974), p. 186.
82 *MECW*, vol. 10, p. 387.
83 S. Avineri, 'How to Save Marx from the Alchemists of Revolution', *Political Theory*, vol. 4, no. 1, 1976, p. 38.
84 Marx, 'The Crisis and the Counter-revolution', p. 431.
85 Marx, *Manifesto of the Communist Party*, p. 486.
86 Avineri, *The Social and Political Thought of Karl Marx*, p. 206.
87 Marx, *Manifesto of the Communist Party*, p. 505.
88 Marx, *The Eighteenth Brumaire of Louis Bonaparte*, *MECW*, vol. 11, pp. 185 and 186.
89 Ibid., p. 181.
90 Marx, *Contribution to the Critique of Hegel's Philosophy of Law*, *MECW*, vol. 3, p. 45.
91 Ibid., p. 47.
92 Ibid., p. 48.
93 Ibid., p. 80.
94 Marx and Engels, *The German Ideology*, p. 90.
95 Ibid., p. 195.

96 Engels, 'The Constitutional Question in Germany', March–April 1847, *MECW*, vol. 6, p. 79.
97 Ibid., p. 88.
98 Marx, *On the Jewish Question*, *MECW*, vol. 3, p. 153; Marx, *Contribution to the Critique of Hegel's Philosophy of Law. Introduction*, ibid., p. 179.
99 J. B. Sanderson, *An Interpretation of the Political Ideas of Marx and Engels* (Longman, London, 1969), develops this point.
100 R. Miliband, 'Marx and the State', S. Avineri (ed.), *Marx's Socialism* (Lieber-Atherton, NY, 1973), pp. 163–4.
101 J. Plamenatz, *German Marxism and Russian Communism* (Longman, London, 1954), p. 151.
102 Marx to A. Ruge, 5 March 1842, *MECW*, vol. 1, pp. 382–3.
103 Marx, *Contribution to the Critique of Hegel's Philosophy of Law*, p. 8.
104 Ibid., p. 7.
105 Ibid., pp. 51 and 72.
106 Ibid., p. 73.
107 Ibid., p. 32.
108 Ibid., p. 77.
109 Ibid., p. 81.
110 Ibid., p. 99.
111 Ibid., p. 98.
112 Ibid., p. 113.
113 Ibid., p. 121.
114 Ibid.
115 Marx, *On the Jewish Question*, p. 166.
116 Ibid., pp. 152, 153 and 159.
117 Marx, *Contribution to the Critique*, p. 29.
118 Ibid., p. 30.
119 Ibid., p. 28.
120 Ibid., p. 121.
121 Ibid., p. 31.
122 Ibid., p. 30.
123 Ibid., p. 119.
124 Ibid., p. 117.
125 Ibid., p. 121. I use the term *Aufhebung* synonymously with 'transcend' in this work, connoting 'to put an end to', as well as 'preserving, but preserving in a new and higher form'.
126 Avineri, *The Social and Political Thought of Karl Marx*, p. 38.
127 Marx, *Contribution to the Critique*, p. 48.
128 *MECW*, vol. 3, p. 186.
129 Ibid., p. 153.

130 Ibid.
131 Ibid., p. 168.
132 Marx, *Contribution to the Critique*, p. 48.
133 E.g., P. Thomas, *Karl Marx and the Anarchists* (Routledge and Kegan Paul, London, 1980), p. 101.
134 R. C. Tucker, 'Marx as Political Theorist', Avineri (ed.), *Marx's Socialism*, p. 150; also R. C. Tucker, *The Marxian Revolutionary Idea* (W. W. Norton, NY, 1969), p. 85.
135 Marx, *Manifesto of the Communist Party*, p. 486.
136 Ibid., p. 486; all emphases are mine.
137 A position taken by Avineri, *The Social and Political Thought of Karl Marx*, p. 49; Lenin, *The Proletarian Revolution and the Renegade Kautsky, LCW*, vol. 28, p. 238; and I. Martov, 'Marx and the State' (1923), T. Anderson (ed.), *Masters of Russian Marxism* (Appleton-Century-Crofts, NY, 1963), p. 113.
138 Marx at The Hague Congress, *MESW*, vol. 2, pp. 292–3.
139 Marx, *The Chartists, MECW*, vol. 11, pp. 335–6.
140 Marx to Hyndman, 8 December 1880, *Selected Correspondence*, p. 314.
141 Ibid., p. 314.
142 Marx, *The Curtain Raised*, in Marx, *The First International and After*, p. 395.
143 Marx, *Doctoral Dissertation, MECW*, vol. 1, p. 64.
144 Marx, *Economic and Philosophic Manuscripts of 1844, MECW*, vol. 3, p. 293.
145 Marx and Engels, *The German Ideology*, p. 438.
146 Marx, *Manifesto of the Communist Party*, pp. 486–7.
147 Ibid., p. 487.
148 The *locus classicus* is the *Communist Manifesto*, which declares that 'The history of all hitherto-existing society is a history of class struggles.' Marx, *Manifesto of the Communist Party*, p. 482.
149 Marx and Engels, *The German Ideology*, p. 77.
150 Marx, *Manifesto of the Communist Party*, p. 514.
151 Marx, *Critical Marginal Notes on the article by a Prussian*, 7 August 1844, *MECW*, vol. 3, p. 199. Marx makes a similar point against Bakunin in 1875: Marx, *From the Conspectus of Bakunin's Book 'Statism and Anarchy'*; K. Marx, F. Engels, and V. Lenin, *On Anarchism and Anarcho-Syndicalism* (Progress, Moscow, 1974), p. 150.
152 Marx, *Critical Marginal Notes*, p. 199.
153 Marx and Engels, *The German Ideology*, p. 49.

154 Marx at the Meeting of the Central Authority, 15 September 1850, *MECW*, vol. 10, p. 626.
155 Ibid., p. 628.
156 Ibid.
157 Marx, *Economic and Philosophic Manuscripts*, p. 294.
158 Avineri, *The Social and Political Thought of Karl Marx*, p. 183.
159 But see also Marx, 'The Crisis and the Counter-revolution', p. 431.
160 Marx, *The Eighteenth Brumaire*, p. 186.
161 Marx, *Second Address of the International on the Franco-Prussian War*, *MESW*, vol. 2, pp. 200–1.
162 Marx to F. Domela-Nieuwenhuis, 22 February 1881, *Selected Correspondence*, p. 318; see also G. D. H. Cole, *A History of Socialist Thought*, vol. 2, p. 519.
163 Marx, *The Civil War in France*, p. 223.
164 Marx and Engels, *Review of E. de Girardin 'Le Socialisme et l'impôt'*, *MECW*, vol. 10, p. 333.
165 Marx, *Critique of the Gotha Programme*, *MESW*, vol. 3, p. 25.
166 Marx, *First Draft of 'The Civil War in France'*, in Marx, *The First International and After*, p. 250.
167 Ibid., p. 249.
168 M. Collinet, *La Tragédie du Marxisme, du Manifeste Communiste à la Stratégie Totalitaire: Essai Critique* (Calmann-Lévy, Paris, 1948), pp. 145–6; P. Ansart, *Marx et l'Anarchisme* (Presses Universitaires de France, Paris, 1969), maintains that Marx held an implicitly anarchist view of the state (p. 423), which was confirmed and strengthened by the Commune (p. 453).
169 E. Kamenka, 'The Paris Commune and revolution today', E. Kamenka (ed.), *Paradigm for Revolution? The Paris Commune 1871–1971* (ANU Press, Canberra, 1972), p. 98.
170 Engels to G. Terzaghi, 14 January 1872, in Marx, Engels, Lenin, *On Anarchism and Anarcho-Syndicalism*, p. 70; a similar sentiment is expressed in his 1873 *On Authority*, *MESW*, vol. 2, p. 379.
171 Miliband, *Marxism and Politics*, p. 180.
172 K. Korsch, 'Revolutionary Commune', part I (1929) and part II (1931), in D. Kellner (ed.), *Karl Korsch: Revolutionary Theory* (University of Texas Press, Austin, 1977), pp. 203 and 206.
173 H. Draper, *Karl Marx's Theory of Revolution*, vol. I, *State and Bureaucracy*, book 1 (Monthly Review Press, NY, 1977), p. 282.
174 W. Leonhard, *Three Faces of Marxism: The Political Concepts of Soviet Ideology, Maoism and Humanist Marxism* (Holt, Rinehart and Winston, NY, 1974), p. 32.

175 Talmon, *Totalitarian Democracy*.
176 Bakunin, *Statism and Anarchy*, in G. Maximoff (ed.), *The Political Philosophy of Bakunin*, p. 284.
177 Marx, *From the Conspectus of Bakunin's Book*, p. 148. Marx's notes must be treated with caution; they were never intended to be published (and thus 'finished').
178 Bakunin, *Statism and Anarchy*, p. 287.
179 Ibid., p. 287.
180 Marx, *From the Conspectus of Bakunin's Book*, p. 150.
181 Ibid., p. 151.
182 Ibid.
183 Ibid.
184 Ibid., p. 152.
185 Marx, *Conspectus of Bakunin's 'Statism and Anarchy'*, in Marx, *The First International and After*, p.337; given in Marx, Engels, Lenin, *On Anarchism and Anarcho-Syndicalism*, p. 152, as 'what a fantastic notion!'
186 Bakunin, *Statism and Anarchy*, p. 287.
187 Marx, *From the Conspectus of Bakunin's Book*, p. 153. I do not agree with Henry Mayer, who claims that this is a reply to the idea that the dictatorship shall only be temporary and brief. H. Mayer, 'Marx on Bakunin', *Etudes de Marxologie*, October 1959, p. 104.
188 Marx, *From the Conspectus of Bakunin's Book*, p. 153.
189 Cf. R. Bahro, *The Alternative in Eastern Europe* (NLB, London, 1978), pp. 41–2.
190 Marx and Engels, *The Alliance of Socialist Democracy and the IWMA*, in Marx, Engels, Lenin, *On Anarchism and Anarcho-Syndicalism*, p. 119.
191 Ibid., p. 120.
192 Marx and Engels, *The Holy Family*, MECW, vol. 4, p. 37.
193 E. Bauer, cited ibid., p. 52.
194 B. Bauer, cited ibid., p. 82.
195 Marx, 'Thesis on Feuerbach', no. 3, MECW, vol. 5, p. 4.
196 Marx, *General Rules of the International Working Men's Association*, MESW, vol. 2, p. 19.
197 Cf. Marx and Engels, *The German Ideology*, p. 394.
198 P. Buonarroti, cited P. Thomas, *Marx and the Anarchists*, p. 110.
199 Marx and Engels, 'Circular Letter', 17 and 18 September 1879, MESW, vol. 3, p. 94.
200 M. Johnstone, 'Marx and Engels and the Concept of the Party', *Socialist Register*, 1967, p. 145.
201 Sartori, *Democratic Theory*, p. 454.

3. ENGELS, DEMOCRACY AND REVOLUTION

1 D. McLellan, *Engels* (Harvester, Sussex, 1977), p. 72.
2 E.g., Engels, *Ludwig Feuerbach and the End of Classical German Philosophy*, MESW, vol. 3, p. 361n.
3 K. Korsch, G. Lukács and A. Gramsci were some of the earliest Marxists to pursue this question, but a neglected work of Sidney Hook, *From Hegel to Marx, Studies in the Intellectual Development of Karl Marx* (University of Michigan Press, Ann Arbor, 1962), pp. 75–6, introduces a similar perspective.
4 Clio, Oxford, 1975.
5 *Marxism, An Historical and Critical Study* (Routledge and Kegan Paul, London, 1971).
6 F. L. Bender (ed.), *The Betrayal of Marx* (Harper and Row, NY, 1975).
7 N. Levine, *The Tragic Deception*, pp. xv and 228.
8 Ibid., p. 174.
9 Ibid., p. 219.
10 Ibid., chapter 13.
11 Ibid., p. 220.
12 Ibid., p. 231.
13 Ibid., p. 183.
14 E.g., H. Marcuse, *Reason and Revolution, Hegel and the Rise of Social Theory* (Routledge and Kegan Paul, London, 1973), pp. 312ff, G. Lukács, *History and Class Consciousness*, and J. Coulter, 'Marxism and the Engels Paradox', *Socialist Register*, 1971, pp. 129–56. An interesting defence of Engels' *dialectics* is mounted by G. Novack, 'In Defence of Engels', *Socialist Worker*, no. 1, 1977, pp. 33–44.
15 Levine, *The Tragic Deception*, p. 50.
16 Ibid., pp. 53 and 56.
17 Engels, *On Authority*, MESW, vol. 2, p. 377.
18 Ibid., p. 378.
19 Ibid., p. 379.
20 Engels, *The Condition of the Working Class in England*, MECW, vol. 3, p. 466.
21 Ibid., p. 466.
22 Engels to A. Bebel, 18–28 March 1875, *MESW*, vol. 3, p. 34.
23 Ibid., p. 35.
24 Lenin, *The State and Revolution*, LCW, vol. 25, p. 444.
25 Marx, *The Poverty of Philosophy*, p. 212; Marx, *Manifesto of the Communist Party*, p. 505.
26 Lenin, *The State and Revolution*, p. 462.

27 Engels, *MESW*, vol. 3, p. 147 (from chapter 2, part III of *Anti-Dühring*).
28 Ibid., p. 147.
29 Engels, *The Origin of the Family, Private Property and the State*, *MESW*, vol. 3, p. 326.
30 Ibid., p. 327.
31 Ibid., p. 328.
32 Ibid.
33 Ibid., p. 329.
34 Ibid.
35 Engels, 1891 'Introduction' to Marx, *The Civil War in France*, p. 187.
36 Plamenatz, *German Marxism and Russian Communism*, p. 138.
37 Marx, *Critical Marginal Notes*, p. 198.
38 Marx, *Review of E. de Girardin*, p. 333.
39 Avineri, *The Social and Political Thought of Karl Marx*, pp. 202–3.
40 One of these examples supports Avineri's claim; the other does not. Marx writes of 'aufheben' in his 'Kritische Randglossen zu dem Artikel eines Preussen' (Marx, Engels, *Werke*, vol. 1, p. 402), but he writes of 'Abschaffung des Staats' in the review of Girardin (*Werke*, vol. 7, p. 288).
41 Marx, *First draft of 'The Civil War in France'*, p. 249.
42 Ibid., p. 250.
43 S. F. Bloom, 'The "Withering Away" of the State', *Journal of the History of Ideas*, vol. 7, 1946, p. 121.
44 R. Adamiak, 'The "Withering Away" of the State: a Reconsideration', *The Journal of Politics*, vol. 32, 1970, p. 3.
45 Ibid., p. 16.
46 R. Bahro, *The Alternative in Eastern Europe*, p. 38.
47 Engels, *Critique of the Draft Social-Democratic Programme of 1891*, p. 434.
48 Ibid., p. 435.
49 Engels to K. Kautsky, 1 April 1895, and Engels to P. Lafargue, 3 April 1895, *Selected Correspondence*, p. 461.
50 Engels, 1895 'Introduction' to Marx, *The Class Struggles in France*, *MESW*, vol. 1, p. 190.
51 Ibid., p. 190.
52 Ibid., p. 191.
53 Ibid., p. 193.
54 Ibid., p. 195.
55 Ibid.
56 Ibid., p. 196.
57 Ibid.
58 Ibid., p. 197.

59 Ibid., p. 199.
60 Ibid., pp. 199–200.
61 Ibid., p. 200; my emphasis.
62 Ibid., p. 201.
63 Ibid.
64 Ibid., p. 202.
65 Ibid., p. 203.
66 Engels, *Critique of the Draft Social-Democratic Programme of 1891*, p. 435.
67 Engels, *The Origin of the Family*, p. 329.
68 Engels to Bebel, March 1875, *MESW*, vol. 3, p. 34.
69 G. Sartori, 'Constitutionalism: a Preliminary Discussion', *American Political Science Review*, vol. 59, 1962, p. 855.
70 Engels, *Herr Eugen Dühring's Revolution in Science (Anti-Dühring)* (International Publishers, NY, 1972), p. 203.
71 Engels, *MESW*, vol. 3, p. 398.
72 Ibid., p. 415.
73 Ibid.
74 Ibid., p. 419.
75 F. Nova, *Friedrich Engels. His Contributions to Political Theory* (Vision Press, London, 1968), p. 49.
76 Engels, *The Peasant War in Germany*, *MECW*, vol. 10, p. 469.
77 Engels, *Marx and the Neue Rheinische Zeitung (1848–1849)*, 1884, *MESW*, vol. 3, p. 167.
78 Marx, *Critique of the Gotha Programme*, p. 25.
79 Marx, *Grundrisse, Foundations of the Critique of Political Economy (Rough Draft)* (Penguin, Harmondsworth, 1973), p. 84.

4. MARXISM AND REVISIONISM

1 Engels, *Speech at the Graveside of Karl Marx* (1883), *MESW*, vol. 3, p. 162.
2 E. Durkheim, 'Revue de Labriola', *Revue Philosophique*, vol. 44, 1897, p. 650; M. Weber, *The Methodology of the Social Sciences* (Free Press, NY, 1968), p. 68; and V. Pareto, *Les Systèmes Socialistes* (Paris, 1965), p. 393.
3 V. Pareto, *The Mind and Society, A Treatise on General Sociology* (Dover, NY, 1963), para. 2183; see also paras. 2244 and 2253.
4 Pareto, *Systèmes Socialistes*, pp. 421–2; my emphasis.
5 G. Mosca, *The Ruling Class, Elementi di Scienza Politica* (McGraw-Hill, NY, 1939), p. 285.
6 Ibid., p. 198.

7 Weber to Midiels, 4 August 1908, cited W. Mommsen, *The Age of Bureaucracy* (Blackwell, Oxford, 1974), p. 59, n.2.
8 B. Russell, *Roads to Freedom. Socialism, Anarchism and Syndicalism* (Allen and Unwin, London, 1966), p. 92.
9 M. Hillquit and J. Ryan, *Socialism, Promise or Menace?* (Macmillan, NY, 1914), pp. 66–9.
10 T. G. Masaryk, *Masaryk on Marx* (Bucknell University Press, Lewisburg, 1972), p. 204.
11 J.P. Nettl, 'The German Social Democratic Party, 1890–1914, as a Political Model', *Past and Present*, no. 30, 1965, p. 73.
12 J. Spargo, *Applied Socialism, A Study of the Application of Socialist Principles to the State* (Melrose, London, 1912), p. 86.
13 T. Kirkup, *A History of Socialism* (Black, London, 1920), p. 223. Kirkup cites both the Erfurt and Gotha Programmes in full.
14 Cited ibid., p. 224.
15 Cited ibid., p. 225.
16 Kautsky wrote more explicitly a decade later: 'So socialistic awareness is something brought into the proletariat's class struggle from outside, not something that has sprung up inside', 'Die Revision des Programms der Sozialdemokratie in Österreich', *Neue Zeit*, XX, 1901–1902, cited L. Basso, *Rosa Luxemburg: A Reappraisal* (Deutsch, London, 1975), p. 163, n.231.
17 Marx, *Critique of the Gotha Programme*, p. 26.
18 K. Kautsky, *The Class Struggle* (Norton, NY, 1971), pp. 90–1.
19 Ibid., p. 109.
20 Ibid., p. 110.
21 Ibid., p. 186.
22 Ibid., p. 188.
23 Ibid.
24 Ibid., p. 191.
25 Ibid., p. 113.
26 Ibid., p. 117.
27 Masaryk, *Masaryk on Marx*, p. 207.
28 A charge made by M. Hirsch, *Democracy versus Socialism, a critical examination of socialism as a remedy for social injustice* (Macmillan, London, 1901), pp. 306–7, and discussed by B. Russell, *Roads to Freedom*, p. 92.
29 L. von Mises, *Socialism*, pp. 84–5.
30 A. Bebel, *My Life* (T. Fisher Unwin, London, 1912), p. 79.
31 T. B. Bottomore, *Marxist Sociology* (Macmillan, London, 1975), p. 21.
32 Bernstein, cited P. Gay, *The Dilemma of Democratic Socialism, Eduard Bernstein's Challenge to Marx* (Collier, NY, 1962), p. 250.

33 W. O. Henderson, *The Life of Friedrich Engels*, vol. 2 (Cass, London, 1976), p. 589.
34 Bebel, *My Life*, p. 287.
35 C. Landauer, *European Socialism: A History of Ideas and Movements from the Industrial Revolution to Hitler's Seizure of Power*, vol. 1 (Greenwood Press, Connecticut, 1959), p. 297.
36 E. Bernstein, *Evolutionary Socialism: A Criticism and Affirmation* (Schocken, NY, 1967), p. 214.
37 Ibid.
38 Bernstein, cited Gay, *The Dilemma of Democratic Socialism*, pp. 76–7.
39 C. Gneuss, 'The Precursor: Eduard Bernstein', L. Labedz (ed.), *Revisionism: Essays on the History of Marxist Ideas* (Allen and Unwin, London, 1962), p. 35. Bernstein also made use of Engels' four letters on 'historical materialism' in his defence (Engels to: C. Schmidt, 5 August 1890; J. Bloch, 21–22 September 1890; C. Schmidt, 27 October 1890; W. Borgius, 25 January 1894 – to be found in *Selected Correspondence* pp. 392–4; 394–6; 396–402; and 441–3, respectively), although they add nothing essentially new to the materialist conception of history.
40 Engels, 1884 'Preface' to Marx, *Poverty of Philosophy* (International Publishers, NY, 1963), p. 11.
41 Bernstein, *Evolutionary Socialism*, p. 97.
42 Ibid., pp. 103 and 106.
43 Ibid., p. 155.
44 J. Jaurès, *Studies in Socialism* (ILP, London, 1906), p. 46.
45 Ibid., p. 53.
46 Ibid., p. 57.
47 G. Sorel, 'The Decomposition of Marxism', I. L. Horowitz, *Radicalism and the Revolt Against Reason* (Humanities Press, NY, 1961), p. 241.
48 Bernstein, *Evolutionary Socialism*, p. 149.
49 Ibid., p. 217.
50 Ibid., pp. 217–18.
51 Ibid., p. 146.
52 Ibid., p. 166.
53 Ibid., p. 167.
54 Ibid., pp. 218–19.
55 G. Sorel, *From Georges Sorel: Essays in Socialism and Philosophy* (Oxford University Press, NY, 1976). p. 175.
56 Sorel, 'The Decomposition of Marxism', p. 215.
57 Gay, *The Dilemma of Democratic Socialism*, p. 224.
58 Bernstein, cited ibid., p. 242.
59 K. Kautsky, *Bernstein und das Sozialdemokratische Programm* (1899), cited R.W. Reichard, *Karl Kautsky and the German Social Democratic*

Party, 1863–1914 (unpublished Ph.D. thesis, Harvard University, 1950), p. 145.

60 I. Auer, cited J. Joll, *The Second International 1899–1914* (Weidenfeld and Nicolson, London, 1968), pp. 93–4.

61 N. Lesser, 'Austro-Marxism: A Reappraisal', *Journal of Contemporary History*, 1966, p. 118.

62 R. Luxemburg, *Social Reform or Revolution* (Young Socialist, Colombo, 1969), p. 12.

63 Ibid.

64 Ibid.

65 Ibid., p. 13.

66 L. B. Boudin, *The Theoretical System of Karl Marx, in the Light of Recent Criticism* (Kerr, Chicago, 1915), p. 11.

67 Cited J. Braunthal, *History of the International, 1864–1914*, vol. 1 (Nelson, London, 1966), p. 265.

68 Luxemburg, *Social Reform or Revolution*, p. 49.

69 Ibid., p. 54.

70 For example, W. Sombart, *Socialism and the Social Movement in the Nineteenth Century* (Kerr, Chicago, 1902), p. 156.

71 Luxemburg, *Social Reform or Revolution*, p. 13.

72 Ibid., p. 60.

73 Ibid., p. 24.

74 Ibid.

75 Ibid., p. 52.

76 Ibid., p. 36.

77 Ibid., p. 29.

78 Ibid.

79 Ibid., p. 30.

80 Ibid.

81 Ibid.

82 Ibid., p. 32.

83 Ibid., p. 33.

84 Ibid.

85 Ibid.

86 Ibid.

87 Ibid., p. 34.

88 Ibid.

89 Ibid., p. 33.

90 Ibid., p. 56.

91 Ibid.

92 Ibid., p. 58.

93 Ibid., p. 60.

94 Ibid.
95 Ibid., p. 61.
96 Ibid., p. 59.
97 Ibid., p. 7.
98 Ibid., p. 37.
99 R. Luxemburg, 'Opportunism and the Art of the Possible', R. Looker (ed.), *Rosa Luxemburg, Selected Political Writings* (Cape, London, 1972), p. 74.
100 Ibid.
101 Luxemburg, *Social Reform or Revolution*, p. 53.
102 Ibid., p. 60.
103 Ibid., p. 67; see also ibid., p. 7.
104 R.S. Wistrich, *Revolutionary Jews from Marx to Trotsky* (Harrap, London, 1976), p. 60; my emphasis.
105 Luxemburg, *Social Reform or Revolution*, pp. 46–7.
106 Ibid., p. 65.
107 Ibid.
108 Ibid., pp. 65–6.
109 Ibid., p. 11.
110 J. P. Nettl, *Rosa Luxemburg* (Oxford University Press, London, 1966), vol. I, p. 223.
111 Millerand, cited A. Fried and R. Sanders (eds.), *Socialist Thought, A Documentary History* (Doubleday, NY, 1964), p. 421.
112 W. Liebknecht, *How Shall Socialism be Realized?*, cited Jaurès, *Studies in Socialism*, pp. 82–3. On Liebknecht's changing views on parliament see G. D. H. Cole, *A History of Socialist Thought*, vol. 2, pp. 253–4.
113 Cited Jaurès, *Studies in Socialism*, pp. 90–1.
114 Cited R. Palme Dutt, *The Internationale* (Lawrence and Wishart, London, 1964), pp. 102–3.
115 Ibid., p. 103.
116 Gay, *The Dilemma of Democratic Socialism*, p. 268.
117 S. P. Orth, *Socialism and Democracy in Europe* (Williams and Norgate, London, 1913), p. 251.
118 Jaurès, *Studies in Socialism*, p. 57.
119 K. Kautsky, *The Social Revolution* (Kerr, Chicago, 1916), pp. 6–7.
120 Ibid., p. 8–9.
121 Ibid., p. 87.
122 Ibid., p. 107.
123 J. H. Kautsky, *The Political Thought of Karl Kautsky. A Theory of Democratic, Anti-Communist Marxism* (unpublished Ph.D. thesis, Harvard University, 1951), p. 268; and Reichard, *Karl Kautsky*, p. 189.
124 K. Kautsky, *The Road to Power* (Bloch, Chicago, 1909), p. 45. This

work is cited many times by Lenin as a model of Marxist analysis, even when Kautsky was being described as a 'renegade' by Lenin. See, for example, *Dead Chauvinism and Living Socialism* (December 1914), *LCW*, vol. 21, p. 94, and *Under a False Flag* (February 1915), *LCW*, vol. 21, p. 147.

125 Kautsky, *The Road to Power*, p. 53.

5. THE RUSSIAN REVOLUTIONARY TRADITION

1 Berdyaev, *The Origin of Russian Communism*, p. 61.
2 S. H. Baron, *Plekhanov, The Father of Russian Marxism* (Routledge and Kegan Paul, London, 1963).
3 Cited A. Walicki, *A History of Russian Thought from the Enlightenment to Marxism* (Clarendon Press, Oxford, 1980), p. 86
4 Cited ibid., p. 89.
5 A phrase coined by Stepan Shevyrev (1806–64); cited ibid., p. 110.
6 Cited ibid., p. 145.
7 A. Herzen, 'Letters from the Avenue Marigny', 1847, cited M. Malia, *Alexander Herzen and the Birth of Russian Socialism 1812–1855* (Harvard University Press, Massachusetts, 1961), p. 357.
8 Malia, *Alexander Herzen*, p. 311.
9 Herzen, 'Letters to an Opponent' (Y. F. Samarin), *Selected Philosophical Works* (Progress, Moscow, 1956), p. 550.
10 Ibid., p. 551.
11 Cited Malia, *Alexander Herzen*, p. 408.
12 Cited Walicki, *A History of Russian Thought*, p. 164.
13 Ibid., p. 178.
14 I. Berlin, 'Herzen and Bakunin on Individual Liberty', E. J. Simmons (ed.), *Continuity and Change in Russian and Soviet Thought* (Russell and Russell, NY, 1967), p. 473.
15 Ibid., p. 498.
16 Cited R. Hare, *Pioneers of Russian Social Thought* (Vintage, NY, 1964), pp. 226–7.
17 Cited ibid., p. 227.
18 Cited B. D. Wolfe, 'Backwardness and Industrialization in Russian History and Thought', *Slavic Review*, vol. 26, no. 2, June 1967, p. 178.
19 Cited A. Walicki, *The Controversy over Capitalism. Studies in the Social Philosophy of the Russian Populists* (Clarendon Press, Oxford, 1969), p. 83.
20 Cited Berlin, 'Herzen and Bakunin', p. 479.
21 N. Valentinov, *Encounters With Lenin* (Oxford University Press, London, 1968), p. 64.

22 M. M. Karpovich, 'N.G. Chernyshevski, between Socialism and Liberalism', *Cahiers du Monde Russe et Sovietique*, vol. 1, 1959–60, p. 583.
23 Cited Walicki, *The Controversy over Capitalism*, p. 85.
24 Lenin, *What is to Be Done?*, LCW, vol. 5, p. 474.
25 P. Lavrov, *Historical Letters* (University of California Press, Berkeley, 1967), p. 139.
26 P. Pomper, *Peter Lavrov and the Russian Revolutionary Movement* (University of Chicago Press, Chicago, 1972), p. 101.
27 Lavrov, *Historical Letters*, p. 138.
28 Ibid., p. 173.
29 S. V. Utechin, *Russian Political Thought, A Concise History* (Dent, London, 1963), p. 131.
30 Cited J. H. Billington, *Mikhailovsky and Russian Populism* (Clarendon Press, Oxford, 1958), p. 91.
31 Cited ibid., p. 95.
32 Cited Walicki, *A History of Russian Thought*, pp. 245–6.
33 Cited ibid., p. 247.
34 Cited ibid.
35 A. Kimball, 'The Russian Past and the Socialist Future in the Thought of P. Lavrov', *Slavic Review*, vol. 30, no. 1, 1971, p. 42.
36 Cited A. L. Weeks, *The First Bolshevik, A Political Biography of Peter Tkachev* (NY University Press, NY, 1968), p. xii.
37 Cited ibid., p. 75.
38 Cited ibid., p. xii.
39 Cited ibid., p. 76.
40 Cited ibid., p. 77.
41 Cited ibid., p. 86.
42 Cited ibid., p. 89.
43 Cited ibid., p. 92.
44 Cited ibid.
45 Cited ibid.
46 Cited ibid., p. 95.
47 Marx to L. Kugelmann, 12 October 1868, *The Letters of Karl Marx*, edited S. K. Padover (Prentice-Hall, NJ, 1979), p. 257.
48 Walicki, *The Controversy over Capitalism*, p. 133.
49 Ibid., p. 134.
50 Tkachev, 'Open Letter to Frederick Engels' (1874), cited A. L. Weeks, *The First Bolshevik*, pp. 115–16.
51 Engels, *On Social Relations in Russia* (1875), MESW, vol. 2, pp. 387–8.
52 Ibid., p. 395.
53 Cited J. H. Billington, *Mikhailovsky and Russian Populism*, p. 66.

54 Marx to the Editorial Board of the *Otechestvenniye Zapiski*, November 1877, *Selected Correspondence*, pp. 293–94.

55 Ibid., p. 292.

56 Marx to V. Zasulich, 8 March 1881, *Selected Correspondence*, p. 319.

57 Ibid., p. 320. W. Weintraub notes that Marx's brief reply to Zasulich was his fifth draft, earlier (and much longer) drafts betraying an even stronger sympathy for the Populists; 'Marx and the Russian Revolutionaries', *The Cambridge Journal*, vol. 3, no. 8, 1950, p. 502.

58 Marx and Engels, 'Preface to the Russian edition of 1882', *Manifesto of the Communist Party*, MESW, vol. I, pp. 100–1.

59 B. D. Wolfe, 'Backwardness and Industrialization', p. 181.

60 W. Bowden, M. Karpovich, A. P. Usher, *An Economic History of Europe Since 1750* (Fertig, NY, 1970), p. 296.

61 Wolfe, 'Backwardness and Industrialization', p. 182; A. Kimball, 'The Russian Past and the Socialist Future', p. 40. Karpovich impies that the commune retarded agriculture, W. Bowden, *et al.*, *An Economic History of Europe*, p. 297.

62 Marx, letter to Jenny Longuet, 11 April 1881, Marx and Engels, *Correspondence 1846–1895*, edited D. Torr (Lawrence and Wishart, London, 1936), p. 391.

63 Engels to V. Zasulich, 23 April 1885, *Selected Correspondence*, p. 362.

64 Engels, 'Afterword' to *On Social Relations in Russia*, MESW, vol. 2, p. 402.

65 Ibid., p. 409.

66 Engels to N. F. Danielson, 17 October 1893, *Selected Correspondence*, p. 439.

67 T. H. Von Laue, 'The Fate of Capitalism in Russia: The Narodnik Version', *American Slavic and East European Review*, vol. XIII, no. 1, 1954, pp. 15–16.

68 A. Gerschenkron, 'Economic Backwardness in Historical Perspective', B. F. Hoselitz (ed.), *The Progress of Underdeveloped Areas* (University of Chicago Press, Chicago, 1963), p. 25.

69 R. Kindersley, *The First Russian Revisionists, A Study of 'Legal Marxism' in Russia* (Clarendon Press, Oxford, 1962), p. 84.

70 Cited ibid., p. 106; see also P. Struve, 'La Théorie marxienne de l'évolution sociale, Essai Critique', *Cahiers de l'ISEA, Etudes de Marxologie*, September 1962, pp. 113–56.

71 G. V. Plekhanov, *Socialism and the Political Struggle, Selected Philosophical Works* (Progress, Moscow, 1977), vol. I, p. 76.

72 Ibid., p. 96.

73 Ibid., p. 97.

74 Ibid., p. 99.

75 Ibid., p. 100.
76 Ibid.
77 Ibid., p. 101.
78 Ibid., p. 104.
79 Ibid.
80 Ibid.
81 Ibid., p. 95.
82 Ibid.
83 Ibid.
84 Ibid., p. 102.
85 Ibid.
86 Plekhanov, *Our Differences, Selected Philosophical Works*, vol. 1, p. 126.
87 Ibid., p. 134.
88 Ibid., p. 145.
89 Ibid., p. 240.
90 Ibid., p. 279.
91 Ibid., p. 288.
92 Ibid.
93 Cited ibid., p. 302.
94 Ibid., p. 310.
95 Ibid., p. 322.
96 See ibid., p. 164.
97 See ibid., p. 336.
98 Ibid., p. 102.
99 Ibid., p. 340.
100 Ibid., p. 339.

6. LENIN AND THE PARTY

1 The best recent study is N. Harding, *Lenin's Political Thought*, vol. 1, *Theory and Practice in the Democratic Revolution* (Macmillan, London, 1977).
2 Akselrod, cited ibid., vol. 1, p. 47.
3 R. C. Elwood (ed.), *Resolutions and Decisions of the Communist Party of the Soviet Union*, vol. 1, *The Russian Social Democratic Labour Party, 1898–October 1917* (University of Toronto Press, Toronto, 1974), p. 35.
4 Lenin, 'The Urgent Tasks of Our Movement' (December 1900), *LCW*, vol. 4, p. 368.
5 Ibid., pp. 370–1.
6 Lenin, *Where to Begin*, *LCW*, vol. 5, p. 17.

7 Lenin, *What is to Be Done?*, LCW, vol. 5, p. 474.

8 Plekhanov, *Our Differences*, p. 139.

9 Lenin, *Where to Begin*, p. 17.

10 Ibid., p. 22.

11 Ibid., p. 23.

12 Lenin, 'Questions submitted to the Union of Russian Social-Democrats Abroad at the "Unity" Conference, 4 October 1901', LCW, vol. 5, p. 230.

13 Subtitled 'Burning Questions of our movement'; first published March 1902.

14 Lenin, *What is to Be Done?*, p. 353.

15 Ibid., p. 375.

16 Ibid.

17 Ibid., p. 378.

18 Ibid., p. 384.

19 Ibid., p. 400.

20 Lenin, 'Our Immediate Tasks', LCW, vol. 4, p. 215.

21 Lenin, *What is to Be Done?*, p. 423.

22 Cited N. Harding, *Lenin's Political Thought*, vol. 1, p. 154.

23 Ibid., p. 170.

24 Cited Lenin, *What is to Be Done?*, p. 384.

25 Ibid., pp. 452–3.

26 Ibid., p. 464.

27 Ibid., p. 479.

28 Ibid., p. 480.

29 Ibid., p. 505.

30 Lenin, 'Letter to a Comrade on our Organisational Tasks', LCW, vol. 6, p. 240.

31 Adopted 5 August 1903, see R. C. Elwood (ed.), *Resolutions and Decisions*, vol. 1, p. 45.

32 'Majority-ites', a term derived from the latter sessions of the Second Congress, when Lenin's followers found themselves in a majority. Acting upon some inexplicable 'death-wish', perhaps, the Mensheviks, or minority-ites, retained their chance title thereafter, irrespective of their size *vis-à-vis* the Bolsheviks.

33 Adopted 21 April 1905, see ibid., p. 56.

34 Cited J. L. H. Keep, *The Rise of Social Democracy in Russia* (Clarendon Press, Oxford, 1963), p. 145.

35 Cited A. Ascher, *Pavel Axelrod and the Development of Menshevism* (Harvard University Press, Massachusetts, 1972), p. 288.

36 'Resolution on Russian Unification', July 1914, cited O. Gankin and H. H. Fisher (eds.), *The Bolsheviks and the World War, the Origin of the*

Third International (Stanford University Press, California, 1940), p. 131.

37 N. Harding, *Lenin's Political Thought*, vol. 1, p. 187.

38 Lenin, *One Step Forward, Two Steps Back (The Crisis in Our Party)*, *LCW*, vol. 7, p. 203.

39 Ibid., p. 253.

40 Ibid.

41 Ibid., p. 254.

42 Ibid., p. 267.

43 Ibid., p. 342.

44 Ibid., p. 380.

45 Ibid., p. 396.

46 Elwood (ed.), *Resolutions and Decisions of the Communist Party of the Soviet Union*, vol. 1, p. 83; in a resolution from the Second All-Russian Menshevik conference in November 1905.

47 V. Akimov, *The Second Congress of the Russian Social Democratic Labour Party*, J. Frankel (ed.), *Vladimir Akimov on the Dilemmas of Russian Marxism, 1895–1903* (CUP, Cambridge, 1969), p. 112.

48 Ibid., p. 115.

49 Ibid.

50 Ibid., p. 124.

51 Engels, 1895 'Introduction', Marx, *The Class Struggles in France*, *MESW*, vol. 1, pp. 199–200.

52 Akimov, *The Second Congress*, p. 135.

53 Cited Lenin, 'Notes on Plekhanov's First Draft Programme', *LCW*, vol. 6, p. 22.

54 Lenin, ibid.

55 Lenin, 'Draft Programme of the Russian Social-Democratic Labour Party', *LCW*, vol. 6, pp. 26–7.

56 Lenin, 'Notes on Plekhanov's Second Draft Programme', *LCW*, vol. 6, p. 49.

57 Cited J. Frankel, 'Introduction', J. Frankel (ed.), *Vladimir Akimov on the Dilemmas of Russian Marxism*, p. 72.

58 Akimov, *The Second Congress*, p. 135.

59 Ibid., p. 136.

60 Ibid., p. 137.

61 Cited ibid., p. 139. There is a significant discrepancy between this citation and the Progress Publishers' rendering of Plekhanov, which reads: '... which permits it to dispose of society's organized force to defend its own interests and to *directly or indirectly suppress* all those social movements which infringe those interests'. Plekhanov, 'The Initial Phases of the Theory of the Class Struggle' (an Introduction to the

Second Russian Edition of the *Communist Manifesto*), *Selected Philosophical Works*, vol. 2, pp. 465–6; my emphasis. Progress would rather blemish Plekhanov's grammar than concede Frankel's translation.

62 V. Akimov, *The Second Congress*, p. 139.

63 Ibid., p. 142.

64 Ibid., p. 152.

65 Ibid., p. 179.

66 Ibid., p. 180.

67 Ibid.

68 Ibid., p. 182.

69 Akselrod, 'The Unification of Russian Social Democracy and its Tasks', A. Ascher (ed.), *The Mensheviks in the Russian Revolution* (Thames and Hudson, London, 1976), pp. 49–50.

70 L. Haimson, *The Russian Marxists and the Origins of Bolshevism* (Harvard University Press, Massachusetts, 1955), p. 188.

71 Cited I. Getzler, *Martov, a Political Biography of a Russian Social Democrat* (Melbourne University Press, Melbourne, 1967), p. 80.

72 B. Knei-Paz, *The Social and Political Thought of Leon Trotsky* (Clarendon Press, Oxford, 1978), p. 176. Trotsky's anti-Lenin writings have yet to be fully translated.

73 Ibid., p. 179.

74 Cited ibid., p. 183.

75 Cited ibid., p. 184.

76 Cited Haimson, *The Russian Marxists*, p. 177.

77 Cited Knei-Paz, *The Social and Political Thought of Leon Trotsky*, p. 195.

78 Plekhanov, 'Speech at the International Workers' Socialist Congress in Paris' (1889), *Selected Philosophical Works*, vol. 1, p. 406.

79 Cited Knei-Paz, *The Social and Political Thought of Leon Trotsky*, p. 199.

80 Cited ibid., p. 204.

81 Cited Baron, *Plekhanov*, p. 246.

82 Luxemburg, *Rosa Luxemburg: Selected Political Writings* (edited R. Looker), p. 95.

83 Nettl, *Rosa Luxemburg*, vol. 1, p. 288.

84 Lenin to A. M. Gorky, 25 February 1908, *LCW*, vol. 13, p. 449.

85 Lenin, *Materialism and Empirio-Criticism. Critical Comments on a Reactionary Philosophy* (1908), *LCW*, vol. 14, p. 358.

86 Lenin, *Two Tactics of Social-Democracy in the Democratic Revolution* (July 1905), *LCW*, vol. 9, p. 48.

87 Ibid., p. 57.

88 Ibid., p. 18.

89 Ibid., p. 22.

90 Ibid., p. 48.

91 Ibid., p. 58.

92 Lenin, *The Revolutionary-Democratic Dictatorship of the Proletariat and the Peasantry* (April 1905), *LCW*, vol. 8, p. 294. This is a response to Martynov's argument that Social-Democratic leadership of a bourgeois provisional government would 'discredit the socialist flag' (see S. M. Schwarz, *The Russian Revolution of 1905, the Workers' Movement and the Formation of Bolshevism and Menshevism* (University of Chicago Press, Chicago, 1967), p. 8).

93 Lenin, *The Agrarian Programme of Social-Democracy in the First Russian Revolution, 1905–1907* (December 1907), *LCW*, vol. 13, p. 421.

94 Ibid., p. 346.

95 Ibid., p. 244.

96 M. Slonim, 'Le précurseur de Lénine', *Revue universelle*, vol. 62, 1935.

97 M. M. Karpovich, 'A Forerunner of Lenin', *Review of Politics*, vol. 6, no. 3, 1944.

98 S. V. Utechin, 'Who Taught Lenin?', *The Twentieth Century*, vol. 168, 1960.

99 Cited V. Varmalov, *Bakunin and the Russian Jacobins as Evaluated by Soviet Historiography* (Research Programme on the USSR, East European Fund, Inc., NY, 1955), p. 6. See also ibid., p. 21, for B. Gorev's 1926 analysis of Bakunin and Tkachev.

100 Cited N. Valentinov, *Encounters with Lenin*, p. 64.

101 See J. Frankel 'Introduction', J. Frankel (ed.), *Vladimir Akimov on the Dilemmas of Russian Marxism*, p. 83.

102 Cited R. Pipes, *Struve, Liberal on the Left, 1870–1905* (Harvard University Press, Massachusetts, 1970), p. 96n. See also Plekhanov's speech at the Second Congress (1903), which implies that the masses may not know their true interests after the revolution, but the party will; Baron, *Plekhanov*, p. 242.

103 Harding, *Lenin's Political Thought*, vol. 1, p. 50.

104 Baron, *Plekhanov*, p. 115.

105 E.g., Lenin, 'How the "Spark" was nearly Extinguished' (September 1900), *LCW*, vol. 4, p. 340.

106 Cited N. Valentinov, *Encounters with Lenin*, p. 182.

7. LENIN AND THE DICTATORSHIP

1 Lenin, *The Socialist Revolution and the Right of Nations to Self-Determination* (January–February 1916), *LCW*, vol. 22, p. 147; earlier,

Lenin had described this division of nations as the essence of imperialism. Lenin, *The Revolutionary Proletariat and the Right of Nations to Self-Determination* (October 1915), *LCW*, vol. 20, p. 409.

2 Lenin, *The Discussion on Self-Determination Summed Up* (July 1916), *LCW*, vol. 22, p. 343.
3 Lenin, *Imperialism, The Highest Stage of Capitalism* (January–June 1916), *LCW*, vol. 22, p. 285.
4 Ibid.
5 Ibid., p. 194.
6 K. Kautsky, *The Dictatorship of the Proletariat* (University of Michigan Press, Ann Arbor, 1974), p. 1.
7 Ibid., p. 4.
8 Ibid.
9 Ibid., p. 5.
10 Ibid., p. 22.
11 Ibid., p. 23.
12 Ibid., p. 29.
13 Cited ibid., p. 36.
14 Ibid., pp. 40–1.
15 Ibid., p. 42.
16 Ibid., p. 43.
17 Ibid.
18 Ibid.
19 Ibid., p. 45.
20 Ibid., p. 46, also p. 31.
21 Ibid., p. 55.
22 Ibid.
23 Ibid., p. 58.
24 Ibid.
25 Ibid., pp. 64–5.
26 Ibid., p. 69.
27 Ibid., p. 74.
28 Ibid., p. 82
29 Ibid.
30 Ibid., p. 97.
31 Ibid., p. 133.
32 Ibid., p. 139–40.
33 Lenin, *The Immediate Tasks of the Soviet Government* (April 1918), *LCW*, vol. 27, p. 268.
34 Kautsky, *The Dictatorship of the Proletariat*, p. 144.
35 Lenin, 'The Proletarian Revolution and the Renegade Kautsky' (October 1918), *LCW*, vol. 28, p. 106.

36 Ibid., p. 108.
37 Ibid., p. 107.
38 Lenin, *The Proletarian Revolution and the Renegade Kautsky* (October–November 1918), *LCW*, vol. 28, p. 231.
39 Ibid., p. 232.
40 Ibid., p. 233.
41 Ibid.
42 Ibid.
43 Ibid., p. 238.
44 Ibid., p. 237.
45 Ibid., p. 235.
46 Ibid., p. 236.
47 Ibid.
48 Ibid., p. 246.
49 Ibid., p. 247.
50 Ibid.
51 Ibid., p. 248.
52 Ibid., p. 255.
53 Ibid., p. 256.
54 Ibid.
55 Ibid., pp. 256–7.
56 Ibid., p. 257.
57 Ibid., p. 263.
58 Ibid., p. 265.
59 Ibid., p. 268.
60 Ibid., pp. 263–4.
61 Ibid., p. 268.
62 Ibid., p. 273.
63 M. Sawer, 'The Genesis of *State and Revolution*', *Socialist Register*, 1977.
64 H. Arendt, *On Revolution*, pp. 256–8.
65 Lenin, *The State and Revolution*, *LCW*, vol. 25, p. 404.
66 Ibid., p. 432.
67 Cited ibid., p. 445.
68 Ibid., p. 445; my emphasis.
69 Ibid., p. 461; my emphasis.
70 Ibid., p. 462.
71 Marx, *Critique of the Gotha Programme*, p. 19.
72 Lenin, *The State and Revolution*, p. 469.
73 E.g., Lenin, *The State* (July 1919), *LCW*, vol. 29, pp. 475, 478 and 480.
74 I. Lapenna, 'Lenin, Law and Legality', L. Schapiro and P. Reddaway

(eds.), *Lenin, the Man, the Theorist, the Leader: A Reappraisal* (Praeger, NY, 1967), p. 248.

75 Ibid., p. 260.
76 Ibid., p. 262. A similar point is made by L. Schapiro, *Totalitarianism* (Pall Mall, London, 1972), p. 33.
77 Cited I. Lapenna, 'Lenin, Law and Legality', p. 255; not in the English edition of *LCW*. See also Lenin, 'Letter to D.I. Kursky with Notes on the Draft Civil Code', 28 February 1922, *LCW*, vol. 33, p. 203.
78 Lenin, *Two Tactics of Social-Democracy*, p. 128.
79 Lenin, *The Immediate Tasks of the Soviet Government*, p. 263.
80 Luxemburg, 'The Problem of Dictatorship', *Rosa Luxemburg: Selected Political Writings*, p. 244.
81 Ibid., pp. 244–5.
82 Ibid., p. 247.
83 Ibid.
84 Ibid., p. 249.
85 Ibid.
86 Ibid.
87 Ibid., p. 250.
88 Ibid., p. 251.
89 K. Kautsky, *Terrorism or Communism, a Contribution to the Natural History of Revolution* (Hyperion Press, Connecticut, 1973), p. 20.
90 Ibid., p. 51.
91 Ibid., p. 74.
92 Ibid., p. 162.
93 Ibid., p. 170.
94 Ibid., p. 171.
95 Ibid., p. 176.
96 Ibid., p. 185.
97 Ibid.
98 Ibid., p. 201.
99 Ibid., p. 202.
100 Ibid., p. 208.
101 Ibid., p. 220.
102 L. Trotsky, *Terrorism and Communism, A Reply to Karl Kautsky* (University of Michigan Press, Ann Arbor, 1963), p. 17.
103 Ibid., p. 20.
104 Ibid.
105 Ibid., p. 21.
106 Ibid., p. 31.
107 Ibid., p. 36.
108 Ibid., p. 42.

109 Ibid., p. 43.
110 Ibid., p. 44.
111 Ibid., p. 45.
112 Ibid., p. 105.
113 Ibid., p. 107.
114 Ibid., p. 108. Lenin's idea of unity complements Trotsky's sentiment: 'But how can strict unity of will be ensured? By thousands subordinating their will to the will of one.' Lenin, *The Immediate Tasks of the Soviet Government*, p. 269.
115 Trotsky, *Terrorism and Communism*, p. 108.
116 Ibid., p. 109.
117 Ibid., p. 141.
118 Ibid., p. 147.
119 Ibid., pp. 171–2.
120 Lenin, *The Trade Unions, The Present Situation and Trotsky's Mistakes*, LCW, vol. 32, p. 24.
121 N. Bukharin, 'The Theory of the Dictatorship of the Proletariat' (1919), N. Bukharin, *The Politics and Economics of the Transition Period* (Routledge and Kegan Paul, London, 1979), p. 36.
122 Ibid., p. 40.
123 Ibid., p. 48.
124 Ibid., p. 49.
125 Ibid., p. 51.
126 Ibid.
127 N. Bukharin, 'Economics of the Transition Period', ibid., p. 161.
128 Ibid., p. 162.
129 Ibid., p. 163
130 Ibid.
131 Lenin, *Deception of the People with Slogans of Freedom and Equality* (19 May 1919), LCW, vol. 29, p. 376.
132 Lenin, *'Left-Wing' Communism – An Infantile Disorder* (June 1920), LCW, vol. 31, p. 45.

SELECTIVE BIBLIOGRAPHY

Extensive bibliographies of studies of Marx and Marxism are widely available. Although it is a little dated, the bibliography attached to D. McLellan, *Karl Marx, His Life and Thought* (Macmillan, London 1973), is one. I do not propose to add to their number. Listed below are the major primary sources of this study, and other works which had been important in its development. In many cases they also contain general bibliographies.

Akimov, V., *Vladimir Akimov on the Dilemmas of Russian Marxism, 1895–1903*, edited and translated J. Frankel, CUP, Cambridge, 1969.

Avineri, S., *The Social and Political Thought of Karl Marx*, CUP, Cambridge, 1972 (first edition 1968).

Bakunin, M., *The Political Philosophy of Bakunin: Scientific Anarchism*, edited G. P. Maximoff, Free Press, NY, 1964 (first edition 1953).

Baron, S. H., *Plekhanov, The Father of Russian Marxism*, Routledge and Kegan Paul, London, 1963.

Berdyaev, N., *The Origin of Russian Communism*, University of Michigan Press, Ann Arbor, 1972 (first edition 1937).

Bernstein, E., *Evolutionary Socialism: A Criticism and Affirmation*, translated E. C. Harvey, Schocken Books, NY, 1967.

Bukharin, N., *The Politics and Economics of the Transition Period*, edited K. J. Tarbuck, translated O. Field, Routledge and Kegan Paul, London, 1979.

Carrillo, S., *'Eurocommunism' and the State*, translated N. Green and A. M. Elliott, Lawrence and Wishart, London, 1977.

Cole, G. D. H., *A History of Socialist Thought*: vol. 2, *Marxism and Anarchism, 1850–1890*; vol, 3, *The Second International, 1889–1914*; vol. 4, *Communism and Social Democracy, 1914–1931*, Macmillan, London, 1954, 1956 and 1958.

Daniels, R. V., *The Conscience of the Revolution, Communist Opposition in Soviet Russia*, Simon and Schuster, NY, 1969 (first edition 1960).

Dunn, J., *Western Political Theory in the Face of the Future*, CUP, Cambridge, 1979.

Selective bibliography

Elleinstein, J., *The Stalin Phenomenon*, translated P. Latham, Lawrence and Wishart, London, 1976.

Engels, F., *Selected Writings*, edited W. O. Henderson, Penguin, Harmondsworth, 1967.

Dialectics of Nature, translated C. P. Dutt, Progress, Moscow, 1972 (first edition 1934).

Herr Eugen Dühring's Revolution in Science (Anti–Düring), edited C. P. Dutt, translated E. Burns, International Publishers, NY, 1972 (first edition 1878).

The Origin of the Family, Private Property and the State, Pathfinder, NY, 1972 (first edition 1884).

Gay, P., *The Dilemma of Democratic Socialism, Eduard Bernstein's Challenge to Marx*, Collier, NY, 1962 (first edition 1952).

Getzler, I., *Martov, a Political Biography of a Russian Social Democrat*, Melbourne University Press, Melbourne, 1967.

Haimson, L. H. *The Russian Marxists and the Origins of Bolshevism*, Harvard University Press. Massachusetts, 1955.

Halévy, E., *The Era of Tyrannies, Essays on Socialism and War*, translated R. K. Webb, NY University Press, NY, 1966 (first edition 1938).

Harding, N., *Lenin's Political Thought*, vol, I, *Theory and Practice in the Democratic Revolution*, Macmillan, London, 1977.

Hook, S., *From Hegel to Marx, Studies in the Intellectual Development of Karl Marx*, University of Michigan Press, Ann Arbor, 1962 (first edition 1936).

Hunt, R. N. *The Political Ideas of Marx and Engels*, vol. I, *Marxism and Totalitarian Democracy, 1818–1850*, University of Pittsburgh Press, Pittsburgh, 1974.

Hunt, R. N. Carew, *The Theory and Practice of Communism, An Introduction*, Penguin, Harmondsworth, 1969 (first edition 1950).

Jaurès, J., *Studies in Socialism*, translated M. Minturn, Independent Labour Party (The Socialist Library), London, 1906.

Kamenka, E., *The Ethical Foundations of Marxism*, Routledge and Kegan Paul, 1972 (first edition 1962).

Kautsky, K., *The Class Struggle*, translated W. E. Bohn, W. W. Norton, NY, 1971 (first edition 1892).

The Social Revolution, translated A. M. and M. W. Simons, Kerr, Chicago, 1916.

The Road to Power, translated A. M. Simons, Bloch, Chicago, 1909.

The Dictatorship of the Proletariat, University of Michigan Press, 1964 (first English edition 1919).

Terrorism or Communism, A Contribution to the Natural History of

Revolution, translated W. H. Kerridge, Hyperion Press, Connecticut, 1973 (reprint of 1920 edition).

Knei-Paz, B., *The Social and Political Thought of Leon Trotsky*, Clarendon Press, Oxford, 1978.

Kolakowski, L., *Main Currents of Marxism, its Rise, Growth and Dissolution*, translated P. S. Falla, 3 vols., Clarendon Press, Oxford, 1978.

Labedz, L. (ed.), *Revisionism: Essays on the History of Marxist Ideas*, Allen and Unwin, London, 1962.

Lane, D., *The Roots of Russian Communism*, Van Gorcum, Assen, 1969.

Lenin, V. I., *Collected Works*, 45 vols., Progress, Moscow, 1960–70.

Levine, N., *The Tragic Deception: Marx contra Engels*, Clio, Oxford, 1975.

Lichtheim, G., *Marxism, An Historical and Critical Study*, Routledge and Kegan Paul, London, 1971 (first edition 1961).

Liebman, M., *Leninism under Lenin*, translated B. Pearce, Cape, London, 1975.

Luxemburg, R., *Selected Political Writings*, edited R. Looker, translated W. D. Gref, Cape, London, 1972.

Social Reform or Revolution, translated Integer, Young Socialist, Colombo, 1969.

The Russian Revolution and Leninism or Marxism?, University of Michigan Press, Ann Arbor, 1970.

McLellan, D., *The Thought of Karl Marx, An Introduction*, Macmillan, London, 1974 (first edition 1971).

Marx, K., *The First International and After*, edited D. Fernbach, Penguin, Harmondsworth, 1974.

On the First International, edited and translated S. K. Padover, McGraw-Hill, NY, 1973.

Grundrisse. Foundations of the Critique of Political Economy (Rough Draft), translated M. Nicolaus, Penguin, Harmondsworth, 1973 (first German edition 1939).

Marx, K. and Engels, F., *Collected Works*, Lawrence and Wishart and Progress, London and Moscow, 16 vols. so far available, 1975–82.

Selected Works, 3 vols., Progress, Moscow, 1976.

Selected Correspondence, Progress, Moscow. 1975 (first edition 1955).

Meyer, A. G., *Marxism, the Unity of Theory and Practice: a Critical Essay*, Harvard University Press, Massachusetts, 1964 (first edition 1954).

Leninism, Praeger, NY, 1963 (first edition 1957).

Miliband, R., *Marxism and Politics*, OUP, Oxford, 1977.

Nettl, J. P., *Rosa Luxemburg*, 2 vols., OUP, London, 1966.

Page, S. W. (ed.), *Lenin: Dedicated Marxist or Revolutionary Pragmatist?* Heath, Massachusetts, 1970.

Plamenatz, J., *Man and Society, A Critical Examination of Some Important*

Selective bibliography

Social and Political Theories from Machiavelli to Marx, vol. 2, Longmans, Green and Co., London, 1963.

German Marxism and Russian Communism, Longmans, Green and Co., London, 1954.

Plekhanov, G., *Selected Philosophical Works*, vols. I and II, Progress, Moscow, 1977 and 1976.

Roth, G., *The Social Democrats in Imperial Germany*, Bedminster, New Jersey, 1963.

Schapiro, L., *The Origin of the Communist Autocracy, Political Opposition in the Soviet State, First Phase 1917–1922*, Macmillan, London, 1977 (first edition 1955).

and Reddaway, P. (eds.), *Lenin, the Man, the Theorist, the Leader: A Reappraisal*, Praeger, NY, 1967.

Schorske, C. E., *German Social Democracy, 1905–1917. The Development of the Great Schism*, Harper and Row, NY, 1972 (first edition 1955).

Shub, D., *Lenin: A Biography*, Penguin, Harmondsworth, 1966 (first edition 1948).

Souvarine, B., *Stalin, A Critical Survey of Bolshevism*, translated C. L. R. James, Longmans, Green and Co., NY, 1939.

Szamuely, T., *The Russian Tradition*, edited R. Conquest, McGraw-Hill, NY, 1974.

Talmon, J. L., *The Origins of Totalitarian Democracy*, Praeger, NY, 1960 (first edition 1952).

Political Messianism, The Romantic Phase, Praeger, NY, 1960.

Thomas, P., *Karl Marx and the Anarchists*, Routledge and Kegan Paul, London, 1980.

Trotsky, L., *Terrorism and Communism, A Reply to Karl Kautsky*, University of Michigan Press, Ann Arbor, 1963 (reprint of 1922 edition).

Tucker, R. C., *The Marxian Revolutionary Idea*, W. W. Norton, NY, 1969.

(ed.), *Stalinism. Essays in Historical Interpretation*, W. W. Norton, NY, 1977.

Ulam, A. B., *Lenin and the Bolsheviks. The Intellectual and Political History of the Triumph of Communism in Russia*, Fontana, London, 1973 (first edition 1965).

Venturi, F., *Roots of Revolution. A History of the Populist and Socialist Movements in Nineteenth Century Russia*, translated F. Haskell, Knopf, NY, 1966.

Walicki, A., *The Controversy over Capitalism. Studies in the Social Philosophy of the Russian Populists*, Clarendon Press, Oxford, 1969.

A History of Russian Thought from the Enlightenment to Marxism, translated H. Andrews-Rusiecka, Clarendon Press, Oxford, 1980.

INDEX

235

DATE DUE